Dead River
— to —
Living Water

My Journey Down this Lifeless River to the
Lifegiving Waters of Christ's Redeeming Grace

Tommy Poole

Fulton Books
Meadville, PA

Published by Fulton Books 2023

ISBN 979-8-88731-430-3 (paperback)
ISBN 979-8-88505-095-1 (digital)

Printed in the United States of America

Comment from Pastor Gary Moyer, VP for Administration / Executive Secretary of the Carolina Conference

"If you need encouragement that God is able to turn your life around for the better, you need to read this book. This is one of those easy, compelling reads I found hard to put down. I've known Tommy for years but never knew the whole, amazing story. Wow!"

Comments from Thomas T. Hardy, Director and Speaker of the Layman's Guidepost, LLC

"What an amazing testimony! Absolutely amazing! I love the river/water allegory and how it remains consistent throughout the book. The opening scene at the kitchen table is incredibly powerful! It drew me in immediately! Your early years were so intensely challenging with so many distinctive experiences. This story is something a lot of people will not be able to put down once they get started. It is almost like a movie!

"Your raw honesty is very earthly and real, making your references to the spiritual concepts more voracious for the consumption of the reader. I love it! The impelling motives you give the reader at the end of most chapters kept me wanting more. Yet the horrors of the alcoholic demon that overshadowed your life gave me great insight about and empathy for your struggle, Pastor!

"This is good stuff! Both interesting and spiritually compelling, this book grips the reader from the outset with scenes of gritty, fallen humanity inspired and transformed by the living waters cascading from the throne of God! The reader is invited to relive the journey of a man caught in the throes of the fallen nature, being miraculously lifted up by the hands of Jesus Christ from His cross.

"Thank you so much for allowing me the privilege of reviewing this book! It has been a personal blessing to me in my faith walk, and I am sure that it will be a blessing to every soul who reads it."

Contents

Acknowledgments

Let me begin by praising my Heavenly Father, his Son, my Savior and Lord, Jesus Christ, and the Holy Spirit of God, for giving me life, a saving knowledge of the Godhead, and bringing me from the dead river of my life to God's *living water*!

Louise Conaway encouraged me to seek God in prayer and later became my initial Bible teacher and fellow student.

The Three Angel's Broadcasting Network aired "Revelation Seminar" classes and supplied the lessons for Louise and me to participate in our first systematic Bible study. The Lord used those classes to give us a firm doctrinal foundation and pointed us to several local congregations to worship with.

Though many members of the Baxley congregation are now resting in their graves, waiting for the return of Jesus, they need to be remembered for opening their hearts to Louise and me. Besides teaching and preaching the truth of God's Word, from the very first service we worshipped with them, their Christian love and friendship made all the difference in us joining their fellowship. It will be wonderful to see them again when Jesus comes to take us home!

Head Elder Gus Nichols and his wife, Julia, never stopped trying to be my friend, and I thank God they did not! Eventually, I found out why...because they were true friends of Jesus and became some of the best friends I've ever had in one of the most difficult times of my life!

I will always appreciate more than I can say, for the faithful delivery of the Lord's message to me through Sisters Noel Bennett and Cletia Seabeck. It gave me the spiritual strength to not let Satan have the victory! The encouragement I received through the years from Sister Alcie Singletary was such a blessing! She never missed sending me a birthday card until the year she died.

Jan and Merlin Wittenberg, daughter and son-in-law of Gus and Julia Nichols, opened their hearts and home when I first arrived at Southern College (now Southern Adventist University). Jan and her friend Mary Morford helped me to get established in a campus apartment and personally hired me for extra work at their homes. Mr. and Mrs. C. R. Lacey believed enough in me to put me to work at the Grounds Department, recommend me for a live-in position with O. D. McKee (founder of McKee Bakery/Little Debbie's Snacks), and aided me in obtaining some additional funding for my education expenses through then—college president Dr. Donald R. Sahly and director of student finance Ken Norton.

In fact, each person I met that was connected with Southern demonstrated their sincere love for God by graciously assisting me in every way they could. And sitting at the feet of my religion department professors: Dr. Jack J. Blanco (then chairman); Dr. Douglas Bennett, Dr. Derek J. Morris (my faculty adviser); Dr. Norman R. Gulley; Dr. Leon I. Mashchak; and Dr. Ronald M. Springett was both a privilege and honor. Each day in their classes was a great adventure as the Holy Spirit used these humble, learned men of God to help me get to know my Savior better through the study of his Word.

O. D. and Thelma McKee (and family) hired me for several months as a live-in helper and, later while we were overseas, helped to support a missionary project.

I am sure this story would have never been written if it were not for a dear Australian lady we met and shared much of our time with while overseas. Since meeting her in Hong Kong, Coral Robbie became a wonderful loving friend, spiritual sister, and counselor. During our time together, the more she came to know of my testimony, the more she encouraged me to share it in a book. With her formal studies in English and linguistics, along with work experience editing for a Hong Kong publisher, Coral volunteered extensive time to this project by helping me organize, edit, and type this manuscript.

Finally, I am forever indebted to my wife, Linda, and daughter Brenda for their love and devotion but most of all for their immeasurable amount of forgiveness for all I have put them through before I met Jesus and since becoming a pastor. Most pastors understand how difficult it is for their family to live in the *glasshouse* of the gospel ministry. Thank you with all my heart, Linda and Brenda!

Introduction

In the early days of my experience with the Lord, I was told, "The best way a Christian can witness is to simply tell others what Jesus has done for you. You do not have to be a polished speaker or gifted teacher. All you need to do is share how God has changed your life and his Spirit will do the rest."[1] Through the years, I have tried to take advantage of the opportunities afforded me to testify of God's *power, goodness,* and *love*[2] in my life, be it with a large audience or in a one-on-one conversation, sharing the answers I have discovered to the questions we all eventually have about life, death, and beyond. Without a doubt, the greatest *peace* and *joy*[3] thus far, has come to me by hearing and accepting God's gospel—good news—which was given to the entire known world in the first century AD. As I came to realize *"the wages of sin is death, but the gift of God is eternal life in Christ Jesus our Lord,"*[4] *peace* and *joy* that I never knew existed was given to me bringing new meaning and direction to my life.

As I participate in this world view of faith, the peace and joy are a continual blessing to me and others I talk with, and this is why I am sharing my story with you. For you who do not have a personal relationship with Jesus Christ as your Savior, I challenge and encourage you to *"taste and see that the Lord is good."*[5] I found Jesus to be *the fountain of living waters,*[6] and he says, *"The water that I shall give him* [the person seeking answers] *will become in him a fountain of water springing up into everlasting life."*[7] For you who already know him, I invite you to partake even more out of his *wells of salvation.*[8]

Just as the Bible stories are presented, so my testimony is given in the context of character, circumstance, and the human condition.

Nothing is white-washed. Both the good and bad of my story is revealed so *that the goodness of God*, which leads men and women to repentance,[9] might be witnessed, recognized, and fully appreciated. For who can improve on the method that God himself chooses to reveal His *goodness*?[10]

The Scriptures also use symbols to teach the wonderful spiritual truths of God. Most of these are the common elements that surround us in daily life. I believe the most fitting symbol I could employ in telling my story is water—more specifically, comparing the lifeless water of this existence with the living water of the Creator, for water, more than any other substance in the natural world, makes the difference between life and death. Most certainly, the living water of our Creator God has been that difference for me and my family!

Here then is the Tommy Poole narrative.

Chapter 1

Insanity

Insanity is doing the same thing over and
over expecting a different result.

—Anonymous

It was early summer in 1987, and here I was, sitting in the dim light of sundown at my kitchen table, looking at a half-empty bottle of liquor as thoughts rolled from my mind and out of my mouth. "Oh no! Not again!" Up to this point in my life, I had lost my family and everything I owned, not once, not twice, but three times! And now for the fourth time, I was a total failure! I had opened my heart to my girlfriend, falling deeply in love with her, and yet I was still consumed by alcohol. This evil drink had caused me to squander away three marriages, everything I had worked for, and now the newest love in my life! It seemed as if the only thing I had left was that bottle sitting on the table staring back at my tear-drenched face.

Minutes before, having returned from town, I pulled into my driveway just in time to see Becky putting the last of her things into her grandfather's car. I could not believe my eyes! Turning the truck off, I hopped out, asking her, "What are you doing? Where are you going?"

This petite young woman looked me straight in the eye and said, "I'm leaving! I can't live with your constant drinking day in and day out! You've squandered away almost all your money, all your property is in HOC, you lost your business and have no hopes of a

1

job, and still, all you do is drink and stay drunk! I do love you, but I've had enough, so I'm leaving you!"

Insanity! That's what this was! Not knowing who originally said it, I had heard the old saying a number of times in my life that "Insanity is doing the same thing over and over expecting a different result." For many years, my life continued to be a failure because of the insanity of putting alcohol as my first priority, something I had sworn never to do because of the problems it caused in my family when I was growing up.

Moving away from home, family, and friends to the Dead River of Montgomery County, Georgia, had not been the solution to all my unhappiness. My problems had not disappeared but were sitting in front of me. After pleading and crying for my girlfriend to stay and watching her pull out of the driveway, I felt I was at the lowest point in my life. I had never felt so crushed. By this time, no one wanted much to do with me as I was, and I could not blame them. And now staring into the darkness, I realized that, for that moment, I was a man without hope and had nobody to blame but myself. In my utter despair, I lay my head on the table and began to weep again, but this time, I never knew a person could weep and sob so uncontrollably eventually calling out to God, "Lord, please have mercy on me and help me!"

It is so amazing how many of us travel down the river of life, waiting until we reach the point of hopelessness until we are willing to ask for help. By then, for many, it is too late—too late because all their worldly resources and relationships are exhausted, and they never have heard of or believed in the redemptive power of the Creator God who can do anything. Hopelessness leads them into the darkness of death. Life becomes a dead river. This is why the world-wide suicide rate is so high and is increasing each day.

For others, immediate death is not an option, and hopelessness leads them into the darkest life imaginable, floating around in the same dead river, and they give up their hope because of their "pride of opinion."[11] It is not because help is unavailable but because they are so afraid of what others will think of them if they ask for help. It will cost them too much to admit they have been wrong! However, for those who are willing to see their wrong and call out to the One who is the *living water*,[12] there is hope and help.

I cried well into the night. Eventually, I found my way to bed but could not sleep. I tossed and turned for several hours, then began walking from one end of my mobile home to the other. All the while, I was nursing my bottle of booze, hoping to ease my heartache and what was starting to be a terrible hangover. By sunup, there was only a couple of swallows left, but somehow, I was completely sober. Understanding that I needed help to quit drinking, I asked myself who I could call. Suddenly, out of the quietness of my mind, I heard these words that weeks later I realized were from the Spirit of God, "*Why don't you call Red Yates? He knows you well and is a recovered drunk, and you will need the help of experience to put this curse down.*"

I went to use my neighbor's phone to call Red who worked security at the Governor's Mansion in Columbia, South Carolina, but I was unable to reach him at home before he left for work on the second shift. After reaching him at work, I told him what was happening and he promised to be at my home the next day, if he could take some vacation days off. I packed my travel bag and slept, waiting for Red to come to my rescue! In the weeks ahead, I would recount over and over how I had come to this point in my life.

Chapter 2

Questions, Answers, and Authorities

Are you the first man who was born? Have you heard
the counsel of God? What do you know that we do not
know? What is man, that he could be pure?

—Job 15:7–9, 14

Each of us eventually seeks to answer the same questions about ourselves: "Who am I? Where did I come from? How did I come to be here? What is my purpose? Where am I going?"

Like most children, I began to accept the simple answers given to me until the reasoning process begin to take hold in my own brain. Accumulating information, I began learning how to test its truthfulness. My observations of life and people taught me how unreliable their truth was; thus, I accepted fewer of their answers at face value. The older I became, the more it seemed each person had his or her own reservoir of truth—their own standards of right and wrong. I realized these different answers for the same questions could not all be correct.

Fundamentally, all humanity has the same basic elements, needs, problems, and desires. For instance, chemically, approximately 99 percent of the human body is made up of just six elements: oxygen, carbon, hydrogen, nitrogen, calcium, and phosphorus. Small portions of twenty-two other elements make up the other 1 percent. "Up to 60 percent" of our body is water and sometimes more.[13]

All of us need food, water, clothing, shelter, and companionship to function at the highest efficiency possible. When these needs are not met in proper balance, the results are sickness of the body and/or mind and even death. Yet even when all our needs are appropriately met, there are the desires and the management of those desires that can have a major influence on our well-being.

We may look different, speak different languages, be born in different countries and cultures, with different beliefs and customs, but fundamentally, we are the same! Our body elements, needs, problems, and desires far outweigh the differences, thus making us the same—human beings!

And since we are the same, it is only logical that the same fundamental questions we all have about ourselves and life should have the same fundamental answers from the same fundamental authority. Who are we? Where did we come from? What is our purpose? Where are we going? Which authority can we trust for these answers?

Originally, I was taught these answers should come from parents and older, wiser family members. In time, answers could come from other authorities approved by my parents—good family friends, school teachers, leaders in church, and the Bible.

This pool of authorities grew in size, and so did the list of differing answers along with the conflicts from those differences. As a youngster, if I questioned a conflicting answer, out of respect for parental rights, most people would say to me, "Maybe you should talk with your parents about that." Yet over time, as society continued to erode, with more people desiring to be the authority for others, consideration for parental rights lessened, and more folks simply gave their opinion and left it at that.

On becoming an adult, the authorities I had come to respect and the answers they had given me became a conglomeration of the world I knew. The answers did not always make sense, but some had proven to be true. Others were valued opinions of people I loved, liked, and trusted while others were simply set aside, with the intention of investigating them further at a more convenient time and place or just forgetting them.

Of course, a few answers came by way of the Bible. Its stories had always appealed to me as a child, but much of it did not make sense, and entering into adult life brought more and more conflict with the biblical answers. It seemed fewer people trusted or even believed in the God of the Bible, but I did. As far back as I can remember, the fundamental idea that God exists and is the Creator of the entire universe and its contents was reasonable to me.[14] After all, there seems to be an endless supply of evidence to substantiate the concept of intelligent design.[15] In fact, so much so, the overwhelming amount of evidence requires very little faith,[16] compared to the enormous amount needed to believe the theories of the so-called "modern sciences"! And yet like most people, I accepted bits and pieces of these theories to answer some of the questions that I thought were not answered in the Scriptures.

I did notice the answers given in God's book almost always conflicted with the various answers of men. I often wondered how I could just accept what the Bible had to say, especially when there were so many other good-sounding options that were less trouble to apply to my thinking. So as I grew up, I adopted various points from the theory of evolution and other ideas that seemed to fit well with portions of the creation picture. If I had to pin my beliefs down, they were probably a mixture of deism[17] and theistic evolution.[18]

Eventually with time, and the multitude of men's bad answers I had accepted (those answers that sounded so good), brought me to recognize a great reality of this life. There are only two answers to each of life's questions: man's and God's. Yes, there are many different answers from the thinking of man, but all of them boil down to being just another opinion of man. However, I found for each question we ask, there is always only one answer from the mind of God.

Thus, the testimony of my life comes from the experiential investigation of answers explained in his Word, after failing time and again by using man's answers. If you will be honest with yourself and make the same investigation multimillions have, you will see how the answers I found to my questions are foolproof, and they come from the One and only True Authority.

Chapter 3

My Four Most Influential Tributaries

He drew me out of many waters.

—Psalm 18:16

For each river represented on a map, between its beginning and ending, tributaries make their contributions of good and bad water toward the river's development and end result. Thus, to fully appreciate what the river becomes, one needs to understand the contributions received along its journey. Since I am just another branch of humanity's river, for you to recognize the value of how my life has been changed, I need to share with you the four main tributaries used in forming my person.

The Poole Tributary

I was born September 21, 1952, to my father, Llewlyn Poole, also known as Hank, and to my mother, Carolyn Godbolt Poole, at the Duval County Hospital in Jacksonville, Florida.

The Poole tributary is deep and long, and we have traced it back nine generations to England.[19] In the seventh generation, my grandfather Alvin Cluese Poole was born. To some, he was known as A. C. or Cluese, but to me, he was Pa-pa. He was raised on a farm and worked the same farm most of his life. Having very little formal education, most of what he knew came from life's experience. However, he did graduate from a barber's college.

Married November 5, 1927, twenty-two-year-old Cluese, with his fourteen-year-old bride, Lacey Estelle Kersey, began their lives together and, within the next year and a half, moved to a farm in rural Montgomery County near the small town of Uvalda, Georgia.

Pa-pa Poole was reared in a hardworking family and raised my father and his siblings in the same manner. Four boys and two girls became typical Poole offspring—tough, hardworking, hard playing, and extremely independent minded. Most, as soon as the opportunity arose, left the farm and went to the city to work and establish their own lives.

Through the Great Depression and World War II, Pa-pa's family had a difficult time. Possessing very little wealth, he constantly tried to reinvest some of his profits to expand his farm. When he died in 1972, at the age of seventy, he had accumulated 365 acres of prime Georgia farmland and timber. Row crops, a big garden, and turpentine from the timber, together with a large number of hogs and some cattle, allowed my grandparents to live comfortably in their later years.

Uvalda was a southern farming town like many that had sprouted up along the railroad. Daddy was born on August 18, 1929, in the same rural community. When I was born twenty-three years later, Uvalda still had only one red light, a bank, post office, feed mill, and a handful of other small businesses.

In 1945, World War II ended, and in October 1946, Daddy enlisted in the United States Army. After basic training and paratrooper's jump school, he served with the Eleventh Airborne Division for seven months in Japan, completing his enlistment in January 1948.

Instead of returning to the farm, Daddy went to live in Jacksonville, Florida, rooming with his aunt and uncle Pickren. He worked selling insurance during the day while attending business college at night until being hired as a billing clerk by R. C. Motor Lines Inc. While attending the church of his aunt and uncle, he met Mama. After dating for a while, they were married on June 5, 1949.

Three years and three months later, I was born. About eighteen months after my birth, Daddy was promoted to be the central dispatcher for the trucking company and was transferred to Columbia, South Carolina.

The Godbold/t Tributary[20]

Carolyn Godbolt was born and raised in the farming community of Wellborn, Florida, of Suwannee County. She was the second daughter of Frank Clark Godbolt[21] and Edna Law Godbolt. Known as Clark, Granddaddy came from the neighboring community of Live Oak, Florida, but after he and Edna were married, they moved to the city of Jacksonville, Florida, where Granddaddy drove a cab and Granny worked in the cigar factory.

Mama and her older sister, Katherine, lived on the farm with Edna's parents while Clark and Edna worked in the city. After moving to Jacksonville, Mama and Aunt Katherine still worked many summers on their relative's farms in North Florida.

In 1938, Granddaddy and Granny Godbolt divorced and a few years later, Granny married Daniel Keene. Two sons, Danny and Jimmy, were born from this union, and the family lived on the south side of Jacksonville.

Throughout most of my years at home, Mama was a mother and full-time housewife, except during the years my younger brothers were in high school when she worked with Daddy at our family convenience store in Columbia.

The Law Tributary

On February 20, 1902, James Walter Law[22] married Lula Odella Croft. They were farmers and had eight children, of which their second eldest was Edna Odella Law, who became my maternal grandmother (Granny Godbolt and later Granny Keene), born on September 16, 1904.

If I have ever known a saint, my Granny Keene (we knew her by her second married name, Keene) was one! She was a fine Southern Baptist lady who loved her Lord. I do not know how much formal education Granny had, but I do know she had a tremendous education of experience with God's Word. Ever since I can remember, she always talked and lived her faith. She was one of a small number of individuals I have ever known who claimed the name of "Christian" that I can honestly say made a constant, positive influence in my life. I wished it had been more! Perhaps then, I would not have veered down some of the treacherous creeks and rivers I eventually chose. I will always remember Granny and thank God for her love for Jesus. She passed away in her eighty-sixth year, November 1992.

She had such a long and prosperous life, perhaps not in material things but in everything else that mattered, and I praise God for that also! No one ever wants to think about people dying, especially loved ones, but it was my prayer that Granny would not have to live in a condition of suffering. She had been faithful to Jesus, and I was thankful when the time was right, she was allowed to rest. I look forward to the Lord's second coming when I will see her again!

The Kersey Tributary

My paternal grandmother, Lacey Estelle Kersey Poole, was known to her grandchildren as Ma-ma Poole. From the community of Swainsboro, Georgia, Ma-ma was the youngest of six children having two brothers and three sisters.

During the years of the Florida boom, most of the traffic heading south came through Swainsboro, and from there, two main roads handled most of the travelers. My great-grandfather Oscar Poole and his family operated a ferry on one of those roads and ferried travelers across the Altamaha River, so he stationed one of his sons Cluese in Swainsboro to direct traffic down the highway that would cross his ferry.

Lacey's family would take in boarders for additional income, and Cluese came to rent a room in the Kersey home. This is how

Cluese and Lacey met and were eventually married. When the boom days were over, the young couple moved to Montgomery County and the farm.

Like Granny Keene, Ma-ma Poole will always have a special place in my heart. I saw her as a pioneer type of woman. Many of the stories I remember hearing were about her in the family's early days on the farm. She seemed to know no limits, working alongside the men in many things. She could fish, hunt, work in the fields, and handle the livestock in addition to the usual responsibilities as a wife and mother.

In particular, I remember the story of how she broke Pa-pa from drinking. Before he became a big farmer in that area, Pa-pa would hire on to work for other farmers when his farmwork was done. One of those things he was known for was making sugarcane syrup. Making enough of the syrup to last a family through the year would take quite a few days and nights, giving the opportunity for a lot of conversation as people came along during his work. And of course, the work, conversation, and long nights seemed to go a lot better when there were some spirits to sip on. But as the years came and went, more sips and less work resulted in a bigger habit developing and less of the extra income in the bank.

The story goes, when Ma-ma was nursing their youngest child, a neighbor came along and told her Pa-pa was down the road making syrup, indulging in the spirits pretty heavy. Hearing this, she decided she had had enough! Leaving the baby with one of her daughters, she took off down the dirt road by herself well after dark. After walking several miles, she finally reached the farm where Pa-pa was working, finding him and several other men sitting around the fire, talking and laughing, passing the bottle of spirits from person to person.

Ma-ma rolled a section of a log up to the circle of men and sat down, waiting for the bottle to come her way. When it did, she took a large swallow, and every time it came back to her, she would take a larger drink than the time before. It was not long before she started embarrassing Pa-pa with her conversation so he decided to send her home but then discovered she could not even stand! He loaded Ma-ma on the mule and took her home.

It was said that after that night, Pa-pa did not have another drink until I saw him take a small one, some thirty years later during a special family occasion. I never knew of him to take another.

I came to discover in my future studies of the Bible that the entire human family is closer than most of us think. This is because *"God, who made the world and everything in it…has made from one blood every nation of men to dwell on all the face of the earth…"* [23] As for me, *"he drew me out of many waters"*[24]—just a small part of this river of humanity. Yet it is the contributions of these four family tributaries that truly help to distinguish me from all others.

Chapter 4

Dead River

For he draws up drops of water, which distill as rain from the mist,
which the clouds drop down and pour abundantly on man.

—Job 36:27–28

Many things about my people, plus the places they lived and worked, cut deep channels of influence into my being. Apart from the different people, farms, and the small towns of Uvalda and Vidalia, Dead River was a great influence on me. I guess this was because, as a youngster, I spent so much time there.

Throughout the years, Daddy, Pa-pa Poole, and my uncles A. C., Jr., and Jim Paul would take me there fishing and hunting. I grew fonder of the place every time I went! Each time of year had its special beauty, and I appreciated every season.

Cypress, Sweet Gum, and Tupelo trees were scattered from the river's edge throughout the surrounding blackwater swamps until the banks and hills, some of clay, others of sand, emerged. Farther up, the banks were covered in huge southern Live Oaks, draped in gray moss that resembled the unkempt beards of trappers and miners of old. Higher up on the hills, there were old saw timber pines, mixed with dwarf palmetto and gallberry bushes. And of course, the abundant wildlife made Dead River a paradise for fishing, hunting, trapping, and just spending time in nature.

Water and Its Cycle

In middle school, during Earth Science class, I learned about water and its cycle. Water is "the most abundant of the essential nutrients in our body... Between fifty and seventy-five percent of our total body weight is water... Water is present in all the tissues of the body as well as in every cell. Even our bones are made up of nearly one-third water... Next to oxygen it is the most essential substance for the preservation of life."[25] It is this way from the simplest to the most complex forms of life.

From my childhood, the basic teaching of a Creator was one that always made sense to me. Having someone responsible for it all was very logical, especially as I grew older and began to hear the variety of this life's philosophies. Logic only dictated that if there was a Creator, he would only create a perfect world, and since life needs water to continue, it seemed reasonable that water, in all its forms, must have been perfect, pure. Dew, rain, snow, creeks, ponds, lakes, glaziers, "*fountains of the great deep*,"[26] and rivers must have all been pure and free of any pollution.

As for the water cycle, it also seemed that the original was basically still in tack. Daily, as the sun heats the various forms of water on the earth's surface, evaporation takes place, causing water vapor to rise into the earth's atmosphere, merging into clouds. Then as the clouds grow heavier from their water content and cooler from low temperatures in the upper altitudes, dew, rain, hail, or snow falls back to the earth replenishing the water that was evaporated.

Additionally, it makes sense that no part of the original water cycle was harmful or destructive in any way; thus, there was always the right amount of water needed for life. Never were there any vast extremes in the original plan. In the beginning, water was truly life-giving or *living water*.[27] Even the oceans must have been perfect in their heavily salted and mineral makeup.

Changes in the Water and Its Cycle

Of course, not being sure about the entire Genesis story, I knew from seeing things the way they are in this present age, something bad happened after creation! Obviously, it had to do with man's misuse and lack of care. Over time, almost all the sources of water, except the polar caps, some glaziers, and aquifers, have become so polluted they cannot be consumed unless they are treated.

Slowly but surely, man saw his perfectly balanced surroundings give way to more and more chaos. Earth's atmosphere began developing areas of unbalance. Greater variances in temperature, humidity, and wind currents produced more marked effects on the earth's surface, altering the perfectly balanced water cycle. The evaporation process varied in the amount of water returning to the earth. Runoff increased in some areas while decreasing in others, producing more stunted crops or others totally failing.

Without the balanced water cycle, man began to look for ways to manipulate the watershed in an attempt to restore the balance. Together with the efforts of man and nature's raw power becoming more erratic, the birth of droughts, deserts, floods, and swamps became part of the norm, as evidenced by the increasing number of these effects today.

Some of these are how the Dead River came to be. Coming out of the northwestern part of Georgia, two of its largest rivers, the Oconee and the Ocmulgee, merge to form the Altamaha. The junction of these rivers came to be known as the forks[28] and "is the most striking geographic feature on any map"[29] of South Central Georgia. For hundreds of years, various Indian tribes, settlements, and trading posts have been found in and around the forks.[30]

The Oconee River is the eastern fork and for almost thirty miles north serves as the present-day western border for Montgomery County. As "water seeks its own level…it generally seeks to flow to the oceans", always flowing downhill,[31] so the Oconee cut its original channel, gently meandering down through the Georgia piedmont and onto the coastal plain, forming an oxbow[32] over its last two miles before the forks. (See appendix A: Oxbow.)

Prior to 1741, the oxbow was open, and the river flowed freely through it. But for several years, heavy winter rains fell in north and Central Georgia, causing the southern Oconee to flood its surrounding lowlands. By the summer of 1742, extra silt and debris had completely closed off the entrance to the oxbow while cutting a more direct route to the junction below. In a very short time, beavers dammed up the southern end, cutting the old channel off completely from the Oconee River, leaving approximately a mile and a half of water that became known as Dead River due to the lack of a current in the oxbow.

With occasional rain and the drainage from the higher timberland and fields, Dead River naturally caught a little water, but its main source continued to be the Oconee River. Though cut off from the Oconee from late winter into early spring, if enough rain fell in the upper state, the lower river would flood, spilling over its banks, and spreading throughout the swamps and low-lying forests that encompassed Dead River.

It was the arrival of these winter rains that brought a temporary rejuvenation to the old channel. The old water, along with the previous year's accumulated forms of death and decay, was flushed out. New fresh water, full of life-sustaining elements, rushed in! Fish and other aquatic animals reappeared in greater quantity with an abundance of new food becoming available for the land animals too. Dead River was momentarily renewed with the seasonal influx of the Oconee's water. Yet when the rain ended, the flooding subsided, and its deterioration soon began causing the old river to die for another year.

Chapter 5

Family Life

I will show them among the peoples...they shall
live, together with their children.

—Zechariah 10:9

Columbia, South Carolina, became the home of my childhood. I attended school there, graduating from A. C. Flora High School in May 1970.

Eventually, I had three younger brothers. Michael was four years younger than I. Danny was four years younger than Michael, and Jeff came along the year after Danny.

A typical middle-class family of the 1960s, we lived in a quiet, pleasant suburb of Columbia. We were not wealthy, but Daddy liked to say, "We have plenty to eat, decent clothes to wear, and a good house to live in. An entrepreneurial, free-market economy was the best system for all people with increased wages and promotions coming as individuals train, apply themselves, and earn them, not because one was a union member."

Religiously, we were considered to be conservative Southern Baptists, strong on the doctrines of "righteousness by faith" in Jesus Christ, "once saved, always saved," and "religious liberty" as the pillars of our faith. In our home, there was an emphasis on personal manners and hospitality.

Daddy worked long hours, especially in the early years, with a peculiar schedule made up of seven days on and three days off, causing his days off to be constantly changing. Yet, even on those days, I do not remember seeing him very much, except sometimes on Sundays he would take me with him to work when most everyone else was off. I loved roaming from office to office, finding the ones not locked and then plundering through their desk drawers, shuffling items in their desks, and fowling up the margins and tab spacing on all the typewriters. Usually, when Daddy was off, he spent most of that time, playing golf or cards and sometimes hanging out at one of the local neighborhood convenience stores drinking beer and playing pool with some of his friends.

There were times when we would use his three-day weekends to visit his boyhood home in Georgia. Throughout my childhood, we visited there four or more times per year, including on legal holidays, causing me to become so fond of my grandparents' country home. Most of my special family memories come from those times! We were often there when at least one of my aunt's or uncle's families were also there, making each occasion seem like to me a family reunion, every two or three months!

There were also the extra special memories of Thanksgiving, Christmas, Easter, and Fourth of July. At Christmas, the children of four or five families would make pallets and sleep on the floor. But first, our mothers would rush shifts of us off to the one and only bathtub, help us put our pajamas on, and tuck us in Ma-ma's nice, soft feather beds. We warmed up the beds until the adults were ready to retire, and then they placed us on our pallets. Of course, by then, most of us kids were sound asleep and didn't know if there was a problem in the whole wide world.

On Easter, as always, Ma-ma Poole had prepared a fabulous dinner. We ate, put on our Easter clothes and took pictures, had a large egg hunt, and enjoyed her beautiful flowers of spring! Often during the spring and summer, a group would dig red worms and go fishing at Dead River or, in later years, to Pa-pa's pond. Many a night, the fisherman came home with several large stringers of bluegill, red-breast, specks (crappie), with a bass or several catfish for good measure! By flashlight, lantern, and truck headlights, we would scale and clean the catch before turning them over to Ma-ma and our mothers so they could fry up a feast of fish, French fries, and hush puppies (balls of corn bread that got their name from being thrown out the back door to keep the hounds quiet while people ate and talked). And someone always had to have a pot of grits and sliced cheddar cheese. All this was topped off with some homemade cake or pie.

After supper, the younger children would head for the living room to watch TV or the front porch to play while the rest of us sat around the table sipping iced tea (of course, most adults would add something stronger to their tea) and sharing any new jokes that were going around or even a favorite story that had been told time and again through the years but was always good for another laugh!

One of the ways Daddy tried to give us more time together was through the game of golf. Growing up, I was always athletic, and so as I approached my teens, he decided to give me a starter set of golf clubs for Christmas. This consisted of a driver, a 5-iron, a 9-iron, and a putter. He added several packages of golf balls, tees, and a few ball markers. Several days when he was off from work, we went outside in the back-yard where he showed me how to hold and swing the clubs. He told me I could practice my short-range shots there until the weather warmed up. The next spring, he took me to a local driving range and helped me get started using the clubs for longer shots. He rented each of us a bucket of range balls, and together, we started practicing our shots from off the tee. After we finished hitting the practice balls, we finished up by moving to their putting green. We had a ball, no pun intended. I only wish we had taken the opportunity to do that more often.

After he saw that I was making good contact with the ball, Daddy began taking me to one of the smaller golf courses in the area, where I would play along with him as he gave me instructions. Of course, like most of the Poole family, his patience would often wear thin when I had to hit the ball so many times per hole to stay up with him and not hold up faster players behind us. Eventually, when he realized that my knowledge of golf etiquette and the rules were adequate, he began allowing me to play by myself as he played with friends of his caliber.

When reaching the seventh and eighth grades, Daddy encour-aged me to try out for the Middle School Golf Team. He had recently changed positions at the trucking company and was promoted to being the sales representative for South Carolina, which meant he would be entertaining freight customers to obtain or keep their business. As a result of this promotion, Daddy was given an expense account to cover these entertainment costs, so he joined the Columbia Country Club, which gave him a very nice place to bring his clients and family. The club consisted of a first-class restaurant, swimming pools, exercise and locker room facilities, and of course, a beautiful, yet challenging golf course with an additional practice nine holes. He met our school golf coach there, and the coach told him to have me come to the tryout he would be holding at the club. I did and made one of the two alternate positions. While never playing in any tournaments, I took advantage of our two practice rounds each week and some of the free lessons the club professional gave us, which did help my personal game for a few years. When I was not playing golf, Mama would take us boys and meet a friend and her girls at the club for an afternoon of swimming and lunch.

The only real negative side of the country club was the drinking and gambling that went on there. In his sales position, Daddy always kept a case or two of liquor in the trunk of his company car. He was giving it away as gifts or treating the guys during card games after playing golf. It was not unusual for him to come home loaded, and on at least four occasions, he would call or have someone else call Mama to come pick him up because he was too drunk to drive home himself. Several other times, we did not have to pick him up at the club; instead, she had to go to the hospital to check on him because he had a wreck coming home! Thank the Lord these accidents were not serious!

Though my family life did have a fair amount of good times in it, I eventually understood that, in fact, there had been as much, if not more, bad as good. I was taught to drink the water of this life's dead river. I learned it well from the Poole clan of Montgomery County. In almost every situation, it was due to alcohol, and for many more years, I would witness this as the river ran its course.

Chapter 6

Someone's Knocking

*Behold, I stand at the door and knock. If anyone
hears my voice and opens the door, I will come in to
him and dine with him, and he with me.*

—Revelation 3:20

I am not sure about the year when I became active in the Baptist
Church. North Trenholm was, and still is, one of the largest Southern
Baptist congregations in the Columbia area. I started attending after
we moved to South Carolina from Florida and Mama and Daddy
transferred their membership. I was in the nursery and preschool
classes then until their attendance began declining. With Daddy's
new job and work schedule, it was easy for the decline to take place.
When he worked on Sunday, since Mama did not have transportation, we stayed at home. Then when Daddy was off on Sunday, he
was sleeping, playing golf, or we were visiting my grandparents in
Georgia.

After a few years, Daddy and Mama bought a house about
two miles from the church, and after making a few friends in the
neighborhood, when Daddy was working on Sundays, we would
ride to church with some friends. When several more years passed,
Michael was now a toddler, and when Mama did not go to church,
I would ride with friends or Sunday school teachers. By the time
I was nine years old, I was attending Sunday school, morning and
evening church services, Royal Ambassadors (similar to Cub Scouts),

and Wednesday night prayer meeting service. Plus, there were always activities for the youth that I participated in, such as baseball in the summer, basketball in the fall and winter, and track and field in the spring. Eventually, I had my own bicycle and would often ride it to many of the church functions. It truly seemed that I was at the church every time they opened the doors! While I did enjoy my participation in all these activities, as I approached twelve years of age, my motives began to change.

I do not remember hearing a lot of theology in those days. I'm not sure if it was because they were not teaching it or if it was too advanced for my young mind, but I do remember the great emphasis on the Bible stories. I learned about Jesus and his love for mankind and his willingness to die for the sins of all. I remember attending every night of a weeklong revival meeting with my Training Union teacher. She would come by my house and take me each evening after supper and then bring me home. I must have been eleven years old then and the preacher was Dr. Rice from the Southern Baptist Convention. I still remember the sermon he preached on the last night of the meetings. In his closing illustration, he explained how "the opportunity to accept Jesus as our Savior is like a rope that hangs from a tree limb which reaches halfway over a great crevice. As you stand on the edge of the crevice, an earthquake suddenly disintegrates the path behind you and the only escape is to cross over the crevice, but you cannot reach the rope! Suddenly, a breeze blows the rope toward you, and the first time it swings to you is the best opportunity you will have to reach out and grab it! As it swings back and forth, each time you do not grab it, the farther it is from you, and eventually, you have lost your opportunity to accept Christ and be saved! Please don't let this happen to you!"

Dr. Rice went on, "For some of you tonight, the rope of opportunity is so close that you don't have to jump! All you need do is reach out and take it. For others here, it is another opportunity to receive salvation, but the rope is not as close as it was before, so please grab it while you still can. Still, others are here tonight who have missed a number of opportunities to receive the grace of God and you can easily see the rope is not coming any closer! You will have to jump for the rope now, but you can make it trusting in God! But the question for you now is, if you don't jump for the rope this time, will you still be able to jump far enough to grab it next time it swings your way? Accept the Lord's call now while you know you can reach his rope of salvation!"

I knew Jesus was knocking at my heart's door, and I did not want to miss going to heaven; thus, Dr. Rice's appeal got me up to answer the door! No adult talked to me or spurred me forward. No one went with me. It was the result of my own thought-out decision and reaching the pastor, I told him I wanted to accept Jesus as my Savior! I believe it was the following Sunday that I was baptized and became a member of the North Trenholm Baptist Church.

There was not much spiritual education during my early church experience. I do not even remember being enrolled in a Bible study or attending a new member's class, I assume because of my young age. It was not long before my first major trial of faith, which came from within the church.

It seems that our pastor had some serious family financial problems and mishandled some church funds. Somehow, one of the church leaders found out and, instead of going to the pastor privately, as Jesus said to do, after talking with other leaders, decided to take the issue before the church one Sunday morning during the middle of the eleven o'clock service. They simply took over the service at the offering time and broke the dam allowing all their ugly feelings to flood the congregation, totally embarrassing the pastor and his family. It reminded me of some western television programs where the whole town would go berserk, and without a trial, they would lynch the accused! They voted the pastor out. It hurt me terribly to see how so many of my fellow Christians who had given me such tender love and instruction were now acting like ravenous wolves toward the pastor.

As a result, I said to myself, "If this is how Christianity treats its own people that momentarily fall from grace, I do not want any part of it!" Eleven years old, I left the church that day, simply dropping out of sight. Being deeply discouraged, I turned away from the Lord's people, and from my middle school years, well into my thirties, my days were full of trouble. I do not remember anyone ever trying to find out why I stopped coming or convince me to return, and I did not talk about it again until many years later. Little did I realize that the course I had now charted would take me into a dead river full of heartache, pain, and misery! I was now running from the Lord, refusing his unconditional love, and unless I came back to the grace of God, I would not make it into his kingdom.

I have often thought back over the years, to the various dangerous situations in which I found myself. It seemed I could always spiritually look back over my shoulder and see Jesus was there. He was patiently following me, calling me, knocking at the door of my heart, reaching out to me, saying, *I know you're hurt. I know the pain you are going through. I understand your struggles. Just take my hand and let me help you. I will never leave you nor forsake you.*[33] But I would not change course. I continued down the river of no return. If only I would have stopped running long enough to talk with the Lord and see what he had to say, I could have spared myself and those who love me so much pain! While I was drowning in life's dead river, the Lord was trying so hard to save me with his living water and I would not stop long enough to drink!

Chapter 7

An Early Education

The eyes of those who see will not be dim, and
the ears of those who hear will listen.

—Isaiah 32:3

My grandparents' house had a screened porch on the front, and when the outhouse was done away with and a bathroom was built on one end of the back porch, they decided to screen that porch in too. Being the second oldest grandchild, most of the others were much younger than me, and we liked different activities for entertainment, and often, I would sit on one of these porches listening to the adults talk about what was going on in their lives—the good times they were having or the problems they were facing. By the time I was ten, I knew more about their lives than they ever dreamed I did. Before long, I was able to conclude the most prevalent problem for many of my family was alcohol.

When Daddy drank, it usually went beyond the point of moderation, and while under the influence, he would become extremely argumentative, arrogant, and dogmatic. As often as I heard him or other family members confronted about their consumption, I never heard any of them admit to having an alcohol problem. Yet through the years, I continually witnessed how alcohol caused or contributed too many hurt feelings, arguments, and hardships. The next thing you knew, they were telling each other off, doing crazy things, and/ or leaving the family gathering.

No matter how great any occasion seemed to be, I could sense something was missing. I could always tell, beneath all the stories of progress and prospering with their jobs and homes, beneath all the alcohol-induced joy, I could feel loneliness and hear emptiness in most of the family's conversations at my grandparents' home. Without actually knowing how to explain it, I realized that it lacked a truly spiritual quality.

One summer, about a week after school let out, Daddy received a telephone call from his youngest brother in Uvalda. After the call, he asked me if I might be interested in going to live and work on the farm with Pa-pa and Ma-ma Poole. Of course, I thought this would be fantastic, but I had just started playing Pony League baseball. What was I going to do about my commitment to the team? He said, "Well, just think about it for a couple of days and we'll talk again before I give your uncle an answer. I'm not going to force you to go, but you should understand that your grandparents are having some problems and you are the only one in the family old enough that can go." So I agreed to think about it and talk with him later.

Two days later, when Daddy came in from work, he asked if I had made up my mind yet. I told him that I really wanted to play baseball, but if my grandparents truly needed me, I was willing to go, but I wanted to know what kind of problems they were having.

We sat down at the kitchen table, and he began to explain that my grandfather had a serious mental illness. In fact, he had the illness for many years. It started out with him being jealous of Ma-ma talking or having much to do with any other men. With time, this jealousy turned into an obsession, and over the years, it caused him to literally go insane. There was never any evidence to prove his belief was true and different ones in the family tried to convince him that he was wrong, but he would not believe them. Therefore, he refused to accept the fact that he had this illness and would not cooperate by seeking treatment. While he was not violent when others were not around, he would mentally hound Ma-ma, and now she was at her wit's end! So the strategy was to bring me in for the summer, and hopefully, his agitations would cease.

I idolized Ma-ma for years because I thought most of her characteristics were fantastic and that she could do no wrong! But through the next couple of summers, I came to know her bad side too. She could make you quite miserable if she wanted to, with her griping, moaning, and complaining. Her tongue could be *sharper than any two-edged sword*,[34] her tactics so devious, and yet, on the other hand, she could be so kind, loving, and sweet! Eventually, she became totally fed up with being falsely accused for so many years that things nearly exploded.

Of course, I realized that baseball was not as important as the family crisis we were facing, so I called my coach and apologized for quitting the team because of the family emergency. Mama and I packed my clothes for the summer, and the next day, Daddy drove me to the farm. We first stopped at my uncle's house so he could update us and explain to me what we should say and do when arriving at my grandparents'. Daddy and I went on to their house, and my uncle followed about an hour later, acting like he had not already seen us. While we ate supper, Pa-pa, Daddy, and my uncle Jim talked about the work I would be doing—some for Pa-pa and some around the house for Ma-ma. Daddy spent the night and left for Columbia the next morning.

Things seemed pretty normal for about a week, and then one morning, Pa-pa took me outside and said he wanted to show me something. I followed him to the cornfield in the back of the house, and there, he showed me some boot tracks in the soft dirt.

He said, "You see this? He's been here last night. Sometimes he'll come out here and just stand for hours hoping to see her on the back porch. I know it's him because I know his boot tracks."

Over the next few days, at various places around the farm, he would show me more tracks, each time saying the man had been there watching him or hoping to see Ma-ma. Before the week was over, I could see they were Pa-pa's tracks. As we would leave each place, I would compare the track he made with the track he was showing me, and they were obviously the same, but I did not dare say anything to him because I was afraid of how he might react.

One morning as we left to feed the hogs, he told me he knew I could handle the .22 rifle he kept in the house, and he wanted me to load it and slip out when I went to my room for the night and keep watch in the cornfield behind the house. If I saw the man, he wanted me to shoot him!

In the meantime, Pa-pa had started psychologically abusing Ma-ma again. He ranted and raged throughout the night, turning on the bedroom lights, slamming doors, and kitchen cabinets, keeping her awake. I slept in the bedroom on the other end of the house but still had to cover my head with a pillow to fall asleep. He never harmed her physically, but I knew things were just about as bad as I thought they could get when one evening before dark, I walked into the house and Ma-ma was sitting in her chair, smoking a cigarette, with a glass of bourbon on the table beside her and the double-barreled shotgun across her lap.

I bellowed, "Ma-ma! What are you doing? Why have you got the shotgun?"

I will not repeat what she said in her response, but simply put, she was going to end her torture that night when Pa-pa came in!

After she talked a few minutes, I started trying to calm her down, telling her she knew that was not the answer. I told her that I would call Daddy and Uncle Jim and they would work something out, but I was not going to let her do what she was planning. She started crying, and I slowly took the gun out of her hands and unloaded it, taking it immediately to my bedroom and putting it under my bed. We got in her car and took the dirt road to my uncle's house, waited until he came in from work, and told him what almost happened about an hour before. Ma-ma and I went back to her house while Uncle Jim called Daddy. The next morning, Uncle Jim came to supposedly have me help him for several hours at his house but told me that Daddy was coming back for the weekend and they were going to commit Pa-pa to the hospital for the treatment he desperately needed.

I asked, "What about me? What am I going to do"?

He said, "You're going to stay with your grandmother and harvest the summer crops before you have to return home for school."

For the next nine weeks, I worked in tobacco fields five days a week, one day for our crop and four days for the neighbors' crops who helped us. My day started an hour and a half before sunrise when Ma-ma would wake me and help me sit up to start getting dressed. She had breakfast ready, and I was usually so tired she would almost have to feed me herself to get me to eat. Quite a few nights I was so tired I did not eat supper! I would take off my dirty clothes and fall in the bed, and most of those nights, I dreamed of working in the hot field. Needless to say, I would wake up with Ma-ma shaking me telling me to get up and it was time for breakfast, and I felt as tired as I did when I went to bed!

Then I filled up the pickup truck with gas and headed down the road to pick up most of our field hands. (Yes, I drove Pa-pa's pickup truck without a driver's license at thirteen years old because Daddy had already taught me how to drive over the last two years. Ma-ma put the word out for friends to keep us informed about any Georgia State Trooper license checks or wrecks, and they would call to reroute me if need be.) As soon as I left, Ma-ma would get ready and head for her job at the sewing factory.

The hands needed to be in the field working two hours after sun rise so we could hopefully finish by 12:00 p.m. or 1:00 p.m. at the latest when I would take the hands back home. After dinner, several field hands would return to help load the tobacco, which had been tied on a five-foot stick, onto trucks and haul them to the barn where we would unload and hang the sticks of tobacco in the barn to cook and cure. This could take from two to three hours.

The rest of the day was spent hoeing weeds out of the cotton field, chasing hogs that escaped their lot and mending the fence where they escaped, or taking cured tobacco off the hanging stick and packing it in burlap sheets to ship to the market. Of course, there were always the various odds and end chores that constantly popped up without warning, and most of the time, I would have to stop what I was doing to handle those things before I could continue the main chores of the day!

When Ma-ma came home from work, she would wash clothes, clean and straighten up the house, and prepare supper, having it ready about 6:00 p.m. When Uncle Jim came home, he'd usually check on me to see if I needed assistance with anything and we would go over what had been accomplished that day, plus what he wanted me to do the next day after finishing my work for our neighbor.

On Saturday mornings, Uncle Jim would pay the hands in town while Ma-ma bought groceries, and I would finish any leftover chores from that week. In the afternoon, I would go fishing at Dead River or our pond. Saturday nights I would go to Vidalia with several of the fellows that worked for us gathering tobacco. Like most of the other kids our age, we would ride up and down the main drag and in and out of the local drive-in restaurant, talking with the girls we would meet. Sundays I slept late and after dinner went to play baseball in the afternoon with the local team from Uvalda made up of former college and high school players in the community.

Several weeks before my summer stay was over, they brought Pa-pa home from the hospital. His case had been so bad they had to give him several shock treatments. He basically did not remember anyone or anything. That day at the dinner table, Daddy, Uncle Jim, and Ma-ma were talking to him and answering his questions about what had happened to him while they had me wait in the other room. When they finally called me into the kitchen, Uncle Jim started to introduce me to Pa-pa when my grandfather suddenly spoke out, saying, "I know who this fellow is. He's the one who's been taking care of my farm while I have been sick." He smiled at me and then stuck out his hand to shake mine, and as I shook his hand, all I could say was, "Yes, sir." With that, we all sat down and ate dinner.

Throughout the summer and the years since, I have often considered the education I received whenever I was on my grandparents' farm. The education we obtain in school is primarily theoretical with some exercises to put theory into positive use. However, the early education I received in Georgia was about the real world we live in. On the surface, it looks one way, but underneath, things are totally different! It's full of the debris and poisons of this world, and the original Creator is the only person who eventually can and will make things right!

Chapter 8

Non-Thirst-Quenching Water Part 1

Whoever drinks of this water will thirst again.

—John 4:13

In my early teens, the rowdy-roaming bug bit me, and my focus was on going and doing, especially without my parents. While this is pretty normal for most guys entering their teens, mine also had to do with my daddy's drinking. When he came home after stopping for a few beers or drinks, he seemed to wear his feelings on his shoulders and the slightest problem at home could make him angry. That meant Mama, Michael, and I had to walk on eggshells the rest of the evening. As time went on, this became more of the norm, and I tried to stay away from the house more and more. This only aggravated Daddy more, and he would often ask me, "Son, why do you always want to go to other kids' houses or go off with other families? Why do you have to go somewhere all the time? You never want to stay home!"

Well, most of the time when he asked those questions, he was drinking and in his mood, so I never got the nerve up to answer his questions honestly. I would simply make up some excuse by trying to tie my desire to a church event or being invited by a friend's parents to go with them somewhere.

By the time I was thirteen, I was venturing beyond the boundaries of good behavior on a daily routine. The more I got away with, the greater my thirst for more, and it did not matter what it involved. I quickly developed a vocabulary that would make the "saltiest sailor" blush! Fighting, lying, stealing, and vandalizing to me were like athletic sports were for others. But worse than all this, I seemed to have a natural ability to plan and execute these activities while making most people think I was a nice, polite youngster.

In seventh grade, I fell head over heels for a pretty girl named Linda Caulder. A remnant of Native American blood gave her a dark suntan-like complexion with almost black hair and large dark brown doe eyes. After several weeks of getting friendly at school, she began giving me all the attention I had ever dreamed about having from a girlfriend. She was crazy about me, and even though I thought I knew it then, it would be many years later until I really knew how much.

Linda came from a lower-middle-class family in Columbia. Her mother was a small, sweet, good wife and mother to Linda and her sister, Sherry, while their father was a tall, wiry, hardworking man employed by the Pepsi Cola Company as a route salesman. He was where the Native American genes game from. All his facial features were handsome and well-sculpted. Just like Linda, his hair and skin tone were dark.

The main issue our families had in common was alcohol. Linda's mother only drank a little, but when she did, a blood defect caused that little amount to go to her head, causing her to lose her good nature. Mr. Caulder was said to be a quarter Indian and a heavy drinker on the weekends. His weekend binges would oftentimes result in bad arguments with Mrs. Caulder and some physical abuse.

In the summer between our seventh and eighth grades, Mrs. Caulder was given a lot at Lake Murray, about twenty-five miles northwest of Columbia, and they moved there. This was a terrible situation for Linda and me because neither of us was old enough to legally drive so all we could do was write letters and, every once in a while, call each other on the telephone.

That was the first summer I went to the farm in Georgia, so the initial excitement helped to occupy my mind for a while, but when I returned to South Carolina, I could not stop thinking about Linda day and night!

About two weeks before school started, a girlfriend of Linda's invited her to come spend a week at her house, so Linda let me know via mail, and that gave us the opportunity to visit a lot. During that time, Linda said her dad was looking to move back to Columbia because of the extra driving time and expense for her dad each work day. We were both excited and anxiously waiting for that to happen!

Several weeks went by, and one morning, as I sat down at the table for breakfast, Mama asked me what Linda's full name was. I told her, and then Daddy handed me his newspaper, pointing to a short article that told about a man with the last name of Caulder, who was living at Lake Murray and he and his wife were in a domestic quarrel over the weekend and had been tragically shot and killed by his wife.

As I read the article, my heart seemed as if it would burst out of my chest, and my mind was flooded with fear and confusion! I did not know what to say or do! Extremely perplexed, I had no idea how I was going to reach Linda to see if she was all right! But after a few days, I was able to speak with her by telephone, and she told me that she, her mother, and sister were moving back to Columbia, and she would be returning to school the next week.

Some months passed, and eventually, a grand jury released her mother due to self-defense. After the case concluded, Mrs. Caulder and her daughters were virtually shunned by her husband's people and many of their former friends. I would soon begin seeing that Linda and her mother were having a terrible time emotionally. Linda was able to work through her difficulties, but her mother would bear a wound that would never heal completely. And trouble from this situation found me too. Immediately, my parents put a lot of pressure on me to find another girlfriend. I now see they were only trying to get me to do what they thought was in my best interest at the time. They could not understand why I needed to associate with a girl who came from such a troubled family. Both of them thought there must surely be many other girls whom I could choose as my girlfriend, but the more pressure they placed on me, the more determined I became to stay with Linda!

Our relationship continued for most of our time through both middle and high school. While we did stay together, we fussed a lot, and it was usually my fault. I became a more demanding person, never having enough of her affirmation and attention. I needed to be with her and away from Daddy as much as possible.

Of course, through all those years, there were times when my demands and our arguments were so bad that we would break up temporarily. Though other girls liked me, I usually found it difficult to be with anyone else. But there were several times when each of us would get to the point where we would start looking in other directions when we split up. After a few days of that, one or both of us would get jealous and send messengers to relay our desire to get back together. By the time we reached the eleventh grade, if we broke up and I tried to get a date with someone else, they would just turn and walk away, saying they knew we were supposed to be together and they did not want to get in the middle.

On the single occasion that we broke up for almost three weeks, Linda acted like she could not stand the ground I walked on, so I got interested in dating this really sweet girl that supposedly liked me a lot. We spent time at lunch and in between classes until I asked her out. She said I would have to come and meet her parents and ask permission for her to date me. So I did! They liked me (not really knowing me) and gave me permission to take her to a movie. We had such a nice time, and the next week I asked her to wear my ring, and she did. Well, all of a sudden, from out of nowhere, a friend comes to me wanting to set up a meeting between Linda and me after school. I consented, and Linda started crying, saying she had made a huge mistake and wanted us to get back together!

Wow! I could not believe it! And I could not say no. I truly hated to break up with that other sweet girl, but she took it really well, telling me that she figured Linda and I would get back together, but she wanted to at least give us a try.

Linda and I stayed together for the remainder of high school. In fact, during all our school years together, I never dated more than five or six different girls, which included the ones in Georgia. Of course, that was the main complaint my parents hammered me with. They were always asking me, "How do you know you like or love her? You haven't given yourself a chance to truly find out who is right for you. You need to be free, not tied down at such a young age!" On and on it went, but the more they hammered, the tighter my grip became on Linda, and the more I thirsted for this life's water. I could not drink enough to quench my thirst.

Chapter 9

Non-Thirst-Quenching Water Part 2

Whoever drinks of this water will thirst again.

—John 4:13

During the early years of middle school and my participation in school athletics, I wanted nothing to do with alcohol. Eventually though, because of the evaporating relationship between Daddy and me and the increasing amount of peer pressure, by the eleventh grade, I was doing some heavy drinking. A number of friends were participating in the use of various drugs, but not me! I would drink most anything, but I would not touch the drugs because I was not going to take the chance of going to jail and having a drug charge on my record for the rest of my life. I simply drank my booze and fell deeper and deeper into its clutches.

Most mornings in our junior year, I would ride with Linda to school since she had her own car. She had an eight o'clock class, but I did not. So she would leave her keys and several dollars with me in case I wanted to buy some breakfast. However, I would take a couple of friends to the grocery store, and with a false ID, we would buy a six-pack of beer. We were so bored with life we needed to get a buzz to face the school day. Often, I attended some classes "as high as a kite." I joined every off-campus activity or field trip the high school sponsored so I could miss some classes and drink as we traveled.

36

It was at this time where the relationship between Daddy and I became totally severed! He now drank more than he ever had, and most of it was liquor. The more he drank, the more agitated and authoritative he would be with me. I did not know why at the time, but Daddy could not understand why I hated living at home. In his efforts to "keep me off the streets," he loved to give me afternoon chores that would take a lot of time when I was not working my part-time job. Then when he would come home, he would put on his inspection hat and, like my future Marine Corps drill instructor, would never be satisfied with any of my results! He would then start some petty argument with me, and I could see how it affected Mama and Michael. He made me miserable, and I was determined that as soon as I graduated, I was leaving!

Being physically larger now, I was feeling my oats more, and when he started in on me, I would not just listen, but now I would argue back, demonstrating my own anger and frustration. I knew that before much longer, if things did not get any better, I was going to bust! And I did!

Since alcohol had become so strong in my own life, I began staying out all night, usually spending the night with several friends whose parents did not keep close tabs on them. As a result of my being gone more, Daddy decided to have me do some painting on the front porch and carport railings, which was a time-consuming project. He said I was to daily paint for several hours, and then if my homework was done and I did not have any other chores to finish, I could then have my free time.

While painting one afternoon, my good friend David Yates came over, and we talked while I worked. Extremely passive in nature, he had a tremendous "gift of gab" and would become my best friend. We would experience many good and bad times together, too numerous to count. Meeting in the seventh grade, we have laughed and cried, loved and fought, helped and hurt each other more than I can recall. I became his only brother while he became closer to me than any of my three brothers.

As we talked, I worked less and less so that David was still there when Daddy came in from work. When he stepped out of the car, he paused and looked at us and fired off a wisecrack, making David so uncomfortable that he stood up and started to leave. I told him to wait because I would be through in a few minutes and we would leave together.

As I was finishing my required work time, Daddy came outside after changing his clothes and having several stiff drinks, starting his usual inspection routine. He was boiling over with anger, verbally chewing me out, challenging and threatening me! Embarrassing David and me, he then told David he would have to leave because he was distracting me from my work and I still had to paint for another hour.

By this time, I had reached my limit and made up my mind that I was not going to take anymore without standing up for myself! I was sick and tired of the continual animosity between us and as far as I was concerned, Daddy was an inconsiderate drunk, and I had no respect left for him! I began my combatant verbal response, which only made matters worse, and I realized there was no use continuing to argue, so I threw down my paintbrush and started to walk away with David when, about that same time, Linda came pulling into the driveway to take me for a ride. Daddy started hollering at me, and Mama came out to see what all the commotion was about when Daddy picked up the yard hose and started whipping me with it, saying that he would "show me once and for all who the boss was!"

It was a terrible situation! We started fist-fighting in the front yard and rolling in the grass! Mama was crying while trying to get us to listen to reason, but Daddy would not stop, so I would not stop until I beat him down to the ground. All the sixteen years of frustration I had stored up inside me had erupted, and I proceeded to dump the whole load of fury on my father!

David and Mama pulled me off Daddy, and when he stood up and gained his breath, he verbally commanded me from the house! I was to take my clothes and leave! If I came around while he was there, he said he would call the police and have me locked up! He yelled, "Since you cannot live by the rules here, you're not living here anymore!"

Deep down inside, I knew I was wrong. My whole attitude was wrong! But I felt like Daddy's mind and heart had become so dulled by alcohol, that he did not deserve for me to honor or respect him anymore. I thought I was a man and was tired of being treated like I was a child. At that point in my life, I hated my father. I left home that day and did not speak to Daddy for the next year. However, the truth of the matter was, after all these years, I had become just like the person I did not want to be like! I simply could not see it yet!

We left Mama and Daddy's, and Linda took us to David's house. His parents were home, so we went in and had a heart-to-heart talk about what had happened at my house. David's dad was also named David, but everyone knew him as Red. He loved to cut the fool, and it was plain that David got his "gift of gab" from his dad who was a used car salesman at one of the larger dealerships in Columbia, and I took to him right away. Red said that I was welcome to move in with them. He would not charge me rent or for meals, but there were a few basic rules I had to live by if I stayed. He would always treat me "fair and square" but would not tolerate any bad manners, especially to women. All of us would share the chores with no argument about what was to be done, and his wife, Judy, would delegate those. Finally, there could be no alcohol in his home, so if I was out drinking, I was not to come home until I was totally sober. He then told me about his history with alcohol and how he had to overcome it to get where he was in life, and he would never allow it, or those who used it, to jeopardize his family's welfare anymore! I agreed because I felt like I was being treated fairly, as an adult and not unfairly by someone who was drinking, trying to overpower me with their authority. I had no way of knowing at the time that some twenty years later, this man would be used to save my life.

As wrong as Daddy had been in the abuse of alcohol and the way he related to our family, I had been just as wrong in my rebellion and raising my hand against him. He did not see me as a young man mature enough to make most of my own decisions concerning my future, and because we had not built a healthy father-son relationship, I could not see him as someone I could trust to give me counsel when it was needed.

When Linda and I were married in October following our graduation from high school, it was my father's youngest brother, Jim

Paul, who came and stood with me. Daddy's absence on the most important day of my life, at that point, as well as my high school graduation, were just other examples of his nonacceptance and lack of affirmation for me and my plans in life. It left a great void, and our lengthy estrangement only added to that void. Yet in the counseling and encouragement from Mama, Granny Keene, Linda, and others, I came to understand they were right. So one evening, I went to their home and approached Daddy, admitting my wrong, asking for his forgiveness, and if we could work things out between us.

He said, "Okay," and we made our peace.

Those were some extremely emotional times for me because I knew at that point in my life, I did love my father! I loved him deeply! I wished all the years when so much hurt and pain was present that it had been different. Oh, we did have some good times together, and I'm grateful that we did, but I wish there had been many more.

I do not believe most parents intend to neglect their families. Yet it is a situation that so many of us seem to get caught up in. Parents are busy trying to earn an adequate living and what little free time they have gets divided with some going to the family and the rest going to self. Then as time moves on, the needs and pressures of family and job build with the expectations of both increasing, consuming more and more energy and time. More energy can be found at times, but there is no more time to be found in each day, so the tug of war begins between family time and personal time. Usually, the family has to give in.

While it was a wonderful event when Daddy and I made our peace with each other, it did not change my course on the polluted river of this life, and I continued drinking its water, never quenching my thirst.

Chapter 10

Uncle Sam

Who has woe? Who has sorrow? Who has contentions?
Who has complaints? Who has wounds without cause?
Who has redness of eyes? Those who linger long at the
wine, those who go in search of mixed wine.

—Proverbs 23:29–30

Linda and I graduated from high school in May 1970, and I then took a summer vacation, via my motorcycle, down through Georgia and Florida, from one relative's home after another. By this time, Mama and Linda really cared for each other and tried to go on vacation with me but could never catch up with me as I stayed several days ahead of them the whole way (due to timely intelligence from my cousins).

In September, I would turn eighteen years old and would no longer need my parents' permission to get married. On the other hand, Linda would not be eighteen until that October, but I could not wait! So with her mother's permission, we were married, beginning our life together, after being together emotionally since the seventh grade.

I thought married life would be a breeze, compared to my school years at home; however, I soon found out it was extremely tough! I thought I had everything figured out! The husband was the boss! He worked a job and handled the money, and maybe the wife worked a job outside the home too. But even if she did, she was to still do the cooking, cleaning, and washing. She was to give most of the affection and understanding because of all the responsibilities the husband had on his shoulders. She was to bare and take care of the children while always looking beautiful and feeling good! On the surface, that was the kind of married life I saw in my home, in the extended Poole family, and in the families of quite a few friends. Surely it was supposed to be that way for me too! Honestly, Linda made a courageous effort to do all those things and more, but my dream world did not last.

Married life for me became miserable. Many years later, I came to know it had become miserable for Linda too. But at that time, I could only feel my misery. Happiness and satisfaction always seemed to elude me, and my drinking continued.

In the eleventh grade, I started experiencing excruciating pain in my hips and lower spine. While living at home, Daddy would not let me go to the doctor. Before I could take that step, I was required to apply the all-purpose Poole family remedy—"soak it!" That and extra homework assignments were supposed to cure most anything that would keep me out of school. However, now being married and working a job with health insurance, I decided to seek a diagnosis and remedy. But my doctors were unable to find what was wrong, and frustration began setting in, and with both the frequency and intensity of the pain increasing, I resorted to more alcohol use. Of course, when I had pain medication, I would abuse it by drinking with it to give me some added relief, but that was only temporary, and my situation worsened. It was many years before I received a correct diagnosis.

After being married and working a year, I was faced with the draft into Uncle Sam's military service. The new National Lottery assigned my birth date as number six out of three hundred and sixty-five days, so I was sure to be drafted, and very soon! This was during the turbulent years of the Vietnam War, and many in their late teens and early twenties were dodging the draft. At first, I decided to do the same and move to Canada, but after talking over the situation with Linda and several good friends, I changed my mind. I concluded the consequences of losing my citizenship and possibly never being able to return home or to my beloved Georgia was too great a price to pay! And besides, I might not be classified as fit for service due to the problem in my back and hips.

I then turned to Mama's youngest brother, Jimmy Keene, and he convinced me the best thing for me to do was to volunteer, and that might get me a choice of jobs and/or duty station. I followed his advice and was able to obtain just a two-year enlistment in the United States Marine Corps but could not negotiate a choice of duties or duty stations. At that time, the Marines were the only branch of service offering a two-year enlistment. Uncle Jimmy had served in the Marine Corps, along with several other extended family members, so I decided that if I had to go in the service, it might as well be the toughest branch in the country.

Growing up, I would fight at "the drop of a hat!"[35] If someone was being bullied or ganged up on, I was glad to jump in and offer my services. I did not care how old or big the others were. I was ready and willing to make them pay a good price for their action! Thus, to me, the Marine Corps was the right place for me to serve, standing up to the world's bullies.

For basic training, I was sent to Parris Island, South Carolina (PI), 120 miles from home. Since that time, I have often said that no matter how bad I disliked someone, I would not wish that experience on another human being. To say "It was tough!" would be an understatement! Boot camp,[36] as it is called, was extremely tough, and the drill instructors (DIs) played no favorites. They referred to me as a Fat Body[37] because, during my senior year, I had gained 55 pounds from drinking, and most of it was fat. I had to quit participating in sports because of the weight and my back pain. When those DIs got a hold of me in that hot, steamy South Carolina coastal atmosphere, I thought they would kill me before I could get out of there! Thirteen weeks later, I had made it! When I arrived at PI, I weighed 205 pounds, and I graduated from boot camp as a "lean, mean, fighting machine,"[38] weighing 165 pounds "soaking wet!"[39] I was in the best shape of my life with my body being as hard as a rock and my mind knowing that nobody could beat me! That was the good news; however, the bad news was that I had not had a drink in three months, and on my Christmas leave, I was planning to catch up!

I went home for two weeks' leave, and in several days, I was arrested for "drunk and disorderly conduct." When that policeman approached my group of friends, he could see I was drunk, and he tried so hard to give this arrogant nineteen-year-old boy a chance to calm down, but I had to force his hand by continuing to curse, and he put the handcuffs on me and took me to jail. We arrived, and they finished booking me. I showed them just how tough a Marine I was—I broke down and started crying because they were going to lock me up. I think I sobered up then because I got so embarrassed over how my immaturity had gotten the best of me in this public situation. The police felt so sorry for me they did not lock me up. I had to stay all night in their office, and they let me leave the next morning when a friend came to pay my fine and take me home.

That incident was indicative of how my life went in the Marine Corps. For the next year and a half, I drank like there was no tomorrow while Linda loved me, took care of me, and tried to advise me, but I could not accept life that way. Eventually, Linda, friends, and even drinking buddies began to tell me of bizarre incidents that were taking place while I was drinking, and I was instigating them. Yet I would not remember anything about the incidents.

Confronting me, they would ask, "Do you remember doing this or that?"

When I said no, they wondered if I was joking while I usually thought they were joking with me. But after these incidents continued to happen and I saw the seriousness in their questions, I realized it was not a joke or some ploy to get me to stop drinking. These experiences were actually happening, and the blackouts were happening more often because when I was not on duty, I was drinking.

During my last eighteen months in the corps, due to my administrative clerk classification, I served as the base chaplain's assistant, and I could never adjust to that duty. Here I was supposed to be this rough, tough Marine, yet the corps (pronounced "core") had me answering telephones, dealing with people who were hurting, and setting up the chapels for the different religious services held each week. For the most part, it was a religious atmosphere every day. I did not have an interest in this type of work, but I had to do it.

My best drinking buddy was my sergeant, Mack Green, who was there on temporary duty. At that time, Mack was my hero! He had a chest full of ribbons and medals for serving three tours of duty in Vietnam and was trying to go back for a fourth tour before the war ended. Mack did not spend much time at home because he had a broken marriage, so we were usually out drinking when off duty.

One day, Mack confronted me about some bizarre things that had been happening when were out together drinking. He said, "I'm telling you as your sergeant and friend, I want you to talk to someone about these problems. I want you to see a doctor!"

I told him I did not want to see a doctor because the first thing he would tell me to do would be to see a shrink, and when the corps hears that I'm seeing a shrink, they will toss me out on my ear! I certainly did not want that after all I had been through to become a Marine! So Mack agreed for me to see a chaplain after he talked to the chaplain first.

The chaplain agreed to speak with me in confidence, and he was very compassionate and understanding, but he leveled with me, saying, "Tommy, you need to see a psychiatrist because you are dealing with more than an alcohol problem. The drinking, to the point of this strange behavior and blackouts, is happening because of a deeper problem. It will take some time in counseling to help you discover what this is." He went on, "I don't want to send you to a military psychiatrist since I know you are ending your enlistment soon. I'm afraid if I do, the Marines will simply discharge you early, and I can't be sure about the terms of that discharge. You have an excellent record, and I want to keep that intact. There is a special counseling program that allows me to send you to a private civilian counselor, and there will be no cost for you and total confidentiality between you, me, and the counselor, but you must attend a minimum of three sessions and then report back to me for his recommendations. Go home and talk this over with Linda and see if it is agreeable with her, then let me know tomorrow and we will go from there."

Linda happily agreed, and the chaplain made us an appointment for that afternoon. After Linda told the counselor some of the things that had been going on, I shared with him incidents others had related to me. We completed the three appointments, and the chaplain gave us the counselor's assessment. It was the same as what the chaplain had told me. The counselor said we needed time to get to the real problem, so we started with two sessions per week. Some were joint sessions, and others were individual. We lived off base, in town, and his office was convenient to our apartment, just a block away.

Four weeks later, he gave us his first evaluation and was straight to the point. "Tommy, you are on the verge of a nervous breakdown. Your excessive drinking causes these blackouts, and when that happens, you seem to lose all control. You lose your understanding of what is right and wrong, and losing this ability to reason is what allows these incidents to happen." He continued, "I want you to stop drinking for the remainder of the time that we work together so I can evaluate you more thoroughly without alcohol in your body between sessions. I cannot follow you to make sure that you do not drink, so do you think you can stop without any problems? I believe we can get to the root of your problem, but you will have to cooperate over the next five or six weeks. Can and will you do this?"

I agreed, and I knew Linda and Mack would support me because they were seriously concerned, and so was I after hearing about some of the things I had been doing.

When the six weeks had passed, there had been no blackouts or incidents. I was then facing a reenlistment appointment with my company commanding officer (CO), and the counselor was aware because I had told him several weeks before, wondering whether or not I might be able to reenlist. When we came in for his final evaluation, he said, "As your counselor, I am first asking you to discontinue using alcohol from now on. Second, I'm recommending that you leave the Marine Corps when your enlistment is finished or change your military job. There is an emotional conflict in your mind from being a Marine and a chaplain's assistant. You find yourself in constant turmoil trying to live up to the perception of these totally different professions, and you drink more and more in an attempt to handle the turmoil, as well as your back pain. Since you were already a heavy drinker before becoming a Marine, the additional emotional stress causes you to lean even more on an alcohol remedy, but as we now know, it's only making your problems worse. By drinking yourself into oblivion, you lose your established self-control, and then the bottled-up emotional frustrations you have inside find their way to the surface, coming out in more violent ways. Thank goodness, they have not manifested into violence on individuals yet, but they will! The only way to stop this from happening before it starts is to stop pouring fuel on the fire and put the fire out! The alcohol is the fuel, and the fire is the turmoil that comes from trying to function in two opposing livelihoods!"

I did not want to stop drinking, at least, permanently. In fact, I had still been drinking most of the time he was working with me but not nearly as much as before. I now knew that I did not want to stay in the corps because I was unable to handle the current situation, and my CO said the corps needed me to stay in my current duty assignment. I had no room for God in my life, so I did not want to take the chance of being a chaplain's assistant any longer by reenlisting! My life was only manifesting itself as a dying river that was continually filling up with the decay of sin, but my finger of blame was only pointing at Uncle Sam and the military assignment he had me stuck in!

Chapter 11

You Are What You Drink

*How much less man, who is abominable and
filthy, who drinks iniquity like water?*

—Job 15:16

On the day of my release from active duty in the Marine Corps, after leaving the base at 10:00 a.m., my first stop was the liquor store. About forty minutes up the road, just outside the small town of Branchville, South Carolina, I pulled off the highway onto a dirt road into the forest to mix my third drink. Pulling back out on the highway, I went around the next curve that brought me to a long straightaway of about three quarters of a mile. As I looked down the road, I could see several cars, the tail lights of one in my lane, and what appeared to be the front end of the other in the oncoming lane. Reaching about the half-mile point, I could tell the cars were stopped, and after another one hundred yards, I could see a South Carolina Highway Patrolman who appeared to be checking driver's license and vehicle registrations. Of course, the first thought I had was turning around, but there was nowhere to turn around, and in that next moment, he turned and looked straight at me, so if there had been somewhere to turn around, he already had a good look at my car!

Rolling to a stop behind the car in front of me, panic struck, and I threw the whole sixteen-ounce drink up under my seat, and at least half of it started flowing back out on my floor mat, under

48

my feet. I figured I was thirty seconds from being arrested for DUI (driving under the Influence) and going to jail!

I rolled down my two front windows, hoping to get rid of enough of the smell to get by the patrolman, but I knew that was probably not going to be the case, so I pulled out my driver's license, vehicle registration, and insurance card as he stepped to my window and greeted me. It seemed like he stood there fifteen minutes before speaking again, and when he did speak, seeing my uniform, he asked if I was on leave, and I said, "No, sir. I was released from active duty this morning, and I am on my way home to Columbia."

He went back to his car, talked on the radio for several minutes, and then returned to my car when he asked, "I smell alcohol in your car. Have you been drinking?"

I answered, "Yes, sir, I have, and when I came around that last curve and saw you standing here, I was sure startled and spilled my drink on the floor beneath me."

He looked behind me to see two more cars coming to a stop and said, "Corporal Poole, please pull your vehicle to the right side of the road and turn your engine off, and I'll be with you shortly." So I did, and after he finished with those vehicles, he came back to my car and asked, "Corporal, I really don't want to take you to jail on this special day, so if I let you go, will you promise me to stop drinking until you get home and be extremely careful the rest of your trip?"

I responded, "Yes, sir, I will!"

Handing my license, registration, and insurance cards back, he said, "Have a safe trip."

Five minutes later, I was coming into Branchville, and I could suddenly hear the train horn blowing as it was heading to cross the road in front of me when, for some strange reason, still not known to me today, I decided not to wait for the train to finish crossing the highway but to beat the train to the crossroad! I floored the accelerator, and without what surely was an angel pushing my car across the track, I would be dead or seriously injured!

Once I realized the train had not hit me, I pulled off the road and got out of the car, thinking I was going to be sick. With the torrential flow of adrenaline coursing through my body, I was trembling beyond control, so I just stood there a few minutes until I could get myself back together and then proceeded on home without another drink, extremely happy to be alive!

As time and my drinking continued, I bounced from one job to another, always trying to find positions that would allow me to keep on drinking—construction, tending bar, cooking in a restaurant, and clerking in the family-owned and operated discount beer and wine store. At times, it seemed like alcohol helped me to get the attention of those I needed to impress to gain a particular job, often in the context of having fun. However, most of the other times, the attention I gained was bad: arguments, fights, causing property damage, and especially when going home to Linda and our baby girl, Brenda, after a Friday or Saturday night of partying or gambling away the week's pay.

Looking back at her efforts many years later, I would see that Linda was very patient with me through our young life together, but at the time, I could not give her that credit. This is because when you are living every day as I did, you see yourself as the one who is right while everyone else who tries to help you see your wrongs, and change is your problem. Yet Linda kept on taking whatever I gave, trying to be the kind of wife I wanted her to be. Oh, we did argue most of the time like cats and dogs, but it was usually me who started it. She would let situations go until she felt compelled to talk with me, and rather than cooperate, I would blow my stack and start the blame game as the way of redirecting the focus of the argument and getting it off me. It was always someone else's fault instead of me or my bottle!

During those days, I never realized what alcohol was doing to me and my family. Mentally, I constantly trained myself to be one step ahead of anyone who might try to talk constructively with me about my habit. Even while drinking, I could see their attempt coming on and interrupt or change the conversation or simply not listen. Should neither of these strategies work, I could always fall back on the blame game because I was never going to take the blame myself or let anyone blame my best friend, alcohol!

In those early years of our marriage, Linda was working as a rate clerk for an insurance company (USF&G), Brenda was in day care, and I attended school using my GI Bill education benefits. Friends jokingly referred to me as a professional student. I bounced from one college to another, changing majors three times. Beginning at the local tech school, I studied basic high school subjects to give me the foundation needed for college-level subjects that I did not get or had already forgotten from high school. From there, I moved on to college credit courses on the freshman level, taking just enough credit hours to draw a full-time monthly check. Whatever schedule or curriculum suited my schedule of personal pleasure was the one I adopted. Just as in high school, I was able to drink and attend class without any rebukes from my professors just as long as I did not call attention to myself or cause any problems. As long as I could maintain this lifestyle and not have many responsibilities, that was all I cared about!

Just like Dead River, my life had been filled with refuse and rubble, impure motives and unclean acts, with very little spiritual nourishment—no inflow of good water and no outflow of the bad. A dam of sin had, for the most part, cut off a continual, renewing supply of the lifegiving water. It has been in the Creator's plan for everyone, that this supply would always be available; however, my efforts to drink my fill have always been out of the wrong river! Over many visits, the desire grew within to one day live on this part of the watershed I had come to love. From a young boy to early adulthood, I found myself scheming and trying almost anything possible to place myself there—even running away once! Unbeknownst to me, I was actually seeking to fill my emptiness with the stagnant waters of a lifeless ditch! Little did I realize then how coming back there, along with most of the things that happened to me there, would eventually help me obtain a clearer picture of our God.

There is an old saying that has come back strong in these recent years where more widespread emphasis is being placed on good health and diet. It says, "You are what you eat." Well, back in those days for me, it could have been said "You are what you drink" because after all the buckets I had consumed of this life's water, it was never enough to quench my thirst or produce a healthy result.

Chapter 12

Foul Water Is Bitter

For the lips of an immoral woman drip honey, and her mouth is smoother than oil; but in the end she is bitter as wormwood, sharp as a two-edged sword. Her feet go down to death, her steps lay hold of hell (Sheol).

—Proverbs 5:3–5

Several years passed, and the relationship between Linda and me continued to go downhill. Linda was not the loving, kind, gentle wife she had been. I could no longer tell her what to do, and she was giving me an ever-increasing amount of rebuke about my drinking, staying out late, and lack of taking responsibility as a husband and father. A barrier was forming between us, and I knew our marriage was in serious trouble!

Her mother and stepfather, Wayne, were hearing more about our troubles from her, and he decided to try to help us out by offering me a business proposition. He owned an amusement machine business and had been looking for another location to put his machines in. He approached me after finding a small strip mall just outside one of the main gates to Fort Jackson US Army base in Columbia and wanted to open a restaurant and lounge there. He proposed that I train and work there for ninety days, and if we both were satisfied with the working relationship, he would take the steps to make it a permanent arrangement. That is, he would take me to the bank and sign the business over to me, paid in full, if I would sign a contract giving him 75 percent of the profit each week from the amusement machines. Should either one of us not be satisfied with the arrangement, we would go our separate ways, with no hard feelings.

As one can imagine, this opportunity was right up my alley! I was certain this situation was for me! I was going to have my own business, be my own boss, and make lots of money! And eventually, I would be able to afford a place of my own in Georgia, down on the river! I could already see that looming on the near horizon. So I went to work remodeling the building, and it was not long before we opened the Trading Post Restaurant and Pub. Things went well from the start, but it would not be long before I totally blew this opportunity.

As usual, I was drinking quite a bit, and since we were open late, I was coming home later and later until I started not coming home sometimes for several days. This was usually because my brother-in-law and several friends would go to other places, successful competition, to shop around for ideas to see what made them so successful. Alcohol, along with some new so-called friends, and my ever-increasing foolish attitude caused me to spend even less time at home, and when I did go home, it was always an argument.

On one of those occasions, we went to a new restaurant and bar that had only been open for several weeks because it was owned and operated by "The Fabulous Moollah"[40] (Lillian Ellison), the long-time Woman's World Wrestling Champion who was a native of the Columbia area. She was also the trainer and booking agent for about a dozen women wrestlers that rented houses from her and worked at the business in between matches. Lillian and some of her girls had charismatic personalities, and they knew how to use that to attract business.

One of those personalities was Mary Donna Alfonsi who wrestled under several ring names, but the most well-known was Donna Christantello.[41] She was ten years older than me and all her adult life was a woman of the entertainment world. She was also Moolah's right-hand woman who trained many of her wrestlers. Together with her longtime partner, Toni Rose, they were the Women's World Tag-team Champions for years. Donna was working as a waitress when we first met, and we seemed to hit it off right from the beginning, and I did not go home that night.

The next day, I could not help but think that she would be the solution to all my domestic problems, but instead, she was only the beginning of deeper troubles. I went back again to the restaurant and then to her place that night. The next day, I went home before Linda left for work and told her I was leaving her for someone else.

I barely knew this woman and was beginning to descend a long series of dangerous, worldly rapids; heartless decisions and irresponsible activities brought me into currents too strong for me to fight! And it would not be long before I was sinking into the murkiness of this dead river, fast becoming engulfed in its depth. Donna was appealing to me because of her understanding attitude and her personal feelings about alcohol. She drank and thought it was wrong for a woman to tell her husband or boyfriend that he should not drink. For that, she had my vote! It was my heavy dependence on alcohol that revealed to those around me how numb to the real world I had become and anyone who would allow me to drink was definitely an ally!

I had absolutely crushed my dear wife! As I look back on that day, I will never forget the hurt on her face as I told her of my plans and drove off down the street. It was one of the cruelest, terrible things I have ever done to someone I love. I came to find out in later years that she went through some horrible, emotional times, and a bitter war developed between us, not only about our failed marriage but about Brenda and the child support and visitation rights I would struggle with.

Of course, when I left Linda and Brenda and refused to return, Wayne voided our agreement concerning the Trading Post. He gave me a month's severance pay, and I gave him my checkbook and keys. Several days later, I was hired by Lillian to run her restaurant and bar since I had the experience and she and the other girls traveled so much.

My health had already begun to decline when I severely aggravated the condition in my back. I was admitted to the hospital for a little while as Linda's and my divorce was pending. It seemed one problem after another kept piling on until it finally came to the point where I had to do something! I felt like everyone, except for Donna, was trying to put all the blame on me, and I was certainly not ready to accept any blame.

The emotional pressure grew until several months later, in drunken blindness, I called Linda and some of her family, telling them I was sick and tired of their control over my life and I was on my way to kill them! I had had enough of their harassments and attempts to punish me, especially using my visitation rights and child support against me. The whole divorce situation had been ugly and very bitter, and I had in my mind that day to put an end to all these problems! I was so drunk I took a friend's borrowed shotgun from my house and left heading through woods to hike the five miles to where Linda and her family had gathered. Somewhere along the trail, I stopped to rest and get my bearings and must have passed out. When I came to, the shotgun was gone (I even went back the next day when I was sober, but it was not there), and it was almost dark. I was feeling pretty sick on my stomach, so I made my way back to the house. Donna was home from work, so I began telling her what had happened. An argument developed, and the situation became quite nasty.

Over the next few months, our relationship was up and down, but we did become closer for a while after my divorce went through, and we got married. It was then we began really trying to settle down to make a life for ourselves. Working for Moolah met my basic financial needs, and things coasted along okay for a while until she and I had a huge falling out. After much discussion, I was able to talk Donna into leaving wrestling and Moolah for a clean, new start. Lillian's emotional makeup was such that she had to control her girls' lives, and since Donna and I were now married, her control was constantly interfering in our personal life. I could not deal with it, and it was too difficult for Donna to juggle the constant friction of control on both sides. So Donna took a dining room supervisor's position at Shoney's where she had worked off and on for years in between matches before Lillian opened her restaurant. The management loved Donna's work and was elated for her to come back on a full-time basis. That gave me the golden opportunity to go back to college. We bought a small house on my guaranteed Veterans Loan, and for the next two years, things went well except for the usual problem—my increased consumption of alcohol. Our relationship eventually hit the turbulent waters of a storm. Working regular hours now, Donna drank less, whereas school allowed me to drink more, and our relationship turned bitter.

Chapter 13

A Friendly Voice Calls

A friend loves at all times, and a brother is born for adversity.

—Proverbs 17:17

It was a hot, steamy Saturday morning in late August, and I was sitting in our living room watching television nursing my bottle of vodka while Donna was at work. With a good buzz on, I had already reached my goal for the day with no other constructive plans, and somewhere in my twisted, distorted thoughts, I was reflecting back on my life as it had been before meeting Donna and the mistakes I had made along the way—primarily how I had allowed alcohol to tear apart my life with Linda and Brenda.

As my thoughts reached back to my original family, the telephone rang. Even in my present state of inebriation, I recognized the voice immediately! It was a voice I had not heard for a number of years, not since I was released from the Marine Corps in 1973. She loudly proclaimed, "Hey, Poole! What is the old 'jarhead' doing these days?"[42]

The woman on the other end was Brenda Green, the ex-wife of my sergeant and drinking buddy from the chaplain's office at PI. She lived in Richmond, Virginia, and when I was discharged from the corps, Linda and I went up there to visit her, hoping to help mend her and Mack's marriage. We remained really close friends with her during those first few years after leaving the military, but after her and Mack's divorce, Brenda's problems and our problems consumed our lives and we did not stay close. After my and Linda's divorce, she and Linda managed to occasionally call each other. Now Brenda Green wanted to see Linda and our daughter, who was named after her, and while in Columbia, she wanted to see me as well.

Brenda had previously explained to Linda that even though there had been a lot of water under the bridge between us, she understood and respected Linda's feelings about not wanting to have anything to do with me. However, she told Linda while she was in town, she intended to call me and make an attempt to visit with me to say hello and reminisce about the old days at Parris Island. She was one of those people you could not seem to tell her no, so Linda agreed for Brenda to call me and visit if it worked out that way.

Then abruptly during her call, Brenda said she would like for the three of us to get together, and she suggested we might share a meal or a drink and visit. I could just imagine what Linda was thinking when that suggestion was made. I wanted to but was hesitant with my answer. I was paranoid about meeting with Linda because, through the years, she had become angry and vindictive toward me about my lack of child support and the visitation issue, especially since I had threatened the lives of her and her family.

I told Brenda about my apprehension and that I was not sure if I could emotionally deal with Linda or her with me, especially since I had to have a drink in me to function in those days. Brenda assured me she did not want to drag me into any type of confrontational circumstance and added, "If Linda is not for it, you and I will get together!" Brenda said, "Hang on," and covering up the mouthpiece of the telephone, I heard their two voices raised, and then she uncovered mouthpiece and added, "She's coming if I have to drag her there!" Finally, I agreed to meet them and told them where.

We met at a nice restaurant and lounge at the mall close to my house. I arrived early to get my courage up, and with the second drink about halfway down, Brenda and Linda arrived. Though Brenda could be demanding, when she wanted to, she could have such a pleasant personality. She seemed to know how to make the situation comfortable between us right off the bat.

The early evening passed and was very pleasant with reminisc-ing. A few drinks, along with Brenda carefully diffusing any tense moments that arose, helped the evening along more than I realized at the time. We enjoyed supper together, and Brenda wanted to go dancing. I think it really stunned Linda from the look on her face, and I know it took me totally by surprise, but after some of Brenda's diplomatic persuasion, we finally agreed to go for a little while.

We went to a club, had several more drinks, and Brenda asked me to dance. While dancing, her scheme started to unfold to my thinking. She asked me about my marriage, and I answered enough for her to get the picture, and then she asked how I felt about Linda. I took the bait, and before I realized it, I was hooked. Brenda then asked me to do her a big favor. She wanted me to be a gentleman and ask Linda to dance and then we would go. I consented, not really expecting Linda to say yes, but she did. As we danced and talked, we both decided right there to get back together again. A few days later, her mission accomplished, Brenda Green left and went back to Virginia.

She met a very nice professional man, an attorney, and they were married. Through the years, we managed to talk occasionally on the telephone, but we never saw Brenda again. Troubled waters came roaring back into our lives a few years later, and we lost touch with Brenda. After trying to make contact, we found she had a stroke and died.

I did not realize it at the time she came to visit, but she had a mission in mind. That mission was to not only plant the seeds of Linda and me reuniting in marriage for the second time but to help cultivate them into a harvest. Many years later, thinking back on the situation, I could not help but wonder if the Lord specifically used Brenda in His search for Linda and me. Typically, as the waters of Dead River periodically do, some fresh water had flooded into my river of death, and life seemed very good for a while!

Chapter 14

Second Time Around

*When the gates of prison open, the path
ahead should lead to a better life.*

—George W. Bush[43]

How many times have I heard people confess they wished they had a second chance? Here was mine with my family: a second time around to change the course from my past life. Could it be done?

When we got back together, our daughter, Brenda, was eight years of age. At that point in her life, she had had very little contact with me since Linda and I had split up about five years earlier. Linda had been so upset and hurt by my leaving she and her attorney made it very difficult for me to see my daughter. Since we did not know each other very well, we had to start our relationship at the beginning. She knew my face as there were pictures around, especially at Mama and Daddy's, and she knew the man in those pictures was called her father, but she did not know me as a person.

Brenda had been accustomed to having virtually all her mother's spare time and attention, except when Linda was at work, but all of a sudden, she was sharing that time and attention with this stranger who was called Daddy. Her mother was giving me a lot more of the time Brenda was used to getting, and this was taking a large emotional toll on her.

Brenda stopped eating her meals, and as time went by, the situation grew worse. We tried all kinds of strategies to get her to eat—talking, coaxing, bargaining, begging, and various types of punishment were to no avail. Someone suggested we see a child psychologist, so we made an appointment, and Linda gave her enough of our family history for her to give us a diagnosis. The child was rebelling! She was not receiving all the attention she was accustomed to getting all her life. With me back in the picture, the amount of attention given to her by her mother had been so drastically cut that she was now willing to accept any kind of attention, be it good or bad. Thus, when we sit down to eat our meals, if she eats, she receives very little attention; however, if she does not eat, she is virtually the center of attention.

We were advised not to allow any snacks in between meals and to go ahead and prepare her plate as normal, but if she does not eat, do not say a word. Do not force her or punish her for not eating, simply let it go. We were to give this a little time, and she would naturally get hungry enough to eat. It was not long before Brenda decided she was going to eat her meals and we had no further problems in that area.

For approximately two and a half years, things went very well for us, primarily because I was not drinking as much, so Linda did not insist that I stop. I was back in college pursuing a business degree in accounting, looking forward to opening my own bookkeeping and tax preparation service. But after I had been in school another two years, my Veterans educational benefits were coming to an end. I transferred to Winthrop University because my brother, Danny, was attending there, playing baseball, and the school accepted all my credits in transfer. I took a double load my first semester there—twenty-six hours. It seemed all I did was go to class, study day and night, and drink, but my grades were good!

As I approached my last semester, I transferred to the University of South Carolina's School of Business to be at home with the family. The university audited my credits and accepted all. On my second day of class, I was called to the school of business office, and they informed me the school of business would not accept my upper-level courses and I would have to take them there if I was to graduate with their university degree.

There was no way I was going to repeat all those courses! I had a very respectable overall 3.57 grade point average with a 3.8 GPA in my accounting courses. So I walked out the door, never to return. A few days later, I found out from my first accounting professor, who was now teaching locally, that I could do bookkeeping and tax work without a degree. All I needed was an IRS Tax Preparation Number and I could go to work for myself. So that is exactly what I did, and after a year, I had built up a fair number of clients with promises from others to give me their business the next year.

My drinking had started to increase, and Linda's and my marriage was back down to mediocre at best, but as long as I was working with some income, things were okay. Yet with the least amount of slackness on my part, our relationship grew worse.

One day, I was approached by a friend who wanted me to handle his income taxes, business books, and family finances; however, he had an unusual profession. He was a bookmaker or "bookie" in the common vernacular. Although bookmaking was legal in some states, it was illegal in South Carolina. He did, however, have a federal gambling license, so as far as the federal government was concerned, he could take bets and or wager himself, so long as he filed his tax returns and paid taxes on his earnings.

Again, I spoke with a previous professor of mine and found out that as long as I kept the books and handled his taxes correctly and honestly, I had nothing to worry about since what I was doing was according to the law. So I accepted the bookmaker as a client and went to work. He paid me a flat weekly salary and a percentage of any winnings that turned out usually to be a good pay day. Through the football season, his business increased so much that he needed me just to handle the tallying of all the wagers he accepted minute by minute, day by day, each Saturday through Monday night. I was making real good money, working forty to fifty hours each weekend. By the end of the season, I thought he needed to invest some of his winnings in a completely legitimate business and begin working himself into a totally legitimate profession. He said the only other way of making a living that he knew was carpenter work, and he was not going back into that line of work. He asked me what I thought he should do, and I suggested making a business out of something he enjoyed. I asked him, "What do you enjoy doing?"

He replied, "I enjoy playing golf, hunting, and fishing. But I can't play golf professionally. Even if I was pretty good, it would take years of practice and lessons to reach the level needed to play on the Professional Golf Association tour! That leaves hunting and fishing. How could I earn a living in those areas?"

I responded, "Open a sporting goods store and supply the things people need to enjoy those areas of recreation."

After thinking and talking about it for a few weeks, he decided to look into the idea. So I began doing research as to what it would take financially to pursue such a venture, and when I had gathered the basic information, we sat down and looked at the possibility. A few days later, he told me he was willing to give it a shot and open a sporting goods store if I would manage it. He told me that he would supply the capital and I would handle the business, and it would be fifty-fifty ownership. I was already sold on the idea, so I accepted his offer.

We found a small building for rent in a strip mall on the busy highway US 1 in Columbia and went to work building counters, shelves, and an office. He had a man that owed him a large amount of money, and the man owned a wholesale business for sporting goods—hunting and fishing gear mostly—so the man stocked our entire store to pay off his debt, and by early spring, the store was open for business and doing pretty good!

During that year, with all the pressures of three businesses on my shoulders and another failing marriage to contend with, my drinking picked up again. I stayed sober when working for the bookie, but I drank while running the store or handling other clients' bookkeeping and taxes. I figured since I was the boss, I could work the way I wanted to, and if someone did not like it, they could go elsewhere!

For the next few months, my and Linda's marriage continued to dissolve, and I seldom went home. It was easier for me to just put a cot in the store office and sleep there, going home the next day when Linda was at work to shower and change clothes, and that way,

I did not have to answer a lot of questions about where I had been all night.

Around midsummer, I received a letter from one of my cousins in Georgia. Her family had fallen on hard times and wanted to sell a piece of property at Dead River. Rather than allow it to be foreclosed on and knowing how much I had longed to live there, they offered the property to me. I could not believe it! What an opportunity! I had been doing well, financially, with the bookie as a client and had saved a nice fat purse, so I took off to Georgia to look at the property.

It was not riverfront property, but it was near enough to what I had always dreamed of owning, so I bought it and began developing it. I would work with the bookmaker Thursday through Monday and leave Monday evening on the two-hundred-mile trip to Georgia. While there, I would stay with my relatives and work my land and head back to South Carolina Wednesday evening. I worked like this for several months, and the property was then ready to accommodate a mobile home. Finding a suitable home, I negotiated a fair price and closed the deal. In a couple of days I had my home delivered and set up at Dead River! I remember thinking that day how I had finally solved all my problems! Everyone thought I had been heading the wrong way, but now I would show them how it had all come to fruition!

It was during this time that I came up with the plan to sell my half of the store to my partner at the end of football season, which would put me into the New Year. Once the season was over and his bookmaking business fell off, I would make the move to Georgia, starting my life over again.

Earlier in the summer when I bought the property, I tried talking to Linda about us moving there after the first of the year. At first, she seemed to be somewhat open to the idea, but as the year went by and I drank more with her seeing less of me, that idea soon faded from her mind, and she finally said that she was not going to move "down in the sticks and swamps."

I pressed on with my plans while working for the bookie, and the fall progressed toward winter. As the holidays drew nearer, hunting season was in full swing, and the pace of the store business really increased. One Saturday morning, just after I opened and my store clerk had arrived, I was preparing to make my way to the bookmaker's house for work when, suddenly, four Richland County Sheriff's vehicles pulled up in front of the store and two uniformed deputies and two plainclothes investigators exited their vehicles and rushed into the store! Presenting me with a search warrant, they ordered me to lock the door and for the store to be temporarily closed because they were going to execute the search warrant. I locked the door, and they began searching the store for gambling paraphernalia. They did not find anything but a small customer football pool, and no charges were made.

I wanted to inform my partner, so I asked if I could make a telephone call, and they said sure.

The bookie's wife answered the phone, informing me that deputies were there searching their home and had just arrested her husband for operating an illegal gambling business. They found and confiscated some cash, all his wager tickets, and other materials associated with the business. Taken to jail and booked, the bookmaker's attorney met him there and posted his bail. I waited for him at the store to find out what to do next.

He told me that he would feel much better about everything if I was to go ahead and take my leave of the store and his business responsibilities earlier than we had planned. He said for me to go ahead and "lose myself in those Georgia woods" so that come court time, the prosecutor would have a difficult time subpoenaing me to testify against him. Other than the fact of losing the good money he was paying me, I was ready to go!

I went to the house, packed my bags, and told Linda that I was leaving her and Brenda again, but I would keep in touch. She was not mad this time because I think she figured I would be back eventually after I got the adventure out of my system.

My partner not only paid me the money he owed me before I left town, but he also paid my base salary for the rest of the year. We agreed that he would pay me half of what we figured the store was worth, and he asked me if he could wait until after his court case to do that. Of course, I agreed. After all, I was leaving South Carolina with more cash in my pocket than I had ever possessed with a home totally paid for waiting at Dead River. I then high-tailed it for the Promised Land!

The US Geological Survey explains that a load of a river is its water, mud, sand, rock, and various refuse. The process whereby a river moves its load from one place to another is called transportation.[44] In that transportation, the load takes on different views and additional substances while fundamentally containing the same content. So it was on the river of my life. On my second time around, I believed an effort had been made to change my course, but in reality, I had not. Instead, my river's load had taken on a much different appearance; it had turned into peacefully deep deception. As a result, I thought it was time for me to simply stretch out on my raft of self-confidence and just enjoy drifting along, now that my former life and its problems were gone…or were they?

Chapter 15

Delusion Is Deep

*And with all unrighteous deception among those who
perish, because they did not receive the love of the truth,
that they might be saved. And for this reason God will send
them strong delusion, that they should believe the lie.*

—2 Thessalonians 2:10–11

When I arrived at my new Georgia home, I unloaded the car and decided to pay my relatives an official visit, announcing my move was complete. Later, unpacking at the house, I began thinking about my next step. Eventually starting a sporting goods business was my goal, but for now, I thought it best to lay low for a while in case the South Carolina authorities were trying to find me. I wanted to make sure that nobody was following me, so for the next two months, I did some hunting and had one big party.

That is where the first problem came from. A full-time party means spending lots of money. And while being absorbed in all that partying, the mind can lose track of where all the dollars go. Most were spent—some given away—while some just disappeared! Under those conditions, it does not take long to blow most of the money you have. That is exactly what I did! I was well into the New Year and nearly broke, but I was at Dead River, and that meant I was in great shape, I thought!

About a month after moving in, I was outside doing some work on the property when I noticed a really cute young woman walking down the dirt road by my house. She looked at me with an inquisitive look. I thought she was probably wondering who I was and what I was doing there. I said hello and kept on working. The next day, she walked by again, and this time, I decided to strike up a conversation with her. She was ready to talk and said her name was Becky. I showed her my place, and by the weekend, we were dating.

Though not divorced yet, I reasoned that for all practical purposes, we were. Linda and I had not completed our legal paperwork, but I justified myself in having a new relationship with this young woman, and by Christmas, we were very involved. Not too long after that, Becky moved in with me.

Her grandparents and mother lived down the road about a mile, and since her grandfather and stepfather loved to hunt and fish, we had a lot of common interests, and I soon got to know them well. While in the store, I had accumulated a good amount of new fishing and hunting equipment, including a boat, motor, and guns, along with other outdoor supplies, and so sharing equipment and knowledge with them only enhanced our relationships while easing any awkwardness concerning Becky and myself.

My easygoing lifestyle included a lot of hunting and fishing and sometimes seven days a week when not too drunk to function. Much of that time was spent with my cousin, her husband, Becky's grandfather, or stepfather. The deception was growing, and life seemed great! It was what I had always dreamed of doing. For the first time in my life, I was truly living! I could do whatever I wanted, whenever I wanted!

Of course, in my new girlfriend, I saw the ideal partner. She was ten years younger than me, attractive, loving, and tender. She wanted to be with me, and she enjoyed doing a lot of things together that I enjoyed. It seemed like she was always looking to comfort me, care for me, and make me happy. Little did I realize then how the devil would later use this relationship to lure me into such a state of vulnerability and then use that state of mind in an attempt to destroy my life! But I had not reached the bottom of the river yet.

One day, while counting my funds, I realized there were just a few dollars left. In those sober moments, I began to think, "What am I going to do now not having any money set aside to start the business?" Operating capital would be needed, and the thought came to me about using my property as collateral for a business loan. My land, mobile home, and car were all paid for, and since Pa-pa Poole had been a longtime customer, maybe his bank would help me out. So I headed for the house to gather my titles and the paperwork of my business plan and then back to Uvalda for a half-pint of courage and from there to the county seat in Mount Vernon where the bank's main office was located.

Parking my car, I had a half-pint left, all my paperwork and documents in hand and not a penny in my pocket. Taking a final shot and no longer shaking, I whispered to myself, "Don't worry! You're going in here and put a sales job on this bank president and you're coming out with the money you need!" I got out of the car and walked into the bank straight to the secretary's desk, introducing myself and telling her that I had no appointment, but I needed to see the bank president when he was available.

She went directly into his office and immediately returned with an elderly gentleman. Extending his hand to greet me, he asked, "Are you any relation to A. C. or Jim Paul Poole?"

I responded, "Yes, sir, I am. A. C. was my grandfather, and Jim Paul is my youngest uncle."

Breaking into a huge smile, he said, "Well, come in and tell me how I can help you."

Sitting in his office, I laid out for him a neatly planned proposition to go into the wholesale sporting goods business. I shared with him my previous experience and the business connections I had established over the southeastern states. I showed him the titles of my property, home, and car and how much I needed to borrow. I finished by saying, "Of course, I need to open a checking account to deposit the borrowed funds in and operate out of."

He looked up at me with another big smile on his face and asked, "Will you need any of those funds in cash today?" When I answered, he stepped to the door instructing his secretary about the paperwork he would need for me, and within twenty minutes, with some blank checks, cash, and loan papers, I was on my way home, in business for myself.

Now Becky had a cousin in Vidalia, about twenty miles away, who was in the wholesale business, and part of the merchandise he handled was basic sporting goods, so after leaving the bank, I picked up Becky, and we went to her grandfather's to ask him to talk with his nephew about my plans and past experience. Papa Durden (Becky's grandfather) went to Vidalia that afternoon and, when he returned, sent word for me to go see his nephew the next morning.

I went to the nephew's place of business the next day, and after explaining my plan, showing him I would not be any competition for him, we worked out a deal where he would sell me his merchandise at a certain percentage of what he sold it to the retail stores for, and I agreed not to sell to any of his accounts. My plan was to travel to various sport shows for the public throughout the southeast on the weekends. Thousands of people came to these shows, and over the weekend, a vendor could sell a large amount of merchandise at just over wholesale prices but much cheaper than in the stores. I had done this with my bookie partner the first winter we were in our store in South Carolina. It gave small business owners the opportunity to move large amounts of merchandise, which we were normally unable to do, thus making it possible to buy from our suppliers in greater lots qualifying us for volume discounts and giving us a better profit margin for what we sold in our store. Becky's cousin loved the idea of my business, giving him greater volume, so we sealed the deal with a handshake.

I began booking booths in various shows and selling my goods. It was going well, and of course now, I had money in my pocket again, and the partying in between shows continued, causing me to become slack in keeping up with my funds. I had the attitude that with a good supplier, my knowledge and experience, and low overhead, I would quickly become a success with little effort.

Three more months went by and business was going so well, but due to a steady intake of booze, I had become overconfident and careless. Well, into the spring and at the bottom of my wallet, I had no shows to attend, very little stock left to sell, and no money to purchase additional stock. With the last one hundred dollars I had left to my name, I continued my normal lifestyle of getting drunk!

Another week passed, and I was so miserable and making life miserable for Becky too. On the last day of the week, I woke up and was terribly sick. Looking in my wallet, I had five dollars left, so I told Becky I would be back in a little while and jumped in the truck and took off for town. After buying a bottle, I started back home on the dirt road, drinking on the way and trying to think of a way to fix my problems.

When I drove into my driveway, I saw Becky loading her grand-father's car with her personal belongings. I could not believe my eyes! Turning off the truck, I hopped out, asking her, "What are you doing? Where are you going?"

This petite little woman looked me straight in the eye and said, "I'm leaving! I can't live with your constant drinking day in and day out! You've squandered away all your money, all your property is in HOC, you lost your business and have no hopes of a job, and still, all you do is drink and stay drunk! I do love you, but I've had enough, so I'm leaving!"

As Becky left that evening, I was face-to-face with a reservoir of delusion, and the dam that had been holding it back had just broken, allowing a flood of all that deception to rush over me, the overpowering current taking me down to the bottom of the river, and I had no idea if or how I would ever reach the surface again!

It would be a little over a year later before I would come to understand why we are ever deceived. The Bible tells us that if we do not receive the love of the truth when it is revealed to us, the only thing left for us to believe is a lie; thus, we are deceived![45] I never wanted to believe that alcohol was controlling my life; instead, I insisted on believing I was in control of the alcohol and my life! Here, I was thirty-four years old before I could admit that most all I had done and said up until then was a lie! Continuing like this for all those years brought me into a deep delusion that I might never be able to escape.

Chapter 16

Trying to Reach the Surface

I sink in deep mire, where there is no standing; I have come into deep waters, where the floods overflow me.

—Psalm 69:2

Red Yates was a unique man. He was born into a high-quality, well-known family but was educated through his own choices in the "school of hard knocks." Knowing what alcohol can do to a family, he had great empathy for me, and I knew he loved me like a son. As I thought back on the fight with my father and being put out of our home, I knew that Red had done for me what he thought the Lord wanted him to do as a Christian and a reformed alcoholic. Taking me into his home when I was seventeen years old, he tried to help in some way to keep alcohol from further ruining my life. Though only a temporary fix, it did get me over a major hurdle, graduating from high school, to the next stage in my life. In that short period, Red did plant some important moral seeds that would eventually sprout and grow.

Now, again, I needed help, and God was bringing Red back into my life to begin a healing and restoration process that, at the moment, I could not yet fathom. As we finished talking on the phone, he gave me some hope, in the middle of my hopelessness, saying, "It will be tomorrow before I can get there, but hang on, I'm coming! I'll help you, and we'll get through this together!" Not much further down the river of life, I would come to the recognition this is just how the Lord is willing to work for each of us. He finds people and ways to say, "I hear you! Hang on. I am coming, and I will help you!" I have often wondered why we wait until we fail or are almost dead before we ask for the Lord's help. The apostle Paul would soon answer that question for me in Romans 3:9–18.[46]

My situation was rather ironic if you think about it. After all the years and efforts to find the life I thought I needed at Dead River, here it was, and it was not what I thought it would be! I had reached the end of my own strength with nothing left to fight with or for, nothing to rely on, and the need for someone else to help me. My problems were not gone! A change of places and circumstances had not done away with my problems. Dead River was not the Promised Land after all! Instead, it had proven to be my wilderness experience, bringing me face-to-face with the reality of my failing life!

The next afternoon, my neighbor hollered for me to come to the phone. It was Red. He was in Uvalda and needed directions to my place. After a few minutes, he and his wife, Kerry, arrived, and we loaded some of my clothes and personal items in his car, locked the house, leaving the key with my aunt, and we headed back to South Carolina. Sleeping most of the five-hour trip to Columbia, not much is remembered except when we got close to town, I started getting sick. Arriving at Red and Kerry's home, he gathered some clothes, leaving Kerry there, and we headed for Lake Murray, just outside Lexington. Red had a house there on the lake, and as he pulled in and turned the engine off, he said, "We're going to lock ourselves in, and we're not coming out until you are completely sober!"

At this time, not having any alcohol for at least twelve hours, I was trembling from head to toe, and my head was banging like a drum! Keep in mind for most of the last two and a half months, I drank day and night, until passing out, only to get up the next morning and start all over again. Each morning, there was a minimum of a half quart of hundred-proof liquor on my nightstand and one unopened can of beer to chase it. This was my "eye-opener" to start each new day, and it was in an endless, hopeless cycle! In some ways,

I wanted to quit but felt I could not quit, unable to think about living without alcohol, and now I was starting to feel the effects of withdrawal!

Red and I talked and cried. He tried to help me eat and drink, but if I did put something in my stomach, it would not remain there long. We would talk and cry again, and then we would sleep awhile. I remember having periods of chills and then sweats like never before. To begin with, the days and nights were tough and ran together. There was the sickness, shakes, and the pain from throwing up so much, but after almost two weeks, reality began to set in. I was not shaking much anymore, and the conversations with Red were beginning to make sense. I was starting to understand some of the serious issues that were pending in my life, and I was thanking God, in my heart, that I had someone like Red who knew what I was going through and was determined, because of his love for me, to help me. (I still thank God for Red and always will and look forward to seeing him and Kerry on the Resurrection Day!)

Approximately two weeks had gone by when suddenly Red got sick. Aching all over and running a fever, before I realized it, he was sick as a dog with a full-blown case of the flu. He had not been out of the house until three days before, when making a quick run to the grocery store, so he must have contracted the flu bug then. I was now taking care of him, and why I did not catch the flu, I have no idea! (I later came to understand that our role reversal was probably part of the ironic rehab the Lord was allowing me to experience.) This was our condition for the next two weeks.

After being in South Carolina for a total of five weeks, I could not free my mind of the situation in Georgia, wondering how my relationship with Becky could be repaired. So desperate to not have our relationship fail after three prior marriages failing, I was constantly obsessed with these thoughts. Red tried very hard to talk me out of going back to Georgia, feeling the situation with its pressures might cause me to fall back into my old habits. I now know from talking with other reformed addicts and alcoholics that if you remove people from out of the environment that was helping to contribute to their habit, the alcoholic or addict stands a much better chance of staying sober. However, with me, almost every environment I had lived in contributed to my habit, so this was not a consideration for me at the time.

During the last week I was there, Red diligently labored with me over this issue, but he finally gave up, realizing my mind was made up and there was no stopping me. I was determined to return and prove myself to Becky and others that I could be a responsible family man and provider!

After arriving back in Georgia, the first step I took was to find Becky and arrange to talk with her, Louise, Papa, and Granny. At that meeting, I assured them I had quit drinking the day before leaving for South Carolina and had not consumed a drop in five weeks. I told them I was back to stay and one way or another, with Becky or without her, was going to put my life together and be a responsible person. I would get a job, pay my bills, and live a decent life. Of course, emphasizing that I loved and wanted Becky to be a part of that life, but if not her, then I would eventually find someone else!

I told Becky she could come with me now or wait and check me out over time and any of her family should feel free to show up unannounced at any time to see if I was sober. They all agreed it would be best if Becky waited a while to see how things went, so I thanked them for listening and told them my efforts would now be focused on finding a job, and I left.

For almost a month, I put in applications and had interviews but still had no job. Maintaining a positive attitude, I continued my search. While at home one day, Becky suddenly showed up. She truly looked startled to see me sober after two months, and she later admitted she could find no signs I had been drinking since returning home. A couple of days later, she showed up again without warning and, after a short conversation, told me she had made the decision to move back in with me, if I still wanted to be with her. I told her that I did, and she moved back that evening. After I ran out of the funds Red had given me, Becky's mother helped me with gas money as I continued to apply for any jobs that were available, which were not many. Louise, Papa, and Granny also helped by giving us a few groceries or letting us eat meals at their homes.

Not long after getting back together, Papa was in Vidalia to visit his nephew. His company sold a large variety of goods that appealed to a small town and country stores around the state. They also handled basic fishing tackle and hunting supplies. In speaking to his nephew, Papa mentioned that I was no longer in business for myself and was looking for a job, so his nephew sent word back to me to come in and talk with him. The next day, I met with him, and while I turned down his offer to be hired as a salesman, explaining that while I was sure I could be successful in the sales position, I was very concerned with being away from home for several days and nights at the time. It would be too easy for me to start drinking again on nights I did not return home, and I needed the steady, daily situation with its accountability much more than I needed a higher income. So I did accept the position of being his delivery man. It paid only five dollars an hour, but I was home every night. We agreed on a thirty-day trial period, and if he liked my work, he would hire me full-time.

I already knew how to deal with the public, so my main focus was to learn the routes quickly. A visit to the county library helped me get started by making copies of the maps of the closer counties I would cover. The ones further away from home, I obtained at the various county seats. With the maps, I was able to discover shortcuts and routes with much less traffic, which allowed me to make better time.

My boss noticed that I not only looked at my position as a job but was constantly looking out for his interest too. Many times, I was able to correct mistakes in the billing slips. which would cut into his small margin of profit, and due to my prior knowledge in sporting goods, I could also sell some things the salesmen had neglected to bring to the customer's attention. After a few weeks on the job, everything was going well, and I was working six days a week, making a small but steady income for the first time in quite a while.

Known as a Christian and family man, my boss had a reputation for being a hard worker who treated his workers fairly. I enjoyed building our relationship as my own self-esteem was rebuilt. He seemed to genuinely respect me and never appeared to be looking down his nose at me like I was some old drunk who was liable to go off the deep end anytime. Neither did he give me a hard time about living out of the bonds of matrimony with his cousin, Becky. He would talk to me occasionally about that in an encouraging way and would thoughtfully, lovingly, share with me that our situation was not God's way. His kind, yet honest manner never made me feel condemned or threatened but always left me willing to consider my circumstances even more.

Life was going well at this point, and I had resolved to live my life according to the reformed drunk's old saying, "One day at a time," concentrating on what had to be done each day to stay sober, being a good employee, and responsible in my relationship with Becky that blossomed even more! People began to have and show more respect for me and believe that maybe I had turned the corner. I was feeling really good, thinking I had pulled myself "up by my bootstraps" and was back on the road to success! What I did not realize then was while God had certainly answered my prayer for help, I had basically forgotten about him. Seeing this as more of a gut effort on my part to straighten myself out, I did not yet recognize there was no way I could be totally successful on my own.

It is such a tragedy how, like myself, most people do not realize this truth for many, many years, and some never do. This shows just how deceptive sin is. The Bible puts it this way, "*Can the Ethiopian change his skin or the leopard its spots?*"[47] Neither has the ability to do this, yet we humans seem to think we can expend some effort and totally change our lives by our own willpower, and I was still convinced I could do just that! Oh, I recognized Red had extended a huge, helping hand at getting me off the booze and back on my feet, but I saw this as more of an occasional helping hand that everyone needs but not something I needed help with on a constant, daily basis.

Almost three months had passed since the dam of delusion had burst, taking me to the bottom of life's dead river, causing me to think I would never reach the surface again. But through a period of "good luck," I could again see light from the surface, and I believed I was almost there! Hopefully my "good luck" would stay long enough for me to make it! Or was it luck at all?

Chapter 17

Life's Dirty Water

*If God puts no trust in his saints, and the heavens are not
pure in his sight, how much less man, who is abominable
and filthy, who drinks iniquity like water?*

—Job 15:16

As my outward life got better, there was still a great deal of emptiness
inside, no matter how I tried to fill the void. These feelings had not
been shared with anyone, and on the surface, all appeared fine. But
no matter how successful I seemed to be in my work or my relationship with Becky and others, this void was not being filled. While it
seemed like my "luck" had changed some, it had not changed enough
to rid me of problems. I had definitely made some good forward
progress, but each time I thought I might get a sustained positive
streak going, something would come along to hinder and hold me
back. Not being sure if it was bad luck, the wrong time, or what it
was, in the course of conversations with Louise, Becky's mother, she
began to sow seeds of spiritual truth in my thinking. She encouraged
me to give my heart to Jesus and seek his presence in my life. She
maintained it was a relationship with the Lord that was lacking in my
life and that would give me the fulfillment I was looking for.

Louise never beat me over the head with the Bible, but whenever the opportunity would arise, she would simply talk to me about
principles in the Scriptures and their applications to my life. At first,
I passed it off without too much thought, not willing to consider

if what she was telling me was true. Eventually, though, I began to entertain thoughts about some of the things she was sharing with me. As I made my deliveries throughout the day, I had a lot of time to think and try to reason things out.

In the course of each day, I would take breaks from my thoughts and turn on the radio to dial in some music or news broadcasts. While traveling, stations would fade in and out, so a lot of time would be spent dialing in new stations, and over the weeks, I realized there seemed to be one network that kept coming through no matter what part of Georgia I was in. Each station had different call letters and varied in locations on the dial, but it was the same Christian network that was being broadcast. Occasionally, I would hear the speaker say something that would grab my attention, so I would stop dialing and listen for a while.

One morning, having a few questions on my mind from talking to Louise the evening before and not coming up with any answers thus far, I dialed in the Christian network and heard the commentator mention the same subject I was wondering about. As I listened, he went to several texts in the Bible, which answered my questions, and I was thrilled to think how "lucky" I was to be dialing the station in at just the right time! But it did not stop there! Over the next few weeks, the same thing would happen more and more! It seemed as if my "luck" was getting better and periodically, I would mention to Louise how these answers would come to me! She would always smile but rarely made any comment. However, after this happened quite a few times, she suddenly asked, "Do you really believe it is 'good luck' that is bringing these timely answers to your questions? Do you realize the Bible never speaks of 'luck,' good or bad? Do you think it is possible that God may be working through the radio stations to get your attention?"

At first, I could not answer and just sat there, looking back at her smiling face. Finally, I spoke up, "Well, yeah, I guess so, now that you mention it. Is that what you think is happening?"

She just continued smiling, finishing her final preparations for supper, as I left wondering and questioning my thinking while heading back home. "Is this just good luck? Is God speaking to me? Is it a coincidence that I'm finding the same programming no matter where I drive each day? Is it a coincidence that every time I have something on my mind, the answer seems to come to me while listening to Christian radio?"

For days, these things bothered me, being unable to grasp them all in faith, so I went back to Louise several times, and we would talk a little more with her continuing to encourage me to seek the Lord in prayer. Finally, after patiently trying for days to convince me to believe that God was reaching out to me, one evening, she just blurted out, "Tommy, you don't have to believe me! Just pray and ask God for yourself! Tell Him, 'Lord, if You are here, please reveal Yourself to me!"

Secretly, I started praying, "Lord, please make Yourself real to me. Please reveal Yourself to me!" I continued to pray this way for days when Louise shared with me a very important passage that made the answer real. She opened her Bible and started reading Hebrews 11:1, 3, and 6. *"Now faith is the substance of things hoped for, the evidence of things not seen... By faith we understand that the worlds were framed by the Word of God, so that the things which are seen were not made of things which are visible... But without faith it is impossible to please him* [God], *for he who comes to God must believe that he is, and that he is a rewarder of those who diligently seek him."*

These verses made good sense to me, but the full brightness of their light was not yet shining. So I continued to pray more each day, in between listening to Christian radio, until one day, I made an application of what Louise and the Scripture had told me. If the Lord was answering me through the things I would periodically get through the radio programs and I did not receive them in faith as his answers, what good would they do me? They would not do me the least bit of good unless I believed them in faith! Well, if I did accept them in faith, what would be next? The thought came to mind that I would act on them! So I asked myself, "How would I act on them?" I thought, "If they were instructions and they were clear, I would follow them! But if I did not understand, I would then ask questions."

Asking Louise what she thought about my reasoning, she answered by reading me a text that said, "*Come now, and let us reason together,' says the Lord, 'Though your sins are like scarlet, they shall be as white as snow; Though they are red like crimson, they shall be as wool. If you are willing and obedient, You shall eat the good of the land.'"*[48] She followed by saying, "Tommy, you are on the right track. Prayer is talking to God as if he is your best friend. Respectfully, of course, reasoning with him, questioning him, and talking to him in a loving, intimate way. God is not trying to keep things from us! God wants to share the abundance of his truth with us! He does not want to trick us! He wants to teach us the truth about everything, especially the truth about who he is and what he is like! If you don't understand him, tell him and ask different questions about what you believe you have heard. Then listen and be alert for his answers. He will answer! (This issue of God answering our prayers would loudly repeat itself in a time of crisis many years later, having to do with my daughter!) Sometimes he may speak to your mind, sometimes through things others say, or things we read, especially in the Bible. But if we stay alert and continue to pray, he will answer us!"

After that conversation, I started thinking about what she said. If luck or its concept is never mentioned in the Bible, then there must not be any such thing. If not, that would mean that God has a reason or reasons for everything he says or does or does not say or do. So there must not be any such thing as coincidence either. There must be a purpose for everything! If coincidence does not exist and God is in control, then he had purposely built a radio network that covered the entire state so that his biblical teaching is available to everyone that wants to listen. If Jesus speaks to people, like me, who have questions about various subjects, this network is a perfect way to accomplish a lot of that, so it is only reasonable that he can speak to me, answering my questions, and the questions of many others! I could not find any excuse to not accept it by faith! And I have to say that with all the dirty water I had drank in this life, this went down pretty well and made me feel refreshed!

I was now realizing that a relationship with the Lord has to be based on faith—a constant faith—faith that he does exist and faith in the idea that he wants me to get to know him by following him, and the result will be a rewarding experience! But without this constant faith-based relationship, I could not know or please God. Only a constant faith in him will bring me to the surface of Dead River, or ultimately, life's dirty water would cause me to drown, never seeing the real *Light*[49] of day!

In the midst of Job's terrible affliction, he asks and answers one of the most profound concerns that every person is eventually confronted with! *"Who can bring a clean thing out of an unclean? No one!"*[50] With the recognition that I could not rescue myself from this torrential flood, nor could I clean up the poisoned, filthy river from which I came, I was suddenly confronted with a state of hopelessness and the question that Louise had already answered, "Where can my total remedy come from?"

Chapter 18

A Drink of Living Water

If you knew the gift of God, and who it is that says to you, "Give me a drink", you would have asked him, and he would have given you living water... but whoever drinks of the water that I shall give him will never thirst. But the water that I shall give him will become in him a fountain of water springing up into everlasting life.

—John 4:10, 14

Continuing to pray each day and not receiving an answer, one day, the thought came to me that I might be praying in the wrong way. Maybe I was already a Christian and should not be asking God if he was real. After all, about the age of ten, during a revival service, I responded to an appeal to accept Christ as my Savior and be baptized in the Baptist Church. So maybe the Lord was offended that one of his children doubted their Father's existence! Based on that thought, I tried to explain myself to him and began asking if I was a child of God.

One morning while driving to work, I resolved to keep praying this way until I had an answer from Lord! In between making deliveries, I would pray and then listen to Christian radio until I heard something that would direct my focus back to prayer.

Midafternoon, as I prayed, something caught my attention in the middle of the two-lane highway I was on. I strained to bring it into focus, and when I did, I saw a dove—a solid white dove! It appeared to be injured, hopping around on the centerline, fluttering its feathers!

The next moment, I saw a semitruck and trailer in the oncoming lane and immediately realized that both of our vehicles would reach the bird simultaneously unless it flew away! Yet it did not fly away and continued hopping in the middle of the road. In just a few seconds, as both vehicles met, the dove lunged straight up into the air of the few feet between us! Trying desperately to hold my truck straight, I looked into my side mirror, expecting to see the bird strike one or both of the vehicles and be killed! Instead, I saw the dove struggling, inching its way upward, all while being blown side to side by the swirling wind from each of our vehicles! Should it veer to the left or to the right, just a little bit, it would meet its death! When it seemed the dove had no more strength left to escape its danger, it was suddenly above both vehicles and disappeared into the sky. Finding what I had just witnessed hard to believe, I asked the Lord to give me understanding. I continued to think on it for a while, but understanding did not come. Continuing with my deliveries for the day, the event gradually faded from my thinking.

One day, the following week, I resolved again to plead with God until he let me know for certain whether or not I was his child. As usual, while making my deliveries, I would alternate between prayer and listening to Christian radio. That particular afternoon, I was listening to Dr. James Dobson's program, "Focus on the Family," and he was sharing the taped testimony of a young Christian missionary. She and her husband had served one of the many native cultures in the South Pacific during World War II.

The Japanese Army invaded their peaceful island, and during the atrocities they committed, her husband was tortured and killed. After his death, she still believed in God but began to doubt God's love for her. Why did a loving God allow this and the other tragedies she faced? Many of the island's inhabitants were shot, hanged, or imprisoned! She and others endured rape and torturous interrogations until finally she was placed in solitary confinement and starved to a point where she pleaded with the Lord for death! However, she still prayed, confessing her previous doubts, demands, and unchristian thoughts.

She recounted each time the Lord had blessed her or the other prisoners and offered him praise and thanksgiving for each blessing! She then closed her prayer by saying, "Lord, if it is possible for me to have one last blessing before I die, all I ask for is one small banana. But if you decide not to give me one, I will continue to love you. Please just let me rest in your loving arms." Closing her eyes, expecting death to come soon, she settled onto the darkness of her cell floor.

She told how in the very next moment, her cell door opened, and it sounded as though someone put something on the floor just inside her cell, and then the door was closed without a word. She began to crawl across the floor toward the cell door when she suddenly felt something she could hardly believe! It was not one but a whole stalk of bananas!

My heart was so touched by God's Holy Spirit and the mercy he was extending to her that tears began flowing from my eyes and I was temporarily blinded! I began to wipe my eyes, and in that moment, realized, I was in the very same place in the road I had seen the white dove the week before! All I could do was continue to weep, and I began seeing the original scene of the white dove in the road replaying in my mind's eye! I was impressed by the narrow space between my truck and the oncoming semi. The dove's only escape was straight up through the turbulent wind currents between our vehicles! Too far to the left or right meant death, and it would need help beyond its own strength to survive!

Suddenly, I clearly saw the enormity of my sinful life and immediately realized that I must have a Savior! Continuing down the highway, I called out for Jesus to cleanse and save me! Instantly, I felt as though my body was lifted off the seat while losing all strength in my arms to steer the truck! A sudden wave of ecstasy flooded over me, and for the first time in my life, I felt truly clean!

Not knowing how long this experience lasted, eventually, the normal feeling in my body began to return. By this time, the radio program had faded out, and I momentarily began to doubt what had just happened. Noticing that I was entering a small, rural community and thinking it best to get some fresh air, I pulled into a small parking lot. Stopping and turning the ignition off, I stepped out of the truck, taking several deep breaths of air. Stepping several paces away from the truck, I turned, looking back at the vehicle, and was stunned at what caught my eye! The left front tire was almost completely gone! Only a few steel and polyester cords with a dozen or so chunks of rubber remained on the rim! The whole experience happened at highway speed with a fully loaded truck, and instantly, I realized God was telling me that I was his child and as long as I was in his hands, nothing could harm me unless he allowed it to happen! I only had to keep my eyes on Jesus!

As I finished my route that day, I could hardly contain myself! When I arrived home, I told Becky that I had met Jesus on the highway and was a new man! I then told her that we could not live together in sin anymore. She would have to move out immediately, and we would have a meeting at her family's home that evening to talk about what had taken place. So without any argument, she gathered her things, and I took her to her grandparents' house where she called her mother to come over for the meeting. Telling them about my experience on the road, I repented of my sins toward them all and asked for their forgiveness. I promised that from then on, I would cease my sinful relationship with Becky and pursue a proper, Christian relationship with her, if she desired. Because of the evidence of true repentance, they all hugged and kissed me while praising the Lord that their prayers for me had been answered! For without a doubt, I had been given a drink of *living water*[51] from the Lord's river of life. Dead River and its poisons would not be my daily drink anymore!

Over the next few weeks, my relationships with Becky and her family grew in a proper way, and we decided to get married when we found a pastor willing to hold the ceremony in his church. After counseling with several pastors who would not perform the wedding, we finally found a pastor of a small congregation just outside Mt. Vernon, Georgia, and after counseling with him and sharing my testimony, he agreed to marry us on October 4, 1987.

Chapter 19

The Remedy for
This Life's Water

*Christ...loved the church and gave himself for her, that he
might sanctify and cleanse her with the washing of water
by the Word, that he might present her to himself a glorious
church, not having spot or wrinkle or any such thing,
but that she should be holy and without blemish.*

—Ephesians 5:25–27

We immediately began attending Sunday services at the little Mt.
Vernon church, and we were treated well, however, with the electric
guitars, drums, and upbeat Southern gospel music throughout the
service. It was more musical than having an opportunity to study and
grow in the preaching and teaching of Scripture. This was the kind
of service Becky and her family were accustomed to in the Holiness
and Pentecostal denominations, but I had come from the Southern
Baptist church, where we believed that church services should be of
a more reverent nature, giving the congregation an understanding
about what the Bible says and how its teachings are to be applied in
our daily lives.

I discussed these differences with Becky and her family and
began praying daily for the Lord to lead us into the truth of his
Word and his will for the church we should attend. This was my
priority from the moment of my cleansing on the highway, for that

day, I admitted to the Lord how limited my knowledge of his Word was, yet through the years, I had learned enough to know that all which was called "Christian" doctrine could not be true. This was only logical since all the different denominations taught so many contradictions! I told Jesus, and now Becky and her family, that I was willing to follow his leading anywhere but only if it was in harmony with the Bible! They all agreed this was the right thing to do, and we never had any arguments about the issue. Soon, I was impressed we should start attending different churches until we found one where both of us felt comfortable, and we could study and grow in our faith. Thus, the Bible became my spiritual compass, and whenever I found man teaching a contradiction to what it said, I followed the holy text rather than man.

In between the Sunday services, I continued daily to listen to Christian radio while making my deliveries. Then most evenings at home, I would go to my mother-in-law's after supper and study basic Bible doctrines. Eventually, contradictions with the group or individual we were studying with would arise, and we would search for the truth. If we could not reconcile the issues, I would ask a pastor or other well-studied believer, sometimes discovering the contradiction was based on a misunderstanding that I or Louise had. Other times, it was obvious the explanations we were given did not come from the Bible or a correct understanding of the passage, and we would lovingly stand on what the Scripture said. We were always willing to help others see a clear point we held, but if that was not their desire, we would simply agree to disagree. I soon came to realize that most other Christians will not accept that their view might be incorrect, even if their view contradicts the weight of scriptural evidence, and so, when disagreements began to cause conflicts, we would politely move on.

Though we were sometimes accused of having arrogance or pride, there was none in our approach—only a prayerful desire about *rightly dividing the word of truth.*[52] It seemed that many folks could not deal honestly with the Bible and/or themselves, holding the opinion that anyone who did not agree with their church's teaching was probably sincere but sincerely wrong!

However, the Holy Spirit continued showing us how Bible doctrines had to fit together, supporting and never contradicting each other. We also found there was a specific method of building each doctrine. Isaiah put it this way, "*Whom will he* [the Lord] *teach knowledge? And whom will he make to understand the message? Those just weaned from the milk? Those just drawn from the breasts? For precept must be upon precept… Line upon line… Here a little, there a little.*"[53] It soon became apparent that all these contradictions in doctrines were the sprouts of three seeds—misunderstandings of the text, the lack of humility, or the pride of opinion. Sometimes what the psalmist said would come true in our experience. He acknowledges to God, "*You, through your commandments, make me wiser than my enemies; for they are ever with me. I have more understanding than all my teachers, for your testimonies are my meditation.*"[54] This was made plain to me one day while reading in the book of Job. In chapter 14:7–9, the Scripture tells us, "*For there is hope for a tree, if it is cut down, that it will sprout again, and that its tender shoots will not cease. Though its root may grow old in the earth, and its stump may die in the ground, yet at the scent of water it will bud and bring forth branches like a plant.*"

Meditating on this passage, several questions came to mind. First, why was this tree cut down? It was cut down because it had died. Second, why did it die? It died because it received no water, and the last verse tells us that just the *scent of water* will cause it to *bud* with new life. Third, will it *bud* with new life if it receives poison water? Obviously, no! So the verses in Job can only be true if they are speaking of noncontaminated, lifegiving water.

Now based on the spiritual truth Jesus shared with the woman at the well, she, like this dead tree, would need *living water*[55] to gain a new life or, as Jesus told Nicodemus, *be born again.*[56] In other words, if the woman, or this tree, were to only be given the poison water of this life, neither would live. I now understood that in death itself, there is no hope, and in deception, one is deprived of the truth. Yet with God, there is hope beyond hopelessness and truth beyond deception.

Misunderstandings of the text—error—come to all of us as we consume the water of this life. Well-meaning parents, other families, teachers, various civic leaders and experts, even pastors and other religious leaders, all give us water to drink that has some poison in it. It is not pure! I do not mean to imply that all these people give us the poisoned water on purpose. Most do not! Yet this makes it even more dangerous because we trust these individuals so much that we do not investigate to see if they are correct! We simply accept it. Eventually, if not corrected by the whole of Scripture, this error—poison—will build up in our reasoning, causing even more error in closely associated doctrines, which only leads to delusion and spiritual death.

In the physical realm, this is the best way to poison someone. You don't give them the whole bottle of poison at once because they will taste it and spit it out, realizing something is wrong with it! But if you continually give them just enough poison that cannot be tasted, eventually, they will take in enough and die!

Little do we realize that much of this life's water—information, instruction, and advice—is tainted, plus the gray matter we use to analyze this input is also diseased. None of us care to admit this is so because, naturally, we lack the humility needed to admit our hopeless or faulty situation.

This was me! Until I met the Lord Jesus, I could not openly admit to being wrong about much of anything. Most of the time, I believed I was in full control of my life, no matter how bad it was going. However, the use of alcohol and the things it caused me to believe, do, and say was the perfect illustration that revealed the lack of my control!

Both before and after becoming a Christian, we must be humble enough to reexamine all we think we know. Without retaining this atmosphere of humility in mind and heart, it is impossible to discover the truth of God's Word and be cleansed from the errors we have already consumed!

This is where the sprout from the third seed is revealed. It is called pride of opinion. I came to realize early in my spiritual experience that pride of opinion is the rampant plague of Christianity that has resulted in almost thirty-three thousand denominations and organizations[57] by this time in my life. A large portion of these groups believe and teach many of the same doctrines, but when their history is examined closely, the differences they have with each other usually came about through the different interpretations their leaders held with each other, which were never reconciled due to personal disagreements, hurt feelings, and the need to personally be correct.

No matter how convinced a Christian may be that his or her doctrine is correct, if they cannot temporarily set that belief aside and thoroughly study the teaching again, asking the Lord to lead their study and correct any part of it that might be wrong, they have "pride of opinion," and the Holy Spirit will not be able to answer that prayer because their mind is already made up. Thus, if there is enough incorrect belief in their mind, their pride of opinion will block God's attempt to correct their understanding, allowing their delusion to lead them into damnation.[58]

Sometime later, I found another text that only compounds the truth and importance of this matter. It is Isaiah 8:20, which speaks about finding the truth: "*To the law* [of God] *and to the testimony* [of his prophets]! *If they* [anyone] *do not speak according to this Word* [of God], *it is because there is no light* [spiritual truth] *in them.*" Those who need to be right will only find ways to disagree with Isaiah's statement of fact.

Thinking on these things, I came to see a pattern throughout the Bible, in how God's people have responded to him, and seeing the pattern, I realized the importance of giving my attention to what Isaiah said. Adam and Eve brought sin into this world by not following God's Word. Later, the whole world was lost, except the eight of Noah's family because they did not follow God's Word to them through Noah. Time and again, thousands and thousands of the Israelites perished and eventually were scattered throughout the world because they did not follow God's Word. When Jesus came to this earth to bring salvation, the majority of God's people, including most of their leaders, were not ready to accept him because they were not following his Word. According to the apostles of the New Testament, and especially John's book, the Revelation of Jesus Christ, the majority of God's people, Christians, will be deceived by the Antichrist and lost in the end because they are not following God's Word![59]

This is why Jesus told Satan, *"It is written, 'Man shall not live by bread alone, but by every Word that proceeds from the mouth of God.'"*[60] Before Satan was exiled to earth, he knew and served Jesus and that Jesus was the prophesied Savior, coming to save mankind, but Satan was not following God's Word and will finally be lost! Thus, regardless of what and how much we think we know and how much we say we believe and accept Jesus as our Savior, if we are not living by God's Word when Jesus returns, we will be lost! James puts it this way, *"You believe that there is one God. You do well. Even the demons believe—and tremble! But do you want to know, O foolish man, that faith without works is dead?"*[61] Most who claim to be Christians think it is simply their belief in Jesus as Lord and Savior that gives them eternal life! However, what most do not understand is, it is our works of faith—living by God's Word—which is the evidence in the judgment that proves our faith is real! Living by God's Word proves that we have genuine, saving faith! Without having genuine, saving faith, we will be lost!

And so I came to understand that *living water*[62] is the only remedy for this life's polluted water and the spiritual death that it brings. In fact, correctly understanding and applying God's Word is absolutely critical, and it was now plain to me that I must continue drinking it![63] For resorting back to the consumption of Dead River's water would only bring eternal death, and this I did not want.

Chapter 20

3ABN

Then I saw another angel flying in the midst of heaven, having the everlasting gospel to preach to those who dwell on the earth—to every nation, tribe, tongue, and people—saying with a loud voice, "Fear God and give glory to him, for the hour of his judgment has come; and worship him who made heaven and earth, the sea and springs of water." And another angel followed, saying, "Babylon is fallen, is fallen, that great city, because she has made all nations drink of the wine of the wrath of her fornication". Then a third angel followed them, saying with a loud voice, "If anyone worships the beast and his image, and receives his mark on his forehead or on his hand, he himself shall also drink of the wine of the wrath of God, which is poured out full strength into the cup of His indignation. He shall be tormented with fire and brimstone..."

—Revelation 14:6–10

A month went by, and I had just added a new route to my work schedule in north Georgia, and because of the distance involved, it required me staying out for two nights each week. So when I returned home and went to Louise's house to study, she had a wonderful surprise waiting for me!

During my absence, Louise and her husband bought a satellite TV system and had it installed. In her free time during the day, she would read the instructions and play with the system, learning how to operate it and find various programming. That first week, she had discovered a brand-new Christian channel called 3ABN (Three Angels Broadcasting Network).[64] The folk who started this network decided on its name by virtue of their commitment to proclaiming the three angel's messages found in Revelation 14:6–12. These messages are the heart of the entire book of Revelation.

One of the programs they produced was a "Revelation Seminar," which guided students through the subjects and prophecies in the book, and we were both extremely excited about this opportunity to participate in a systematic Bible study. I had never studied any prophecies, and Louise had only studied a few, many years earlier. Each class used a printed lesson guide and the King James Version of the Bible, so she called 3ABN and ordered two sets of the lessons, which would arrive in several days. She also bought some blank videotapes to record the classes for me to watch.

Of course, I reminded her about my commitment to the Lord in seeking only His truth of the Scriptures, and she agreed that if we were led into anything contrary to what the Bible said, we would call them with our questions, and if the answers were not from the Bible, we would put the lessons aside and move on to some other studies!

So with that, we agreed to wait until the lesson guides arrived before viewing the class videos. Meanwhile, I bought some more blank videotapes so Louise could continue taping each class while making additional notes of the teacher's comments not included in the guides.

When the guides arrived, we began the studies, looking up each text in our Bibles to obtain the fill-in-the-blank answers. Plus, we made note of any questions we might have as we moved through each lesson. After completing the lesson, we watched the class video to see if our answers were correct and clear up any questions we had on the subject. What impressed me the most about these studies was how they were arranged. Starting with the basic subject about how to understand the book of Revelation, each study was like laying bricks to build a wall. Each new brick (subject/doctrine) expanded on the studies before it while bringing in a new subject to incorporate it into the whole wall of truth.

We learned that Revelation (in Greek is *apokalypsis*) means "an unveiling."[65] Thus, the book is about Jesus unveiling or revealing himself to his churches and the world using many symbols and Old Testament imagery. So if you do away with the Old Testament as many Bible students are taught to do, it is impossible to fully comprehend John's visions. As Lesson RS-001 says, "The amazing *key* to understanding Revelation is the study of other Bible writers, especially those of the Old Testament."[66] In other words, for us to unlock the meanings of the symbols and prophecies, we needed to find out what John and the other Bible writers said about the same subjects.[67] In this way, we would allow the Bible to interpret itself. "Twenty-six of the thirty-nine Old Testament books are quoted from in Revelation, and of the 404 verses in the book, 276 are borrowed or copied from other Bible authors."[68] In the Scriptures, we are given four vital keys to help us understand its meaning:

1. *"But the natural man does not receive the things of the Spirit of God, for they are foolishness to him; nor can he know them, because they are spiritually discerned."* (1 Corinthians 2:14)
2. *"I will give of the fountain of the water of life freely to him who thirsts."* (Revelation 21:6)
3. *"Be diligent to present yourself approved to God, a worker who does not need to be ashamed, rightly dividing the Word of truth"* (2 Timothy 2:15). *"They received the Word with all readiness, and searched the Scriptures daily to find out whether these things were so."* (Acts 17:11)
4. *"Blessed is he who reads and those who hear the words of this prophecy, and keep those things which are written in it..."* (Revelation 1:3) *"If any man will do his will he shall know of the doctrine whether it be of God."* (John 7:17)[69]

It is fascinating to me how John's Revelation and Daniel's book complement each other in speaking about the Messiah. John uses such detailed word pictures to confirm seeing the very same person of Jesus before his birth as a man, his earthly life, and beyond his death and resurrection—events which are confirmed by many other

Bible writers. Daniel's seventy-week prophecy[70] (which equals 490 prophetic days,[71] which is actually 490 literal years)[72] reveals exactly when Jesus was to be anointed for his ministry and die on the cross.[73]

This same period ended in AD 34,[74] closing the probationary time that the nation of Israel had to accept Jesus as Messiah and his gospel.[75] Since Israel, as God's chosen nation did not accept Christ, it then marked the time for the gospel to be taken to the Gentiles beginning with the stoning of Stephen.[76] This prophecy leaves no doubt that Jesus is the Messiah![77]

As we continued our studies, it soon became apparent that if an honest person had any doubts or misunderstandings about the gospel (i.e., the good news about God), Revelation and Daniel could clear them up! God's love for mankind is ever-present in these visions, as well as his justice, and by revealing Jesus the book of Revelation fully shows the details in the plan of salvation.

The most consistent encouragement I witnessed in the book was how John's testimony, from beginning to end, gave me the assurance of my salvation while also making it crystal clear that I, or any believer, could turn from and give our salvation back to Jesus! He will not force us in any fashion to be saved, even after making our decision for him! We use our God-given free will to accept his gift of salvation, but God does not take our free will away after we accept his gift. Instead, through our same free will, the Lord gives us the right to turn down his gift of eternal life. One day, I sat down and went through the whole book, finding some 125 verses that assured me of salvation while also finding 44 clear verses that pointed out that I could also lose my salvation! In fact, the whole of Scripture is this way! If not, then some portions are contradicting other portions, making God a liar! But He is not a liar![78] Everything in the Scripture must fit and agree with no contradictions!

And just like the rest of Scripture, Revelation is not always written in chronological form, which is another common mistake made in its study. John will tell us about an overall period and then pauses to closely focus our attention on key points within that period. This is very important to keep in mind as we read the book! If we do, the pieces to this prophetic puzzle will fall correctly into place, answering our questions that naturally arise without any contradictions. Carefully notice in the next five paragraphs how the end-time information comes to a reasonable, logical conclusion!

Revelation thoroughly reveals Jesus, and it also teaches us much concerning Satan and the war between them (known to some as the great controversy between Christ and Satan), which started in heaven. And when the devil fell into sin from his lofty, right-hand-man position, he and one-third of the angels that he deceived were cast out of heaven to this earth, bringing sin and its many temptations to the human beings God had created here, until he and all the wicked are cast into the lake of fire (which is the unveiled glory of God)[79] that comes down from God out of heaven (hellfire).[80]

Our studies in this book confirmed teachings we found in the rest of Scripture:

1. Jesus will return soon but not in secret.[81] He brings the reward for the saved and the lost with him,[82] and of course, there are few signs of his soon returning left to be fulfilled.[83]
2. (See note 83 for biblical/historical signs fulfilled.)
3. False Christs will appear.[84]
4. Satan is a real angelic being. He still has great power but is not stronger than the Father, Son, or Holy Spirit, or any child of God trusting in Jesus![85]
5. The Great Controversy is the war about who God's created beings will worship.[86]
6. Only those keeping the commandments of God and having the faith of Jesus will be saved.[87]
7. Heaven is real![88] The New Jerusalem will be real![89] Earth, recreated, will be real![90]
8. When Jesus returns, it will be the most glorious day ever![91] These and many other teachings are found throughout the Bible!

Revelation verifies there will be two resurrections[92] and two rewards:[93] the first results in the saved taken to heaven[94] and the second results in the wicked, Satan, his evil angels, death, and hell (the

grave) being destroyed in the lake of fire.[95] In between these two resurrections is one thousand years known as the millennium.[96] During
that time, Jesus and the saved are not on earth but in heaven, looking
over the books with the Lord, answering our questions about who is
there and who is not there, verifying that God's judgments are fair
and just for each person that has ever lived.[97] Our God is a reasonable, trustworthy Ruler, and wants us to know this in every detail of
his judgment! This knowledge will be the insurance policy that sin
will never rise up again![98] *"He will again have compassion on us, and
will subdue our iniquities. You will cast all our sins into the depths of the
sea"* (Micah 7:19).

During this millennium, the earth sits in total devastation[99] as
the devil is bound by his chain of circumstances, being unable to
tempt anyone because the wicked are dead.[100] All that Satan and his
evil angels can do is to contemplate their final judgment.

After the thousand years are over, the New Jerusalem is brought
down to this earth with the saved in it.[101] The wicked are then resurrected and kneeling before the great white throne, together with
Satan and his cohorts, receive their final judgment and its execution
in the lake of fire.[102] After that, the Lord recreates this earth as it was
in the beginning.[103] Praise his name!

Of course, this was not everything we learned in the Revelation
Seminar. There was much more *living water* to drink! And when
Louise and I finished this series of studies, we both understood more
from the Scriptures than we ever did! Not only did we learn about
the fundamental Bible doctrines, but for the first time in our lives,
we understood that only the Spirit of God, over some 1,500 years
and through many different writers, could have inspired this book,
called the Word of God, so that every truth fit perfectly together with
all the others, never contradicting one point from beginning to end!
For whenever someone thinks they have found a contradiction, part
of their understanding is in error! God cannot contradict himself or
lie![104] His Word is the truth![105]

Following and consuming this life's dead river had given me
a desperate thirst for good water! It is the same for everyone even
though we may not yet recognize what will satisfy our thirst. If we

would only *"taste and see that the Lord is good. Blessed is the man who trusts in him!*[106] *For I will pour water on him who is thirsty."*[107]

Due to my own decisions, I was in one of the most rural areas of South Georgia—a dirty river bottom swamp that almost everyone outside that small county had no knowledge of. As an irresponsible drunk, I had lost everything and most everyone before I was thirsty enough to admit I was drinking the wrong water, and when the Lord gave me a cup of his *living water*, it quenched my thirst as nothing had ever done before! Yet I wanted more, not because I had to have it but because it was so good! It was then, through His providence, the Lord used 3ABN and his three angel's messages of Revelation 14 to bring me *"a pure river of* (the) *water of life"* from his throne,[108] and it continues to refresh me to this very day!

Chapter 21

The Seal of God Part 1

Then I saw another angel ascending from the east, having the seal of the living God. And he cried with a loud voice to the four angels to whom it was granted to harm the earth and the sea, saying, "Do not harm the earth, the sea, or the trees till we have sealed the servants of our God on their foreheads."

—Revelation 7:2, 3

Caution: What many of you are about to read in the next four chapters explains the greatest spiritual deception in history! It reveals something totally different from what most of you have been told or taught. It was for me! In my early days of Sunday school and church, like most people, I simply accepted what I was told by those who were in a teaching authority over me, never considering they may not know any better than me. Of course, I never dreamed any of them would be telling me something untrue. Yet as a new adult Christian seeking Bible truth, I discovered many errors in what I had been taught, which drove me to more in-depth study and prayer. This is my prayer for you!

As you consider the "different" information, please don't respond like most do, especially, other Christians. God will judge each of us based on the truth we know or had the opportunity to know. Therefore, each of us owes it to ourselves to study the Bible and verify the information whether it comes to us by way of a deacon, elder, pastor, theologian, your parents, or grandparents…or even me!

In my early days as a Christian, the pastor I learned the most from used to always say, "I don't want you to trust and follow me! Write the text references down, go home, and check me out in your own Bibles and encyclopedias! All this truth is there! If what I am telling you lines up with the Bible and documented history, then you can take it to the bank! If not, then don't believe me! Go elsewhere to be spiritually fed!"

As you read, read it with your Bible (not with your Bible notes and commentaries because they are not inspired), and if it does line up correctly, then pray and ask the Lord if he wants you to live by what his Word says *or* by what somebody else has taught you, which is contrary to God's Word? If you are determined to do God's will, He will answer and tell you to "*follow my Word.*"

Nine weeks had passed since beginning our lessons in the Revelation Seminar, and each one was more exciting than the one before! The tenth lesson was entitled, "The Seal of God," and I could hardly wait to start what sounded like a very important study. Little did I know just how important it would be!

As usual, when I arrived home from work, Becky and I would eat supper, and I would head down to her mother's house to study. I usually invited Becky, but she rarely showed any interest.

That evening, Louise was nice, but from my arrival, she seemed different. In fact, the atmosphere during our study seemed a bit tense. It was as if she was "walking on eggshells" as she led me through each question and answer; however, I did not say anything about her strange manner because I figured she might have had a difficult day, so I tried to just focus on the lesson.

The lesson began by asking these five questions:

1. "Would you be surprised to learn that God has a special sign, seal, or mark that he places on his people?" (Keep in mind, the Scripture will often use these terms interchangeably: Ezekiel 9:4, Romans 4:11, Ephesians 4:30, Revelations 7:2–3.)

2. "Would you be startled to learn that unless a person bares this mark at Jesus' return, he cannot enter God's kingdom?"

3. "Would you be shocked to discover that most people [including most Christians] are totally unaware of God's mark, and thus ignore it?"

4. "Would you be amazed to suddenly realize that God is much displeased that men are ignoring his carefully selected mark?"

5. "Would you be dumbfounded to find out that one great prime purpose of Revelation is to identify and restore God's mark to His people?"[109]

The only mark I had ever heard of was *the mark of* the beast,[110] and since I had not heard of a mark or seal for God's people, I wanted to know more. The lesson went on to say that few things were as important to God as his mark, and currently, as he looks around the globe, he sees very few of his people that have his mark! Looking back down the corridors of time, approximately five millennia ago, God saw this to be the case and made note of it for humanity.

Revelation 7:3 points out why God delays the destruction of this world. "*Do not harm the earth…till we have sealed the servants of our God on their foreheads.*" Before the Lord destroys this earth, his people must receive his mark or seal! Chapter 14:6 says the "*everlasting gospel* must go *to every nation, tribe, tongue, and people…*" And verse 7 directs us to his seal by telling us to "*worship him* [the Creator] *who made heaven and earth, the sea, and springs of waters.*"

Like many words in various languages, a lot of words in the Bible have multiple meanings and can be used in different ways. Thus, "a seal may stand for a truth or a requirement of God. It may also indicate his ownership and approval. A seal may also be used to authenticate a document."[111]

For thousands of years, kings, queens, and their most trusted members of the government have used seals to sign the vast numbers of documents emanating from their decisions. These seals typically include three pieces of information: the official's "[a] name, [b] title, and [c] territory."[112] Plus, some of the laws that govern these officials usually designate the information that is in the official's seal. Probably the most common seal used today is that of a notary public.

His/her "name" is John/Jane Doe, the "title" is notary public, and the "territory" is the state/province that is served. All three parts are in the seal and the laws concerning the notary public specify this information must be included in the seal.[113]

So the obvious question is, Where is God's seal to be found in Scripture? Isaiah 8:16 tells us to *bind up the testimony, seal the law among my disciples.* Then logically, we asked, *do any of God's laws include these three items required in a seal?*[114] We found that in the whole of Scripture there is only one law of God that includes this specific information. It is in the heart of the Ten Commandments. In fact, it is the fourth commandment that reveals the seal of the one and only true God, our Creator! *"Remember the Sabbath day, to keep it holy. Six days you shall labor and do all your work, but the seventh day* is *the Sabbath of the Lord your God. In it you shall do no work: you, nor your son, nor your daughter, nor your male servant, nor your female servant, nor your cattle, nor your stranger who* is *within your gates. For in six days the Lord made the heavens and the earth, the sea, and all that is in them, and rested the seventh day. Therefore the Lord blessed the Sabbath day and hallowed it."*[115]

His name is *the Lord your God* (v. 10). His title is a given (Creator) because He *made* (v. 11) everything, and his territory is "*the heavens and the earth*" (v. 11), the universe. Is this true? Of course, it is! The fourth commandment is the only law of God that contains all three pieces of information required in an official seal; thus, the seventh-day Sabbath is God's sign, seal, or mark that he is both Creator and Redeemer![116] And yes, every word of this is true! (But please don't put this book down now because there is much more clear Bible evidence for your consideration.)

The prophet Ezekiel confirms that God's seventh-day Sabbath was to be a sign between himself and his people, *that I am the Lord your God*[117] *who sanctifies them.*[118] And *his people* does not only mean the nation of Israel—the Hebrews—because Jesus said in Mark 2:27, *The Sabbath was made for man...*—that is, mankind. Plus, Revelation refers to those who will be saved as those *who keep the commandments of God.*[119] Therefore, in the first angel's message of Revelation 14:7, we are instructed to *worship him* [as the Creator] *who made heaven and earth, the sea and springs of water*, which is a quote from the fourth or Sabbath commandment.

As we progressed through the study, it was becoming evident that Louise was growing more and more cautious at each major point. Yet I stayed focused and did not inquire about her behavior.

The next question inquired as to "where will God's sign or seal 'be placed on a person'"?[120] Of course, the answer is, *their foreheads.*[121] Romans 7:25 supports this by saying that we serve God *with the mind*, and the mind is in the forehead. Ephesians 1:13 tells us that after we heard the gospel, we then believed it with our mind. Thus, before human probation closes, and we hear His Word of truth about the sign or seal for his people and consent with our mind to keep God's seventh-day Sabbath, we receive God's seal or mark of authority in our forehead.[122]

The lesson then asked, "When did God make the Sabbath?"[123] Scripture says he created the Sabbath on the seventh day after creating the first six days.[124] "From what did God make the Sabbath?"[125] He made the Sabbath out of time—the final twenty-four hours of Creation week. And just like the first six days of the week, he gave certain instructions for its use. The first six days are for man's work—caring for the world, his garden, the animals, and his family needs, etc... The twenty-four-hour period of the Sabbath is for worshiping God and developing a deeper personal relationship with him as we rest from our six days of work. Of course, we should spend some time with the Lord every day. Yet it is only the seventh day that he rested on, blessed, and sanctified (i.e., set it aside for our holy use).[126] Therefore, his Word makes it clear that he wants his people to sit by his still, *living waters* to rest, be blessed and refreshed, using its holy time with him throughout eternity![127]

Let us *remember* that God gave the seventh-day Sabbath to Adam and Eve before sin existed on this earth.[128] After sin came into this world, man was to still keep it. When Israel came out of more than four hundred years of slavery in Egypt, the Lord reminded them to keep the Sabbath, and they reinstituted it into their lives;[129] however, throughout the Old Testament, they struggled to remember it, and on most occasions, that is why God became angry with them;

all or part of his anger was due to them forgetting to keep his seventh-day Sabbath holy.

During the time of the New Testament, Jesus and his apostles kept the seventh-day Sabbath.[130] After Jesus died, was resurrected, and returned to heaven, his apostles and the new Christian church continued to keep the seventh day. When Jesus was answering his followers' questions about when the end-time would come and the destruction of the temple, looking prophetically some forty years into the future, he told them, *"Pray that your flight be not in the winter or on the Sabbath."*[131] Obviously, Jesus expected the church to be keeping the seventh-day Sabbath through the destruction of Jerusalem!

John tells us in Revelation 1:10 that he was *"in the Spirit on the Lord's Day..."* We know this is the seventh-day Sabbath because there again, in Matthew 12:8, Jesus stated he *"is Lord even of the Sabbath."* It is the Lord's Day, and nowhere in the New Testament does Paul or any other apostles tell us that the Sabbath of the Lord, his original weekly day of worship for his people, was changed!

Sunday, the first day of the week, is mentioned only eight times in the New Testament, and never in these verses, or their context, do they say the Sabbath has been changed.[132] Some teachers try to make the verses say this, but a close, careful reading proves otherwise!

Isaiah reveals that when the people of God get to his kingdom, *"it shall come to pass that...from one Sabbath to another, all flesh shall come to worship before me, says the Lord,"* keeping his seventh-day Sabbath throughout eternity![133] In this rest with God, we *"shall be like a tree planted by the rivers of water that brings forth its fruit in its season, whose leaf also shall not wither; and whatever he does shall prosper."*[134]

Speaking for the Lord, Ezekiel says, *"Hallow my Sabbaths, and they will be a sign between me and you, that you may know that I am the Lord your God."*[135] Based on God's Word, is the seal or sign of God important to him and his people? Of course it is!

Keep reading because in the next chapter God performs a modern-day miracle to help me see the importance he places on his sign!

Chapter 22

The Seal of God Part 2

Then I saw another angel ascending from the east, having the seal of the living God. And he cried with a loud voice to the four angels to whom it was granted to harm the earth and the sea, saying, "Do not harm the earth, the sea, or the trees till we have sealed the servants of our God on their foreheads."

—Revelation 7:2, 3

It was at this point that I asked Louise, "But a lot of churches today claim that the Ten Commandments were done away with when Jesus died on the cross! So if they are done away with, that means the Sabbath commandment is no longer binding on humanity! Correct?"

Louise then pointed me to what Jesus said in Matthew 5:17, 18. "*Do not think that I came to destroy the Law or the Prophets* [the writings of the Prophets]. *I did not come to destroy but to fulfill* [to keep them, not to do away with them]. *For assuredly, I say to you, till heaven and earth pass away* [has this happened yet?], *one jot or one tittle* [i.e., not even the dotting of an "i" or the crossing of a "t"] *will by no means pass* [be done away with] *from the law till all is fulfilled.*"

Louise then said, "These moral laws were given to us, by God, to identify sin.[136] And as they point out our sins, they help us see our need of a Savior and therefore lead us to Jesus![137] If these ten laws were done away with, as many teach them to be, mankind would no longer be able to know what sin is! In fact, this is why there is so much lawlessness in our world today! Preachers have told the people for hundreds of years that God's moral law has been done away with and that obedience to the Ten Commandments is legalism. The results are plain to see! Society, more and more, does what it wants to do; sin—unrighteousness—increases year after year." (Note: Those who teach that God's moral law no longer exists for the Christian, promote the condition of "antinomianism," which means "opposed to law." They are spiritual outlaws! Jesus fulfilling the moral law could not mean doing away with the Ten Commandments! To interpret these verses this way would, in essence, make the Lord contradict himself when he said, *"I did not come to destroy the law, but by fulfilling it to abrogate [abolish] it"* [Matthew 5:17]. In Isaiah 40:8, the prophet confirms God's moral law has not and will not be erased: *"The grass withers, the flower fades, but the word of our God stands forever."* Are there any people in society today opposed to law?)

Speaking up, I asked, "Then what law has been done away with?"

She answered, "Colossians explains that when Jesus forgave our sins, he wiped out the charges for our sins that were against us, nailing them to his cross. It further explains, since Christians understand that the ceremonial laws, *which are a shadow of things to come,*[138] are no longer to be kept due to the Lord's sacrifice, we are not to let others [legalists] fool us into doing so. Meat and drink offerings, special Old Testament holiday ceremonies, or annual ceremonial Sabbaths are no longer binding on God's people.[139] This is because Jesus's own death took the place of these offerings, ceremonies, and yearly Sabbaths. When the Lord went back to heaven, he became our High Priest, ministering for us in the heavenly sanctuary. Thus, all these earthly priest functions were no longer needed on earth. It is God's Ten Commandments (the moral law) that are still enforced and binding on the Christian because of their eternal purpose. Keeping them has everything to do with our love for God and our neighbor! Commandments numbers 1–4 deal with how we love God and commandments numbers 5–10 deal with how we love our fellow man. After all, Jesus said, *'If you love me, keep my commandments.'*[140] It has nothing to do with earning our salvation, but keeping them is simply the natural result, the evidence [i.e., the proof that our love for and faith in Jesus is genuine]![141] We have been misinformed by those who have been misinformed or, in some cases, purposely lied to by some teachers." (If you pin them down privately, many Protestant pastors will admit to knowing that the Ten Commandments are still in force for Christians, and some will actually admit that if they taught this, along with keeping the seventh-day Sabbath, they would lose their jobs!)

What Louise said rang the bell of remembrance in my mind. I could remember when my brothers and I were young, Mama would tell us that if we loved her, we would do as she told us to do.

I saw that the fourth commandment is very clear, and someone would have to try hard to misunderstand it! In fact, all the Ten Commandments are easy to understand, and Jesus gave mankind a perfect example in keeping each one from the motive of love. Did Jesus have any other gods but his Heavenly Father? No. Did he make any graven images and bow down to them? No. Did he use God's name in vain? No. Did Jesus dishonor his Heavenly Father or earthly father and mother? No. Did he kill anyone? No. Did he commit any sexual sins? No. Did he steal? Did he lie? Did he covet (desire) anything belonging to others? No! No! No! Well then, if Jesus did not break any of the other nine commandments, what valid reason would he have for breaking the fourth commandment and telling us it's okay to do the same thing? Especially since it is the only one out of the ten that begins by telling us to *remember* it?

As I listened and read the Scriptures, I could see where it was all consistent and fit Louise's and the lesson's reasoning perfectly! Plus, she began to share some history about the legal action taken by a Roman emperor to change the Bible Sabbath to the first day of the week.[142] This was amazing to hear again after so many years, and it is all documented in history!

Reaching the end of the study, we just sat there momentarily, in silence, looking at each other. She had the strangest look on her face, and I did not know why!

She then spoke abruptly and asked, "Well?" as if she was expecting a huge response from me.

I came right back, asking, "Well, what?"

She further asked, "Well, what do you think?"

I replied, "Do you mean, 'what do I think about the lesson?'"

Almost hollering, she said, "Yes! What do you think about this lesson?"

I broke into a smile as I asked once more for clarification. "What do I think about the seventh-day Sabbath?"

This time, she did holler, "Yes!" Most Christians get upset and do not want to hear anything about the seventh-day Sabbath! Their pastors have taught them wrong and convinced them to not listen to anyone who shares the seventh-day Sabbath with them or even consider all this evidence from God's Word and history, but it has not seemed to bother you at all!"

I calmly replied, "Louise, ever since my ninth-grade world history class, I've known that Saturday was the seventh day of the week or what the Bible calls the Sabbath."

She just sat there, looking at me with such astonishment on her face, and then asked, "Really? You have known that Saturday is the Bible Sabbath all these years?"

I answered, "Yes, but I have never really thought about it until just a few minutes ago. I was brought up to worship on Sunday. Saturday was never an issue in my mind, so I never really thought any more about it!"

Louise went on questioning me, "Well, how did you come to know in the ninth grade that Saturday was the seventh-day Sabbath?"

"Well, let me answer you by explaining what just happened as we were finishing the lesson. As you began sharing some of the history of the Sabbath, you came to the part about the Roman emperor, Constantine the Great, creating a law [the constitution of Constantine, AD 321) to change the seventh-day Sabbath for Christians to Sunday.[143] Well, I learned in ninth-grade world history, Constantine had become a Christian and declared the religion legal throughout the Roman Empire, and to draw more Roman citizens into the faith and not be associated with the Jewish faith, he changed the day of worship from the seventh-day Sabbath to Sunday![144, 145]

"As I told you a moment ago, I've never thought about learning that in public school until you started talking about it in this study, and the moment you did, God started playing a video memory of me learning it in my history class. In our textbook, subarticles were written down the side of most pages, giving additional information on key parts of the chapters. My mind was playing a video of that subarticle in my textbook. I could once again see a painting of Constantine, on his horse with his army all around him, as they were fighting a battle. Constantine was looking up into the sky, seeing a vision of the cross that he believed was a sign from the Christian God."

Louise burst out, "You were seeing that?"

"I saw it just as clear, several minutes ago, as I did years ago sitting in that classroom, and it is obvious to me that God was answering my prayer from the day I encountered Him on the highway!"

She asked, "God was answering your prayer? What prayer?"

I then reminded her, "Remember a few weeks ago when I had an experience with the Lord on the highway and came home a different man? I was born again that day and told the Lord that I knew there had to be a church teaching the truth of the whole Bible. I told him that I did not know where it was or what it was called, but if he would lead me and direct me in the way he would have me go, I would follow! And that is exactly what he has been doing! Everything we are learning is straight out of Scripture and documented history!"

She was totally astounded and continued to stare at me!

I then added the following, "Louise, I hated world history, and I cut class all the time! I did anything I could to get out of that class, including forging my mother's signature on excuses, and yet on one of the few days I attended, our great God saw fit to plant that seed of knowledge in the back of my mind because he knew that years later I would need confirmation of his truth as he was trying to lead me into a new life with him.

"All this has not just happened! It was like a light bulb being turned on! I had been in a dark room, and the Lord flipped the switch, turning on the light of his Word, answering my prayer about where I should go! I have no doubt about it! Whoever teaches these lessons is being used by the Lord to lead us where he wants us to go, and I believe we should find out if there is a church around here teaching these same Bible truths, and if so, we need to visit them!"

Louise spoke up, "There is that toll-free number on the screen during their programs. I'll call them and see if they know of a church around here." The next day, she did call, finding out there were two churches about thirty miles away, in opposite directions, so she obtained the phone number for each pastor.

The next few days, I was out of town again, but when I returned, Louise told me there was one church north of us in Dublin, Georgia, and another southeast of us in Baxley, Georgia. I did not know much about Dublin because I made no deliveries there, but I was acquainted with Baxley, so we decided to visit there that coming Saturday, and we called the pastor for directions and the time of their service.

Pastor Alan Williams and his family had not long before this came to the Baxley-Alma Church District. He was so elated when we shared with him our story as to how we came to call him, and he could hardly wait to meet us! He gave us directions, and we told him to look for us that coming Sabbath, starting at 9:30 a.m. for Sabbath School study.

Thus, by drinking more and more of God's *living water*, this is how I began keeping the seventh-day Sabbath, *the Lord's Day* of the Bible, and would eventually be sealed with the seal of the Living God.

Chapter 23

The Unwanted Mark Part 1

Then a third angel followed them, saying with a loud voice, "If anyone worships the beast and his image, and receives his mark on his forehead or on his hand, he himself shall also drink of the wine of the wrath of God, which is poured out full strength into the cup of His indignation. He shall be tormented with fire and brimstone in the presence of the holy angels and in the presence of the Lamb…whoever receives the mark of his name."

—Revelation 14:9–11

After a few more studies into the series, we came to a lesson that led us to discover a mark that the Bible warns against receiving—the *mark* of *the beast*![146] Yet in a more positive way, it clarified our understanding of *the seal of the living God*.[147]

Like many raised in a Protestant denomination, I gained a general understanding of the doctrine of *righteousness by faith*.[148] As I grew older, I began to see more clearly that what most of us are taught and what the Bible teaches of this fundamental doctrine are different. For example, if Jesus is our Savior by delivering us from all aspects of sin, then as our Lord, is he not entitled to our wholehearted, total obedience to his Word, *bringing every thought into captivity to the obedience of Christ?*[149]

This understanding is very different for most or at least practiced differently from how most Christians live. The difference is found in the last item of the above question, *obedience*. The majority of Catholics and Protestants will tell you they believe a Christian is obligated to obey all three persons of the Godhead: the Father, Son, and Holy Spirit. They will also profess that Christians should obey God's Word, the Bible. Yet if you were to question them specifically about what parts of God's Word they do not have to obey, their answers may surprise you! Yet both the seal of God and the mark of the beast have everything to do with both *righteousness by faith*[150] and *obedience* to God's Word, which includes His moral law, the Ten Commandments.

Righteousness by Works versus Righteousness by Faith

Studying my Bible each day whenever I had a few minutes, I came to understand that those who inherit salvation—eternal life—must be righteous before God. Many are taught that in the Old Testament, righteousness came by God's people, keeping His law (righteousness by works), and in the New Testament, righteousness comes by believing in Jesus as your personal Savior and Lord (righteousness by faith). But this is only halfway correct!

No one has ever obtained salvation by keeping God's law, yet this is a huge misunderstanding throughout Christendom! "*Knowing that a man is not justified by the works of the law but by faith in Jesus Christ...for by the works of the law no flesh shall be justified.*"[151] The saved "in all ages have been saved by grace [through faith in the Savior and His gracious promise]."[152] "This *'grace...was given us in Christ Jesus before the world began."*[153] The law points out our sin, thus *by the law is the knowledge of sin.*[154] It is only Christ who can save! "*Nor is there salvation in any other name* [or way] *under heaven given among men by which we must be saved.*"[155] "*That having been justified by his grace we should become heirs according to the hope of eternal life.*"[156]

113

"Noah *found grace* (Genesis 6:8); Moses *found grace* (Exodus 33:17); the Israelites in the wilderness found grace (Jeremiah 31:2); and Abel, Enoch, Abraham, [Sarah,] Isaac, Jacob, Joseph, [Rahab,] and many other Old Testament worthies were saved *by faith* [in God's gracious promise of the Redeemer and] *obtained a good testimony*."[157] Because of his grace to them, they were to be saved by looking forward to the cross, in faith! Due to the same grace of God toward believers since Jesus's death, we are saved by looking back at the cross, in faith!

"The law is necessary because, like a mirror, it reveals the 'dirt' in our lives. Without it, people are sinners but are not aware of it"[158] unless it is revealed to them. "However, the law has no saving power! It can only point out sin"[159] and help us to understand our need of a Savior.[160] "Jesus and he alone can save a person from sin! This has always been true, even in Old Testament times [Acts 4:10, 12; 2 Timothy 1:9]."[161]

As I continued to study, I also found there is another extremely important point about God's law that most Christians fail to remember! While pointing out what sin is, the Ten Commandments, God's moral law, helps us know what is right! Yet so many lose sight of this dual purpose in God's commandments because they have been taught incorrectly that his law has been done away with![162]

Paul opens and closes his letter to the Romans pointing out that we have received God's *grace…for obedience to the faith* (Romans 1:5, 16:26). Here, "faith means…that habit and attitude of mind by which the Christian shows his loyalty and devotion to Christ and his dependence of Him. Such faith produces obedience… The great message of…Romans is that righteousness comes by faith [chap. 3:22; etc.]." Paul…"regards his apostleship as a commission to bring about the obedience that springs from faith among all the nations."[163] He is talking about the same natural results in 6:16: "*Do you not know that to whom you present yourself slaves to obey, you are that one's slaves whom you obey, whether of sin leading to death, or of obedience leading to righteousness?*"

I saw in Hebrews 8:7–10 where the difference between the old and new covenants is explained. It says the first covenant failed because of the weakness of God's people to keep their promise to obey his law. However, due to God's great love for Israel (and all people); he gave the second [new] covenant based on his promise to fulfill his law and write it in our hearts! As we see God's love for us, we are drawn closer to him, and the closer we come to him, the more we open our hearts to him, desiring to obey his Word from the love we have for him and not from a legalistic fear to obey the Lord's rules. This is *obedience to the faith* or *obedience of the faith*.

"God's purpose in proclaiming his law to Israel, and eventually all people, was to reveal to them their sinfulness [Romans 3:20] and their need of a Savior [Galatians 3:24]. But the Jews had perverted God's purpose and had used the laws, both moral and ceremonial, as the means of establishing their own righteousness by their own attempts at legalistic obedience. Christ came to bring this mistaken abuse of law to an end and to point the way back to faith. Such faith does not abolish law but rather establishes it [see Romans 3:31] and makes it possible for men to fulfill its requirements,"[164] not as the means of obtaining salvation but as the evidence of having received salvation! Paul was teaching that Christ had come and died to bring an end to his people, trying to keep the law to earn their salvation when that was never God's intention for giving the law!

As for Ephesians 2:14, 15 and Colossians 2:14, 16, 17, these verses speak of the ceremonial laws being no longer needed because Christ became our only needed sacrifice and our heavenly High Priest. It is these laws that were ended at Christ's cross. When Jesus died, this is why "*the veil of the temple was torn in two from top to bottom*" (Matthew 27:51). The ceremonial laws were ended, but *the law of liberty*, God's Ten Commandments, will never come to an end! They will always be the basis of his character, the foundation of his government, the principles of morality, and the definition of right and wrong! These are the reasons he will write the Ten Commandments, his everlasting covenant, upon the tables of our heart (Jeremiah 31:31–34; Hebrews 8:8–12)!

Obedience versus Disobedience to God's Word

I then realized the Bible gives us the perfect illustration about the importance of the Christian's obedience to God's Word in the example of our spiritual father, Abraham. What did the Lord originally instruct Abraham to do? "*Get out of your country, from your family and from your father's house, to a land that I will show you*" (Genesis 12:1). How did Abraham respond? "*So Abraham departed as the Lord had spoken to him*" (v. 4). Then what was the fruit of Abraham's faith about what God said to him? Abraham's obedience was the fruit of his faith! "*By faith Abraham obeyed when he was called to go out to the place which he would receive as an inheritance. And he went out, not knowing where he was going*" (Hebrews 11:8).

What did the Lord much later command Abraham to do? "*Take now your son, your only son Isaac...and offer him there as a burnt offering on one of the mountains of which I shall tell you*" (Genesis 22:2). What then was the evidence of his faith in God's promise to make him the father of many nations? (17:4; 22:10–12). Due to Abraham's love for God, the evidence of his faith in God's promise was his obedience—his heartfelt decision to offer his only son as a sacrifice to the Lord! "*Was not Abraham our father justified by works* [the evidence] *when he offered Isaac his son on the altar* [in his mind]? *Do you see that faith was working together with his works, and by works faith was made perfect?*" (i.e., *complete*; James 2:21–22). *Faith* here is *conviction, trust.*[165] Our love for God, plus the faith he gives us, acted upon by our free will, *produces the righteous obedience of faith*, which is the evidence of our salvation! In the judgment, this evidence proves to the universe that we are justified before him. "*For in Christ Jesus neither circumcision nor uncircumcision avails anything, but faith working through love*" (Galatians 5:6).

So is there any part of God's Word that is okay to disregard? Yes! Christians may disregard the parts of God's Word that were completed by Jesus at the cross. These are the ceremonial laws concerning "*food* [offerings]...*drink* [offerings], *or regarding a festival or a new moon or* [annual Ceremonial] *sabbaths, which are a shadow of things to come, but the substance is of Christ.*[166] All these are biblical *shadows* or *types* of Christ's various ministries that have come and were fulfilled. However, the weekly seventh-day Sabbath [not mentioned here] is nowhere in Scripture called a *shadow* or *type* (tupos) in the original language.[167] Therefore, the weekly seventh-day Sabbath was not done away with at the cross! It is still here just like the other nine commandments!

I asked Louise, "Then why do most Christians reject the fact that the seventh-day Sabbath is still valid and binding on them just like the other nine commandments?"

In a kind but straightforward manner, she said, "They reject it because their Bible teachers have confused them by teaching two false doctrines. First, as I previously explained, they teach them that God's Ten Commandment Law has been done away with at the cross. Second, they teach them that God's seventh-day Sabbath was changed in the Bible. And when you have been told the same thing over and over and over again, and almost everyone you know follows it in some way or another, it becomes what you accept and believe without question!"

Ever since that night's study, I have often thought about Louise's answer, and I have seen time and again the evidence of its truth play out in the lives of people everywhere, not just about God's Word but about almost any subject you can think of. Yet there comes a time in all our lives when we are thirsty for the truth, and at that point in time, God brings his *living water* to quench our thirst. He will not force us to drink. The decision is ours. If we accept the *living water*, he will give us all we desire! *"For I will pour water on him who is thirsty, and floods on the dry ground"* (Isaiah 44:3).

I was continually thirsty, not because my thirst was not being quenched but because I had never tasted water that was so delicious! After each lesson, I could hardly wait to partake of the next one! And God was fulfilling his promise, pouring floods of his *living water* upon a dry ground that was soaking it up! In his next cup would be the final evidence for the mark of the beast.

Chapter 24

The Unwanted Mark Part-2

Then a third angel followed them, saying with a loud voice, "If anyone worships the beast and his image, and receives his mark on his forehead or on his hand, he himself shall also drink of the wine of the wrath of God, which is poured out full strength into the cup of his indignation. He shall be tormented with fire and brimstone in the presence of the holy angels and in the presence of the Lamb...whoever receives the mark of his name."

—Revelation 14:9–11

Growing up, I remember hearing people periodically express ideas about who the beast of Revelation 13 is, also known as the Antichrist.[168] Their ideas varied about individuals, institutions, and conspirators not yet known were suggested to be the great end-time enemy of God's people: Antiochus IV Epiphanies; Roman emperors Caligula and Nero; dictators Napoleon, Hitler, Stalin, and Saddam Hussein; different popes; and the New World Order, just to name a few. Yet no matter who or what is believed to be the Antichrist, usually only one or two reasons are given for these opinions.

I never realized until Louise and I became immersed in God's Word, the last day prophecies of Daniel and Revelation give a specific list of characteristics about the beast enabling honest Bible and history students to clearly recognize this power. As we studied, it became evident that only one power had all the characteristics given by Daniel and John the Revelator. Even though many modern Bible scholars do not believe the book of Daniel was authored by him, Jesus gave reference to the prophet's testimonies,[169] and that is good enough for me to accept the book as true and penned by Daniel.

Daniel, writing in the sixth century BC while John writing close to the end of the first century AD had a historical gap of approximately 665 years.[170] For such a long time, we followed the lesson's comparison of Daniel's fourth beast (which evolved into the Little Horn) with John's first beast and verified as much historical information as we could. Since the lessons maintained that both powers are Rome, we began there to see if the evidence accurately fit Rome.

Chapters 2, 7, and 8 of Daniel describe two different dreams and one vision that are parallel in much of their content. While the prophet does need help from the angel Gabriel in understanding the different symbols used in each dream or vision, there are enough common points to match, with historical facts, for us to identify the kingdoms involved.

In chapter 2, the king of Babylon had a dream of a great image, and God revealed the dream and its meaning to the king through Daniel. The head of the image was fine gold, its chest and arms were silver, its belly and thighs were bronze, its legs were iron, and its feet were partly iron and clay. Daniel told the king his kingdom was the head of gold. After him, another kingdom would come symbolized by the silver. Then a third kingdom would come represented by the bronze with a fourth kingdom symbolized by the iron. A fifth kingdom, partly strong and partly weak, was seen as iron mixed with clay that would eventually break into ten pieces, represented by the ten toes.[171]

In chapter 7, Daniel has a dream, and in it sees four great beasts come up out of the turbulent sea of humanity that is filled by the dead rivers of this life. Allowing the Bible to interpret itself whenever possible, Revelation 17:15 explains that many of the waters we see in prophecy *are peoples, multitudes, nations, and tongues.* Thus, these beasts are coming out of the populations of the then-known Mediterranean world. He was told the beasts are kings or kingdoms:

the first is represented as a lion with eagle's wings; the second was a bear raised on one side with three ribs in his mouth; the third beast was a four-headed leopard with four bird's wings. The prophet is especially interested in the fourth beast since it is unlike the previous three, and he seeks greater understanding. It is described as *"dreadful and terrible, exceedingly strong. It had huge iron teeth; it was devouring, breaking in pieces, and trampling the residue with its feet. It was different from all the beasts that were before it, and it had ten horns."*[172] Daniel watches until the beast is slain and destroyed (v. 11). Yet he is troubled because he does not understand the meaning of the dream, so he asks a heavenly being what it all means (vv. 15, 16). The first kingdom was identified as Babylon in chapter 2, and as chapter 7 begins, Daniel is serving a different king but the same kingdom. Plus, according to archeology, the winged male lion was a common figure used in Babylon's art, especially at the city's main gate.

Chapter 5 ends, and chapter 6 begins with the second kingdom, led by Darius the Mede. Chapter 6 ends speaking of Cyrus the Persian king and his rule; thus, the second beast is the combined kingdom of Media-Persia, confirmed in the interpretation of chapter 8:20–21. These verses also identify the third kingdom as Greece under Alexander the Great and his four generals who divided his empire after Alexander's death. According to history, the fourth kingdom can only be the pagan Roman Empire!

Daniel and Revelation predict, and history confirms a major change taking place in pagan Rome.

Daniel says, *"After this I saw in the night visions, and behold, a fourth beast...and it had ten horns. I was considering the horns, and there was another horn, a little one, coming up among them, before whom three of the first horns were plucked out by the roots. And there, in this horn, were eyes like the eyes of a man, and a mouth speaking pompous words"* (7:7, 8).

"I, Daniel, was grieved in my spirit... I came near to one of those who stood by, and asked him the truth of all this... So he told me... "'Those great beasts...are four kings...'" (vv. 15–17).

"Then I wished to know the truth about the fourth beast...and the ten horns that was on its head, and the other horn which came up, before

which three [horns] *fell, namely, that horn which had eyes and a mouth which spoke pompous words... I was watching; and the same horn was making war against the saints, and prevailing against them, until the Ancient of Days came, and a judgment was made in favor of the saints of the Most High, and the time came for the saints to possess the kingdom* [of heaven]" (vv. 19–22).

"*He...shall persecute the saints of the Most High and shall intend to change times and law. Then the saints shall be given into his hand for a time and times and half a time*" (v. 25).

The prophet sees a little horn come up among the ten and next, three of the ten were plucked out. The little horn has the eyes of a man, speaks "*pompous words*" (v. 8) against God, and persecutes God's people. Daniel even tells how long the little horn has this power and that he will "*intend to change times and law*" (v. 25).

Pagan Rome with its Caesars and emperors grew into the largest, longest-lasting, of these four kingdoms through its military might. It was always against Christianity until Emperor Constantine expressed his faith in the Christian God and legalized the religion. Eventually, its religious power grew as its military characteristics were shrinking. Church bishops began struggling among themselves for influence and power until the church split with the European clergy and members coming under the control of the bishop of Rome and the Asian clergy and members coming under the control of the bishop of Constantinople. Rome declared its bishop to be a papal king or pope. (See appendix B1.)

In order for the church to attract the pagan citizens of the empire into their membership, Rome kept many of the pagan gods and merely renamed them as biblical characters, using their statues and other artwork of these gods in the same manner. The church also maintained many of the pagan festivals and feast days by substituting Christian holidays and celebrations—the greatest substitution being the "venerable Day of the Sun—the first day of the week, Sunday— for the seventh-day Sabbath. "The English noun Sunday...which itself developed from Old English [before 700] Sunnandæg (literally meaning 'sun's day')... In Roman culture, Sunday was the day of the sun god. In pagan theology, the sun was the source of life, giving warmth and illumination to mankind. It was the center of a popular cult among Romans, who would stand at dawn to catch the first rays of sunshine as they prayed."[173] Sunday as the Christian Sabbath was instituted on March 7, 321, AD.[174] Though given its power, seat, and authority by the empire, papal Rome claimed it all came directly from the apostle Peter and Christ.[175]

The papacy continued to grow into a worldwide power from 538 BC to AD 1798. During this period is when the additional characteristics prophesied by Daniel and John are revealed. The worst being the persecution of God's people! The papacy openly admits and brags about this! (See appendix B2.)

In order for papal Rome to gain more power over the kings and kingdoms of Europe and Christendom, it began to interpret Scripture in ways that were blasphemous "*against God...to blaspheme his name, his tabernacle, and those who dwell in heaven.*"[176] Rome instituted a policy of harsh corporal punishments and war through the civil government as their arm of enforcement for getting rid of those who did not accept its dogma, highlighted by the three kingdoms that were *plucked out*; the Heruli,[177] Ostrogoths,[178] and Vandals.[179] They believed the doctrines of Arianism,[180] which taught that Jesus was not of the same substance as God but a created being exalted above all other creatures.

The pope and his priests claimed to be able to forgive sins[181] and then, in AD 1190, began claiming the power to sell indulgences for sins. He also receives worship (Revelation 13:4, 8) and "is the supreme judge of the law of the land."[182] "Hence, the pope is crowned with a triple crown, as king of heaven and earth, and purgatory (Infernorum)."[183] In the worship service—the "Mass"—their clergy claim to create the actual body and blood of Jesus for the communion service.[184]

Gregory VII, pope from AD 1073–87, wrote the following dictates:

> 9. that all princes should kiss his (the pope's) feet only...
> 12. that it is lawful for him to depose emperors...

122

18. that his sentence is not to be reviewed by anyone while he alone can review the decisions of
all others…
19. that he can be judged by no one…
22. that the Romish Church never erred, nor will
it, according to the Scriptures, ever err.[185]

(On March 12, 2000, Pope John Paul II admitted the papacy killed many Christians and others who would not agree to follow the papacy's interpretations of Scripture and commands; so much for the papacy's infallibility and claim to never err!)

Daniel 7:25 tells us the little horn power controlled the people of God *for a time and times and half a time.* But what does the term *time* mean in prophecy? In Numbers 14:34 and Ezekiel 4:6, we find the prophetic key for the term *time.* At God's instruction, Moses sent twelve spies, one from every tribe of Israel, into the Promised Land to gather information to plan their entrance. When the spies returned, ten were so frightened by the successful large kingdoms they saw they gave bad reports due to their lack of faith. The Lord decided to bar Israel from entering Canaan and sentenced them to roam the desert forty years until all that generation had died, except Joshua and Caleb who had given good reports due to their faith in God. The Lord told Israel, *"According to the number of days which you spied out the land, forty days, for each day you shall bear your guilt one year, namely forty years…"*

In Ezekiel 4:1, the Lord instructs his prophet to give a message to Israel and Judah through an object lesson. First, Ezekiel was to build a simple model of the city of Jerusalem being under siege. Second, the seer was to lie in his bed on his left side. God then tells him in verses 4–6, *"According to the number of the days that you lie on it* [his left side], *you shall bear their iniquity…three hundred and ninety days… And when you have completed them, lie again on your right side; then you shall bear the iniquity of the house of Judah forty days. I have laid on you a day for each year."*

Continuing to let the Bible be its own interpreter, we asked ourselves if there is another place in Scripture where the phrase *a time and times and half a time* is used. There is in Revelation 12:14. In this chapter, the *dragon* of verse 13 is identified in verse 9 as *that serpent of old, called the Devil and Satan* (v. 14). Then *the woman*, who is the church, is given two wings to escape the devil's persecution during that same time, *a time and times and half a time*. In this verse, most Bibles will give a reference pointing the reader back to verse 6, where it defines what this phrase means *one thousand two hundred and sixty days.*

We then apply the *day for each year* principle just like the Bible did in Numbers and Ezekiel, and we can then understand how long the little horn power of Daniel 7:25 will persecute and war against God's people. The angel tells Daniel, "*The saints shall be given into his* [the little horn's] *hand for a time and times and half a time*" or "*one thousand two hundred and sixty days*," which are prophetic days and applying the *day for each year* principle, gives us the actual time of *one thousand two hundred and sixty years*. We know this application is correct because if it were only a literal meaning of *one thousand two hundred and sixty days*, it would only equal a little more than three and one half literal years into the second beast's (Media-Persia) rule, whereas the interpretation is about the little horn which comes on the scene after the fourth beast (pagan Rome).

At this point in the lesson, our attention was taken to the time mentioned in Revelation 13:5. Since the conversion of prophetic time to actual time was fresh in our thinking, we also considered the same verse because it revealed a very important point of identification! We were told in verse 5 that the first beast of this chapter was given authority over *the saints* (v. 7) *for forty-two months.*

> In biblical eschatology (end-time events) a prophetic year or prophetical year is sometimes regarded as being different from an ordinary year, namely a 360-day period of *time*, a 360-year period of *time*, or a 360-year period of *time* composed of 360-day *years*.
>
> (The fact that the prophets understood a year as 360 days is clearly understood) and

"can be seen in the prophecies of Daniel and Revelation as in the use of '*time, times and half a time.*'" (i.e. [*time* = 1 prophetic year of 360 days] + [*times* = 2 prophetic years of 720 days] + [*half a time* = 0.5 prophetic year of 180 days] = 3.5 prophetic years), or "1,260 days" or "42 months." These references represent a period of 1,260 days (based on the 360-day Jewish [prophetic] year multiplied by 3.5). Divide 1,260 days by 42 months, and you will get a 30-day month, as 12 months of 30 days equals 360 days in a year.[186]

Therefore, the two time periods expressed in Daniel 7 and Revelation 13 are the same, only expressed in different terms. (Example: twelve months/one year.)

The next identification point says the little horn *shall intend to change times and law.*[187]

A. How has the papacy tried to change God's laws? In three different ways: In its catechisms (books that teach official church doctrine) it has (1) omitted the second commandment against veneration (a feeling of deep respect and reverence) of images, and (2) shortened the fourth (Sabbath) commandment from ninety-four words to just eight. The Sabbath commandment (Exodus 20:8–11) clearly specifies Sabbath as the seventh day of the week. As changed by the papacy, the commandment reads: "Remember that thou keep holy the Sabbath day." Written thus, it can refer to any day. And, finally, she (the church) (3) divided the tenth commandment into two commandments."[188]

B. How did the papacy attempt to change God's times? In two ways: (1) It has changed the time of the Sabbath from the seventh day to the first day. (2) It has also changed God's "timing" for the beginning and closing hours of the Sabbath. Instead of counting the Sabbath day from sundown Friday night to sundown Saturday night as God mandates (Leviticus 23:32), it adopted the pagan Roman custom of counting the day from midnight Saturday night to midnight Sunday night. God predicted these 'changes' would be attempted by the beast or antichrist.[189]

The following boastful quotations reveal the mindset of the papal Antichrist:

> They (the Catholics) allege the Sabbath changed into Sunday, the Lord's Day, contrary to the decalogue, as it appears; neither is there any example more boasted of than the changing of the Sabbath day. "Great," say they, "is the power and authority of the (Catholic) church, since it dispensed with one of the Ten Commandments." (Augsburg Confession, Art. XXVIII.[190] [*Boastful quotes* continued in appendix B3])

In AD 538, the Ostrogoths, the reigning Arian power in Italy, was defeated in the siege of Rome. This opened the door for the papacy to expand its power in the western church. It serves as the starting point for the *time and times and half a time* prophecy of Daniel 7:25 and the *forty-two months* prophecy of Revelation 13:5. Thus, AD 538 + 1,260 years = 1,798—the very year the papal institution was *mortally wounded* (Revelation 13:3), after a long series of events that progressively weakened the papacy. On February 10, 1798, Napoleon's General Berthier entered Rome, taking the pope prisoner, and he died in exile the next year at Valence, France.[191]

In 1929, *his deadly wound was* beginning to be *healed* (13:3). "The Lateran Treaty restored temporal power to the pope, who was given the rule of Vatican City, a section of the city of Rome about 108.7 acres..."[192] "However, the prophet [John] envisioned a much greater restoration. He saw the wound completely healed, as the Greek implies. After the healing he saw *all that dwell upon the earth,* except a faithful few, worshiping the beast (v. 8; cf. GC 579)" and receiving his mark. "This is still future."[193]

Daniel then tells us that he "*watched till the beast was slain, and its body destroyed and given to the burning flame*" (7:11) while John confirms this, saying, "*the beast was captured, and with him the false prophet* [apostate Protestantism] *who worked signs in his presence, by which he deceived those who received the mark of the beast and those who worshiped his image. These two were cast alive into the lake of fire burning with brimstone*" (Rev. 19:20 and 20:10).

John then gives us the last point of identification in Revelation 13:18. "*Let him who has understanding calculate the number of the beast, for it is the number of a man: His number is 666.*" Supposedly in AD 331, Emperor Constantine, in a document entitled *Donation of Constantine*, first referred to the pope in Latin as "VICARIUS FILII DEI" or "Vicar of the Son of God."[194] Though the document was later determined to be a forgery, the use of this title began a long time precedent. "The legitimacy of the title as a papal claim cannot be questioned for the term VICARIUS CHRISTI, Vicar of Christ is used for the pope. It was made an official title of the pope by Innocent III."[195] Therefore, if "the pope claims to be the 'Vicar of Christ,' he is claiming to be the 'Vicar of the Son of God'."[196]

In the twelfth century, an Italian priest named Gratian used the *Donation of Constantine* in his writing, the *Decretum,* which was never voted as an official statement of the Catholic Church but "has been quoted constantly through the centuries," like most official documents have, especially in "seminaries for the instruction of priests."[197] VICARIUS FILII DEI was then used by the Jesuit encyclopedist of the eighteenth century, Ferraris, in his *PROPPTA BIBLIOTHECA* ("Handy Library"), in the article "Papa."[198]

Yet "the most striking use of the title occurs not in Latin but in English. Cardinal Manning, a convert to Roman Catholicism… during the Oxford Movement of the early nineteenth century, wrote a book called *The Temporal Sovereignty of the Pope*. In this book, eleven different times he calls the pope the VICAR OF THE SON OF GOD."[199] "It cannot be said that this book expresses the opinion of a man. When cardinals write they need no imprimatur [an official license by the Roman Catholic Church to print an ecclesiastical or religious book]. As princes of the church, they speak for the church."[200]

But what is the significance of this papal title, besides being blasphemous? One of the early church elders, Irenaeus (c. AD 130–202) "identified the beast [of Revelation 13] as the Antichrist, and believed that the numerical values of the letters of his name would add up to 666… Since Irenaeus' day 666 has been applied to many names. The number alone cannot identify the beast…"[201] "Roman numerals are a numeral system that originated in ancient Rome and remained the usual way of writing numbers throughout Europe well into the Late Middle Ages. Numbers in this system are represented by combinations of letters from the Latin alphabet."[202] (Go to appendix B4.)

All these identification points given in Daniel and Revelation, point to the same figure in history. If this last one points to the same entity, we can be sure that the little horn power of Daniel and the first beast power of Revelation are one and the same Antichrist spoken of by the apostle Paul too! *"Let no one deceive you by any means; for that Day* [the second coming of Jesus] *will not come unless the falling away* [the great apostasy] *comes first, and the man of sin is revealed, the son of perdition, who opposes and exalts himself above all that is called God or that is worshiped, so that he sits as God in the temple of God* [as head of the church, not a rebuilt temple in Jerusalem], *showing himself that he is God… And now you know what is restraining, that he may be revealed in his own time. For the mystery of lawlessness is already at work.* [In Paul's day, the fourth beast power of pagan Rome was on the world scene before the little horn—papacy—was born]; *only he who now restrains will do so until he is taken out of the way. And then the lawless one will be revealed, whom the Lord will consume with the breath of his mouth and destroy with the brightness of his coming"* (2 Thessalonians 2:3–8).

Revelation 13:11–18 then told us that a second beast (the most powerful government in the world at the end-time and the only one to be established around 1798)[203] on the world stage would exercise all the power of the first beast (Antichrist), causing the whole world to worship the Antichrist (by merging church and state through a congressional Sunday law) who deceived them. This is the main reason why there is a considerable movement in the United States today to prove there has never been a separation of church and state.[204] Ever since the Antichrist blossomed into the religious entity of the papal system, it needed civil muscle to force the world to worship and obey it. In the end-time, just as the first beast did, it will join its leadership and religious authority with governmental power requiring all to worship according to its dictates.

Now when you worship someone or something, there is usually a designated time to do so. What day would you expect the papacy to require worship until Christ returns? For centuries, the Catholic Mass has been held daily, but the designated day of worship is Sunday ever since Constantine's edict. At this time (October 2020), the papacy is holding private, high-level meetings with world leaders pressing them to legislate Sunday as a worldwide day of rest and worship to save the earth from the effects of climate change![205] All Christians (and non-Christians alike) who do not realize they have been deceived about the Sabbath/Sunday truths will automatically follow the papacy, supported by the world governments, receiving the mark of the beast!

At this moment, the most important question in your (the reader's) life is, Are you open enough to the possibility that you have misunderstood God's Word about his seventh-day Sabbath, the seal of God, and the mark of the beast? Because if you are not open enough to consider this a possibility, you may have already believed the greatest lie in history!

As we finished this lesson, Louise then gave me a most serious look and asked, "Is it clear to you what the seal of God and the mark of the beast are?" But without giving me the chance to answer, she said, "In case you have any doubts, let's go back and reread the quotes from the Catholic leaders and their documents! Let the papal system tell us again what the mark of its authority is [the mark of the beast] [reread appendix B3 and B4] and then let the Bible and documented history tell us again what the seal of God is! If we don't consider this evidence again and not reexamine it before moving on, we will be sticking our heads in the sand and ignoring God's Word and documented history!" (Reread *The Seal of God Part 1*.) Amazing as these worldwide deceptions were to me, I did not need to reread the Bible texts or the historical evidence because they were very clear!

How about you? Are God's Word and the relevant world history clear to you? I pray so! While it is certainly true that Christians, since believing the gospel, are *sealed with the Holy Spirit of promise, who is the guarantee of our inheritance until the redemption of the purchased possession.*[206] It is also just as true that due to the beast's deception, an additional end-time, testing seal is needed (not for God but for the judgment record) to distinguish between those who are truly God's remnant people[207] and the many false Christians who will receive the mark of the beast with the other wicked living during the time of trouble.[208] The end-time seal of God is the belief and acceptance of God's seventh-day Sabbath truth, calling this world back to the way the Creator set life up in the beginning before sin. The mark of the beast will be the belief and allegiance to the papal lie of Sunday sacredness! Attempting to change God's unchangeable law by changing man's Sabbath will snare many by giving the mark in or *on their right hand* for convenience so they can buy and sell. The rest will receive the mark on *their foreheads* because they actually believe the lie they were taught (Rev. 13:16–17). The testing seal is not for God to know who belongs to him because he has always known those that are his, but it is for true Christians and non-Christians alike, plus the witnesses of the judgment, to know for sure who is part of his remnant…to know who will stand for the Lord's truth though the heavens may fall…to know who will be saved from those living in the last days!

"If anyone worships the beast and his image, and receives his mark on his forehead, or on his hand, he himself shall also drink of the wine of the wrath of God, which is poured out full strength into the cup of his indignation. He shall be tormented with fire and brimstone in the presence of the holy angels and in the presence of the Lamb...whoever receives the mark of his name." (Revelation 14:9–11)

However, *"if you turn away your foot from the Sabbath, from doing your pleasure on my holy day, and call the Sabbath a delight, the holy day of the Lord honorable, and shall honor him, not doing your own ways, nor finding your own pleasure, nor speaking your own words, then you shall delight yourself in the Lord; and I will cause you to ride on the high hills of the earth, and feed you with the heritage of Jacob your father. The mouth of the Lord has spoken."* (Isaiah 58:13–14)

This life's dead river will end with the mark of the beast and those who receive it being eternally lost! But the *living water* of Jesus will lead this last generation to receiving the seal of God and life that flows eternally! After completing the last few studies, I knew without a doubt which sign I wanted in my life and the refreshment it would continue to give me from now on. (For additional information about the differences between Catholic and Protestant doctrines, see appendix C.)

Chapter 25

The Baxley Church

*For I will pour water on him who is thirsty, and floods
on the dry ground; I will pour my Spirit on your
descendants, and my blessing on your offspring.*

—Isaiah 44:3

The next Sabbath morning after first speaking with Pastor Williams, following the directions he gave us, Louise and I traveled to Baxley, Georgia. Baxley is on US Highway 1 between the towns of Vidalia and Alma. It is a small rural farming town and the county seat of Appling County, which is in the southeastern portion of the state of Georgia.

Arriving at the little Seventh-day Adventist Church, I mentioned to Louise that I had never heard of the denomination before. She had but did not know too much about them. She did say that the members were supposed to believe in and follow the Bible closely.

As we drove into the parking lot, I remember feeling ashamed of my clothing because I did not have a suit and Louise did not have a nice dress, but we wore the best clothes we had. I had always been taught to wear what Mama and Daddy always called "our Sunday best," which usually meant for us a suit. Louise wore a clean white blouse and plain dark skirt she had washed and ironed with a pair of black flat shoes while I wore a fairly good pair of blue jeans, a short-sleeved casual shirt with socks and tennis shoes. She reassured me that God was interested in our hearts and would change everything else for us as he desired to and blessed us.

Arriving at the entrance, we saw an older woman with a warm smile, greeting people and handing out church bulletins. She graciously welcomed us, invited us to sign the visitor's ledger, and encouraged us to make ourselves at home, sitting anywhere in the sanctuary we desired. She informed us where the restrooms were located and told us that Sabbath School would be starting in a few minutes.

We found a seat, and in a few moments, Pastor Williams came along, introduced himself, and took us around to meet a few of the members. Not knowing anyone, he said he would like to briefly share with the congregation how we came to their church, so after the opening prayer, he began to interview us from the podium. Hearing our answers, before long, the members grew very excited and also asked us some questions! Some expressed having no doubt that God had led us there because of what had happened to me meeting Jesus on the highway just a few weeks before and asking Him to lead me where the truth of his Word was being taught. As the pastor brought the interview to an end, someone gave us two Adult Sabbath School Quarterlies, and we proceeded with the Sabbath School lesson.

Pastor Alan Williams was a "short but powerful spark plug"! He was a Southerner with a grand smile, a large sense of humor, and how he could preach the Word! As we got to know each other, I could see where we shared quite a few experiences from our preconversion days, which made it much easier for me to relate to him as a person and not just my pastor. I especially loved to go visiting with him, and I could tell that the members enjoyed our visits as well. Alan was married to a sweet wife, Terry, and they had two girls.

It was so obvious that our arrival gave the little church "a shot in the arm" since they did not have many young adults and only a handful of children of mixed ages. We brought new blood, and they were elated, and yet our arrival was especially interesting to them because we had come by way of the Three Angels Broadcasting Network, which was one of their church's evangelistic organizations that many of them gave freewill offerings to. While 3ABN was physically located in Southern Illinois, they were seeing some of the fruit of that ministry appear in their own backyard, and it was a special blessing to them!

When the services were over, we did not want to leave! Somebody invited us home to lunch, and we accepted their gracious invitation, but we did not stay too long because we had to return Papa's car. The Baxley congregation was so kind and loving we could hardly wait until the next Sabbath!

Through the remainder of that year (November 1987) Louise and I continued with our studies and most every week attended church unless she was not well or my vehicle would not run. Every Sabbath was a wonderful experience! The people of the church were so hospitable, and different ones would take us home for dinner almost every Sabbath, and we would spend the afternoon with many of them. During those afternoons, they would answer many questions we had about the church, its history, and various points of doctrine we brought from our home Bible studies. They would also expose us to the various methods they used to keep the Sabbath a delight rather than having a boring, legalistic afternoon full of "I can't do this or that."

I personally came to see Jesus in a whole new way than I had seen him before. The Sabbath experience opened up so much more meaning about resting in Christ for my salvation! Since those early days of keeping the Sabbath, I have never looked at keeping it as some type of regulation to earn or ensure my salvation. I keep it because it is the truth of God's Word, and it is the Lord's Day[209] that he ordained for man[210] to have a special communion with and worship him from the very beginning in the garden of Eden![211] The prophet Isaiah says everyone will come to worship him on each Sabbath in eternity.[212] And so it only makes sense that he intended *man* to continue keeping the seventh-day Sabbath from his resurrection until ours!

All my wilderness wanderings in this world, all my blunders and failures throughout my life, had now taken on a new perspective. How could God the Father forgive such a worthless sinner and give me such new hope and assurance of his salvation? Truly, His grace is amazing, and now the eternal blessing of his seventh-day Sabbath—his Memorial of Creation—has revealed to me the Creator's amazing grace like never before!

Chapter 26

Death, Burial, and Resurrection

Therefore we were buried with him through baptism into death, that just as Christ was raised from the dead by the glory of the Father, even so we also should walk in newness of life.

—Romans 6:4

I began to joyfully share the truths I was discovering in our Bible studies with family, friends, and work associates. Most people were initially glad to see the positive changes in me, knowing the wicked lifestyle I had lived for so long. They were amazed I had given up alcohol, tobacco, and the use of foul language in such a short period! I told them it was not by my own willpower but through the power of God's grace! And I would go on to explain how that same grace had provided me a steady job and was preparing me to be a responsible family man and Christian citizen. Many bragged on me and wanted to know the details of each change. However, it did not take long before the newness began wearing off for most. This usually happened not long after telling them I was keeping the seventh-day Sabbath rather than Sunday and that I was studying with the Seventh-day Adventist Church.

I started to meet with all types of scriptural misrepresentations and slanders. They were not directed at me personally but at the Seventh-day Adventist Church and what it taught. Initially, most of these folk said they were simply trying to warn me. They believed my experience with Christ was genuine, but because I was an "immature babe in Christ," I was being misled to keep the old Jewish Sabbath. They would tell me the Ten Commandments of God were no longer binding on New Testament Christians. I would then attempt to share with them where Jesus said He had not come to do away with God's law but rather to fulfill it, which is, to live it and show to man its true, important use in his life. If Jesus had done away with the commandments, man would then have nothing to reveal right from wrong. I would then tell them that is why Jesus went on to explain that no part of God's commandments would be changed or done away with until heaven and earth passed away.[213]

I would point them to the Apostle Paul's explanation that no one could be justified by obeying God's law because the purpose of God's law is not to save people but to point out sin.[214] I would continue by explaining that many Christians have been told that because we are saved by faith, the law of God has been done away with, but Paul says that is not true.[215] He asked us a point-blank question, *"Do we then make void the law through faith?"* And he answers it, *"Certainly not!* [God forbid!] *On the contrary, we establish the law."* For those who were still listening to me at that point, I would tell them, "I have made up my mind that it is safer for me to listen to and follow the Lord Jesus and His Apostle Paul than it is for me to follow the crowd."[216]

Eventually, people started taking a step back when they would see me coming, and it was so obvious how they would find something to do or start talking to someone else. They were still nice and cordial but would not give me an opportunity to start a conversation for fear I might try to witness to them. And when I did try to confront several individuals with whom I felt we had a good enough relationship that I could talk frankly with them, they would deny avoiding me. "Oh, you are imagining this," some would say, and others would simply answer, "No, I was thinking about something else."

Time moved on, and we continued keeping the Sabbath while studying and growing in the Lord and the knowledge of his Word. I was having an awesome spiritual experience! I could not get enough of the Word of God! I was consuming it in daily readings and personal Bible study at home and did not want to watch very much television. Other than my regular chores, my spare time was only about studying the Bible. Soon, people began to talk and make accusations about me, comments such as, "You're becoming a fanatic! You've got to watch out for those Seventh-day Adventists!" Yet we pushed forward receiving daily encouragement from the Lord Jesus.

As 1987 moved forward, Louise and I were ready to set a date with Pastor Williams for our baptisms. We wanted to be baptized by the beginning of 1988, but the church sanctuary was under renovation and had the baptismal pool pulled out to have it placed in a new location. During the early months of that year, the pastor approached me several times, saying he would be more than willing to make arrangements to use the baptismal pool at another nearby church, or if we would rather go to the river or someone's pond or swimming pool, it would be fine with the church too should we desire to go ahead with our baptisms. After talking with Louise, I explained to the pastor that we wanted to wait and be the first new converts in the church's new baptismal pool. He agreed, and we put off our baptisms until May, which was the target for the completion of the sanctuary.

On Sabbath morning, May 7, 1988, in the newly remodeled sanctuary of the Baxley church, Louise and I were baptized by Pastor Alan Williams during the worship service. He then gave a rousing message about what it means to become a member of God's last-day church! We had invited my wife, Becky, along with her grandparents, to attend the special service, but Becky was the only one to attend. After the service, we shared a fellowship dinner and some testimonies from other members. On the way home, and then at Papa's and Granny's house, Louise and I recounted how that day went and that it was one of the greatest blessings of our lives!

Chapter 27

Persecution

He drew me out of many waters. He delivered me from
my strong enemy... The Lord rewarded me according to
my righteousness... For I have kept the ways of the Lord,
and have not wickedly departed from my God.

—2 Samuel 22:17–18, 21–22

During September 1987, my boss (one of Becky's cousins) had come up with an idea to increase his sales volume while taking advantage of my retail sporting goods experience in South Carolina. He opened, in my name, a sport shop in a small town about twenty miles west of Vidalia. He stocked it with inventory from his wholesale business, and Becky operated it while I was making his wholesale deliveries. This arrangement was implemented just a few weeks prior to the strong conviction of the Holy Spirit on my heart that I needed to take a stand for the Lord's Sabbath! We were rapidly approaching our baptismal day in May, and after talking with Louise and praying about the decision, I went to talk with my employer.

He had a reputation of being a hard but honest worker. He expected a full day's work out of his employees for a full day's pay, and he liked me because I believed and worked the same way. Due to the type of business we were in, I might not get back to the warehouse until late, about six or seven o'clock in the evening. This came to be a problem for me on Friday afternoons because of when sundown would occur. The Bible teaches that Sabbath should be kept from sundown each Friday through sundown each Saturday and no work or business is to be handled during that twenty-four-hour period.[217] This time is holy and sanctified,[218] for worshipping,[219] spending special time and resting with the Lord.

I discussed my situation with the boss, who was known to be a born-again, God-fearing deacon in a local Baptist Church. He had been very cordial with me from the first time we met and seemed to be happy and supportive when I had my experience on the highway with the Lord, started studying my Bible, and looking for a church to attend. But when I began attending the Adventist Church regularly, he let me know very quickly that I needed to be careful and not be deceived! He said it was his Christian responsibility to warn me about being deceived by cults and the possibility of "going off the deep end!" That was all he said about the subject until I went to talk with him about taking a stand for the Sabbath.

I told him I had been studying for months, and as I read the Bible, I was now thoroughly convinced that the seventh-day Sabbath was what God wanted me to keep. I was not being pressured by anyone, but I had a deeply held personal conviction that the weekend trade shows I occasionally worked, and my deliveries on most Friday evenings after sundown were going against my conscience. I informed him in a kind but firm manner that working the trade shows or at the sport shop on Saturdays were no longer something I could do. I was very willing to work extra hours on other days to make up for my lost delivery time on Fridays. Expressing that I fully respected his views about keeping Sunday, and since I was a hardworking, honest, and steady Christian employee, I thought it only fair for him to do the same for me in keeping the Sabbath so that I would not have to give up a good job I enjoyed, nor would he have to give up a good employee that always looked out for his interest! At first, to my surprise, he agreed, as he handed me a little booklet about Sunday to take home and read. I did, and the next day, he asked if I had any questions about its contents, and I told him, "No, it was all very clear."

He then wanted to know if any of its material changed my mind about the subject, but when he saw that my convictions were firm, he told me he changed his mind about respecting my decision to keep Saturday holy. Feeling that he had rushed into the decision without giving it much thought, he wanted to think and pray for a few days about the situation and then talk with me again. After several days had passed, he told me he would like for us to talk after work, so when closing time came, we locked everything and went to his office.

He said he had worked up a compromise and wanted to share it with me for my consideration. "If you will be willing to stop handling the deliveries," he said, "and switch over to being a full-time route salesman, I believe I can accommodate you regarding your Sabbath. Plus, I will give you the store and continue stocking it with some of all the sporting goods I carry on a consignment basis, giving you my usual wholesale price, less 10 percent, across the board and will not require any payment until after you sell each item." He continued, "Becky can run the store while you work an established sales route in one of my territories adjacent to plenty of new area around several lakes in North Georgia. I'll buy a large new walk-in panel van that will carry several times what you carry in the delivery van so you sell directly off the van. If you have to stay out overnight to cover all your territory, I'll pay for your night's lodging. You and Becky can then run the store as you please, closing on Saturday and keeping your Sabbath."

I felt like stopping him right there and reminding him that the Scripture said it was the Lord's Sabbath, not mine! I only kept it because it belonged to Jesus, and he told me to keep it holy! But I held my tongue for fear of making him mad and messing up a really good deal for both of us!

The boss went on to remind me, "Of course, we will miss a lot of business by you closing the store on Friday evenings and Saturdays, but maybe if you open on Sundays, you could possibly make up some of the lost sales, but that is up to you. As a salesman, you will make substantially more income than as my delivery man, plus whatever Becky clears in the store."

I went home that night and first talked to Becky. Over the next few evenings after supper, we both talked with her mother, Louise, and her grandfather about her cousin's offer. Then after praying over the weekend, and since the Lord did not give us any indication not to say no, we agreed to give it try, and I told the boss our decision on Monday.

That little one-stoplight community did not know what to think about having a store that sold hunting, fishing, and camping supplies! To purchase their outdoor gear, they usually had to drive twenty miles or more to the nearest sport shop, depending on which direction they were heading. And if we did not have what they wanted in stock, it was in stock the next week or we could order anything they wanted for a reasonable but smaller price than the larger stores would think of doing. We even obtained a federal firearms license and started selling hunting weapons and ammunition, plus state hunting and fishing licenses and live bait!

We did really well in the fall, and soon customers started buying gifts for Christmas because we started a layaway. However, like all businesses, as soon as Christmas was over, sales took a "nose-dive," yet we were still doing enough business to make ends meet until the spring hunting and fishing seasons arrived! Traditionally, Friday evenings and Saturday mornings have always been great retail business times for those who loved the outdoors, yet because of my stand regarding the Sabbath, we decided to follow the boss's suggestion to open on Sundays, and sure enough, the Lord blessed our efforts by making up almost all the sales we were losing being closed on the Sabbath, honoring His day!

This success truly got under the boss's skin! He thought that not only was he missing out on large bulk sales from the winter trade shows I used to work for him, but due to my Sabbath accommodation he was giving me, he had an employee/partner taking off on some or all the main business days of each week!

Yet instead of seeing and appreciating all the positive benefits for both of us working this way, he could only focus on the little bit he felt he was missing out on! The truth of the matter was twofold: first, the Sabbath blessing my wife and I received placed him under conviction, and second, he was plain greedy!

We continued working according to our agreed arrangement, and God continued giving us His blessing for being faithful to his Word. About a month later, he said that we needed to talk. After seeing that all his salesmen and the deliveryman were on their way, we went to his office, and he said, "You are breaking our agreement, and because you are, I am withdrawing my consignment inventory from your store unless you pay me for it right now at the 10 percent less than wholesale I agreed to."

I asked him in return, "How am I breaking our agreement?"

He responded, "By not opening during the hours we agreed to."

I said, "We never had an agreement as to what hours I would open the store! In fact, you said if I went to work for you as a salesman, the store was ours and we could run it as we saw fit!"

Yet he argued that doing business during the hours I wanted to be closed was a given! It was supposed to be understood. And the new arrangement we made was him giving me the store in return for me selling on the road, off the new van, and developing the territory around the North Georgia lakes. He insisted that having the Sabbath off was only about me not running my route that day but not closing the store! He claimed that was in the first agreement, not the second one!

I truly could not believe what I was hearing! I appealed by reminding him that ever since I had studied the seventh-day Sabbath, I had been attending church in Baxley each Saturday morning and not working anymore on that day. He knew this, and I reminded him again of the original and second agreement we made and had been following for a month! I asked him, "If I was not living up to the agreement we both made, then why did it take you a whole month to say something about it?"

But he stuck to his story, not wanting to address the specific point I was asking about. Now it seemed that he had only two possible motives for "pulling the rug out from under my feet." One was greed. The second was, there was such a heavy conviction on him about the seventh-day verses Sunday, he felt he needed to take a stand to justify himself not giving me my day of worship.

With no working capital and no credit available to me from banks or other wholesale companies, it looked like the end of our store. Over the next couple of weeks, we returned his inventory and closed the store. I was so confused and hurt I quit working for him, and that ended my relationship with Becky's cousin.

At that point, besides not having income from the trade shows and the prospering new route sales territory, he had lost his best retail store along with an honest Christian employee/partner! I have often wondered if he ever realized the extent of what he did to himself by attempting to make my biblical decision hurt me. For a while, I often let the experience get me down, but I found several verses of Scripture that I would draw strength from when it did. In Genesis 12:3, the Lord says to his child and friend, Abram, "*I will bless those who bless you, and I will curse him who curses you...*" Speaking through his prophet in Isaiah 58:13–14, the Lord gives a wonderful promise to his people! "*If you turn away your foot from the Sabbath, from doing your pleasure on my holy day, and call the Sabbath a delight, the holy day of the Lord honorable, and shall honor him, not doing your own ways, nor finding your own pleasure, nor speaking your own words, then you shall delight yourself in the Lord; and I will cause you to ride on the high hills of the earth, and feed you with the heritage of Jacob your father. The mouth of the Lord has spoken.*" I have found these promises to be so true! God has let me know I made the correct decision and that he was still in control. He would honor me for honoring his holy, unchangeable Word.

Unfortunately for my ex-boss, not too long after we parted ways, I heard his business went under.

Chapter 28

Heaven's Open Windows

Bring all the tithes into the storehouse, that there may be food in my house, and try me now in this...if I will not open for you the windows of heaven and pour out for you such blessing that there will not be room enough to receive it.

—Malachi 3:10

There I was, with no job, no income of any kind, and in several days, Becky had landed square on my back! She could not understand why, since all things were going so well through Christmas, I had to be so rigid about keeping the Sabbath! She did not understand the heavy conviction I felt for standing on God's truth. The others in her family, except for Louise, did not seem to understand either!

Because of my stand, we were back at the bottom of the financial ladder. I went from pillar to post to take what little work I could find. We lived for several months on odd jobs I found with family and friends, but soon, their help faded. In between jobs and when I had no appointments to apply for jobs, I started walking the roads, gathering discarded aluminum cans. Taking them home, I soaked the ones covered in dried mud, cleaned them, and bagged them until I had a large enough load to take and sell at the scrapyard.

Papa—Frank—also collected scrap metal but on different roads than me. I always let Frank sell his cans first, and the next day or so, I would sell mine. He could never understand how my cans would always get a much better price, sometimes close to double, which always had him scratching his head. I told him that cleaning them added a few cents to the price, but most of the increase came from the Lord, blessing me for returning a faithful tithe on every cent I earned. He usually just looked at me and mumbled something like, "Yeah, I guess so. It is in the Bible," and he would walk away.

Since the day I encountered the Lord on the highway, I was faithful in returning his tithe. It did not matter if I had an income of $5 or $2,000 per week! The Lord's tithe was put aside first until my next church attendance, and we paid our bills out of what funds were left. In spite of all the criticism given to me by Becky, her family, and some of my family and friends, it did not matter. I put the Lord first, and he would always provide for our needs! In fact, on some occasions, Jesus would even use the people criticizing me to bless us![220] They could see I was trying to be honest and faithful to Jesus and would suddenly become overwhelmed with compassion as they realized our need.

The first payday after my experience on the road with God, I cashed my check on the way home. When I arrived, Becky met me in the driveway to let me know our next-door neighbor—Sue—was inside. She told me it was the old lady's birthday, and she was so sad because none of her people had even acknowledged she was alive, much less her birthday. Becky knew I had been at war with the lady because she had always given me a fit about my drinking, and since my conversion, I still had not reconciled with her. Becky did not want me to walk inside and seeing the neighbor there and blow my stack! But I assured her that was all in the past and I would apologize to the lady.

Becky made the comment, "I know our budget is very tight, but do you think we could spare a few dollars to buy her a small cake and have her for supper to celebrate her birthday?"

Responding to her idea, I said, "Yes, sure!" In fact, since we had not started attending a church yet and returning our tithe, being ignorant of the appropriate way to handle the situation, I continued, "You take our tithe and go to town and buy her a small cake and gift from us, and we will celebrate her birthday together!"

That tiny frail woman was so shocked to hear me apologize to her for mistreating her in the past, and then being invited to supper and celebrating her birthday with cake and a gift, she cried like a baby and could not stop thanking us for showing that we cared about her! I told the wife afterward that I knew the Lord was pleased with our decision of how to use our $17.50 tithe because he had blessed it far more than I ever dreamed! The next evening when I arrived home, Becky told me our stove was not functioning properly, so she turned off the gas until we could have it seen about. She then told me that Sue had taken her to town and insisted on buying us a microwave oven.

As the odd jobs dried up, it began to seem like Dead River was trying to live up to its name again. But I just kept going to the Giver of *living water* who would keep opening the windows of heaven so he could pour the buckets of his blessed water to meet every need! One day, Becky took Granny to town and came home, telling me she had found a job working in a Dollar General store and would begin the next Monday morning. I praised the Lord for his continual blessing!

These kinds of blessings came to us all the time! After breaking up the business and work relationship with Becky's cousin, it was not too long before I lost my mobile home, land, and truck. It was a terrible feeling, having a home one day and no home the next, but I prayed and claimed the promise in Malachi 3:8–12 again. Before dark, Louise came while we were loading our car with our personnel items and told us we could have the two-room camper trailer behind Papa and Granny if we wanted it. It was hers but had not been lived in for a number of years because the roof had an awful leak. They had built a shingle roof on a frame over the trailer, but it began to leak too. About that time, her husband was hired for a better-paying job, so they bought a full-size mobile home, putting it on a different lot just down the road.

The next day, we went to town and bought two tubes of roofing cement and a gallon of cool seal. Taking those items home, we painted the trailer roof with cool seal and planned on waiting until it rained to discover the leak in the shingle roof. However, when it rained, it poured, and not a drop leaked through the shingles! Oh, what a God!

The camper was very small with the first room being a sitting room and kitchen all in one, and the second room was a little bedroom; the two were connected by a four-foot-long hall and combination bathroom. The tub/shower was really three feet long so that a one-foot wide toilet could fit at the end of the tub. When using the facilities, we had to close a sliding door at each end of the hall. After the first night, I told Louise that we needed to build another room or two on the backside where her husband had put in a sliding glass door leading out to a deck. She said we could do anything we wanted because she gave it to us.

My mind truly started working overtime about how I could build two rooms without any money, and so I prayed again, claiming the same promise. Later that day, I was at Louise's for our Bible study when her husband came in from work and we started talking about my building idea. I told him that with the tools I had and my past experience building custom wood fence, I was sure I could build the rooms, but buying lumber and having no truck to haul the lumber were my primary problems.

He asked Louise if she told me about the scrap lumber they give away at the sawmill, and she said, "Oh my, I forgot!"

I cut in and asked, "Where is this place? Are you sure they give the scrap away?

They simultaneously answered yes, and Louise explained how to get there, adding that it was probably fifteen miles, one way. She then asked how I was going to haul the lumber home.

Her husband spoke up and said, "If our little Chevette in the front yard was running, you could haul some in that because it has fold-down back seats and a hatchback door."

I asked him what was wrong with the car, and he told me the timing was off, the valves were rattling bad before it quit, and the battery was dead and probably no good now. The tires were almost bald, and he did not know what else was wrong.

"It has been sitting there for more than a year! I got so frustrated trying to repair it that I quit messing with it! If you can get it running, you can have it!"

I sent Becky down the road to another neighbor's house to borrow his battery charger, and I put it on a deep cycle charge overnight. We came back in the morning, and I disconnected the charger, pulled out the four spark plugs and cleaned them, put a little gas in the carburetor, and turned the motor over. It took about fifteen or twenty seconds, but it started right up!

Louise started crying and praising the Lord! Becky was standing there astounded while I could not say anything but "Thank You, Lord," over and over and over! We took it for a ride down the river-side dirt road, and other than backfiring a little and skipping some, it drove surprisingly well. Borrowing $2 from Louise, we drove to town and almost filled the gas tank.

Arriving back at Louise's, her husband was standing in the driveway, wearing a huge smile. He had several tools in his hand and told me not to turn it off because he wanted to adjust the carburetor and set the idle. While he did that, he kept telling me that it was impossible for the car to be running. He could not believe it! And after things quieted down, I told him what I usually told Papa concerning the promise in Malachi. Like Frank, he just looked at me for a moment and walked off, shaking his head in unbelief!

The next day, we went to the sawmill. Every time someone came to pick up scrap wood, they had to sign in at the office, get a vehicle pass, and sign out as they left. We signed in and were directed to the scrap pile. All the lumber was six feet long or less, with widths of eight, ten, or twelve inches and a full two inches thick. Rough cut is what they called it before being kiln dried and run through a finish saw. It was all pine, and many pieces had splits or knotholes in them, so I would have to rummage through the pile to find the best boards. I also discovered that many of the boards could be repaired with wood glue and finish nails, and I could then use them on the outside walls.

The thought came to mind that I could make a drawing of the rooms and figure out how many two-by-fours I would need to complete all the framing. Next, I would find out how much it would cost to rent a table saw per day. Then I would get busy picking up cans to pay for my gas, oil, and rental. Working several weeks, I finally obtained enough money to rent the saw and buy several boxes of different-sized nails and some wood glue. After that, I started hauling lumber.

Stopping the hauling only long enough to buy gas, pick up and clean the cans, plus eat and sleep, before realizing it, I had a stack of boards six feet high, six feet long, and six feet wide. I managed to reach the rental shop just before closing, and because I had so far to drive, the manager told me as long as I returned by 8:00 a.m. the day after tomorrow, he would only charge me for one day. That enabled me to cut boards from sunup until dark, which gave me an extra three and a half hours of cutting since I did not have to leave early enough to reach his shop by 5:00 p.m. closing! When the stack was cut, I had more than enough to finish all the framing.

One evening while I was framing the rooms, Becky had just arrived home and called me inside. She said, "We are out of can money and in between my paydays. Today, I spent the last I had for gas. We are out of groceries, except some bread and butter. But we do have the tithe from my last check and the cans you last sold. What do you want me to do for supper?"

I said, "Well, I do not know about you, but I can eat some toast for supper and we can have prayer and ask the Lord to please help us in our situation."

Angrily, she said, "I don't see why we can't use the tithe money until we get paid! It's just going to sit here until after we are paid again! This is silly! The Lord doesn't want us to go hungry!"

I told her, "I agree! He does not want us to starve, but we are not starving. We can eat toast tonight and pray for his assistance. Have some faith! How soon you and your family forget the way Jesus has faithfully helped us in the past! Let's pray."

She did not like my answer, but she bowed her head as I prayed, reminding the Lord of his promise to us in Malachi and our faithfulness to him in tithing. I asked Jesus to once again keep his promise by providing for our need for groceries for the next week or so. When I said amen, she still wanted to argue for a few minutes until there was a knock at the door. It was one of our neighbors with several sacks of frozen items, meats and vegetables, from their extra freezer that had just gone on the blink. He asked me if we could use some of the food since they were not going to buy another freezer and keep so much extra on hand from now on. "This food will only go bad if someone did not use it," he said.

Without telling him our situation, I sincerely thanked him then and the Lord after he left and went back to my framing without saying anything to Becky. I thought it would be a good exercise for her to reflect on the open window of heaven pouring out more *living water* as God, again, kept his Word to his people!

Chapter 29

God's Call

And how shall they hear without a preacher? And how shall they preach unless they are sent?... "How beautiful are the feet of those who preach the gospel of peace."

—Romans 10:14–15

In January 1989, I had been attending church for about fourteen months. During that time, the Lord began speaking to me in various ways about the full-time gospel ministry. At first, as these thoughts and impressions became stronger, I was more determined to discount and ignore them. I had never been an outgoing type of person who liked crowds. One on one or with two to three people, I was all right, but crowds made me feel uncomfortable, and I was certainly not the type to get up and speak in front of a group.

Yet the thoughts persisted. At times, they would simply pop into my mind from out of nowhere. Other times, I was reading my Bible, and the Holy Spirit would use what I was reading to prompt my thinking on the subject. On other occasions, I would be sitting in church or at home, working, and I would see or hear something that would bring these ideas to mind.

Eventually, church members began making periodic comments about me becoming a pastor. It was as if the Lord was taking conversations, whatever they were about, and somehow using a word, phrase, or sentence to communicate directly to me. Ultimately at times, it would sound in my head like God was speaking on a public address system! He was speaking to me, and the person he was using had no idea the Lord was using them to reach me!

One example happened the week after sharing my testimony in church. I saw one of our senior members, Sister Mabel Clark, drive into the parking lot, and I went out to greet and assist her in getting out of her car. She used a walker, and as she stood up, she reached into a cloth bag attached to the walker and pulled out a book. Handing it to me, she said, "God wanted me to give you this book. I can't help believe I'm going to see you in the pulpit one day." The title of the book was *Prophets Are People Too*. (Of course, the use of the word "prophet" in the title and the book was about God using regular people to be his mouthpieces—preachers. I certainly do not profess to be a prophet, in the usual meaning of the word.)

Helping her make her way into church, I was thinking, "Surely to goodness, Lord, you really are not speaking to me like this! I believe this dear sister means well, but she does not know me well enough to make this assessment." Her comment and my thought scared me to no end!

It was not too long until the pastor asked me to take the service in Alma, Georgia, at the smaller church in the district, and after giving me a few pointers with my sermon preparation, he later wanted me to take another service in Baxley. He and the other elders began having me help them serve on the platform regularly. As it came to my one-year anniversary as a member, they ordained me a deacon. The next thing I knew, they had me teaching the Earliteen Sabbath School class. I was thoroughly involved in my church and getting used to it, loving every minute of it! But I still did not want to be a pastor!

As the prompting continued, I began to gently entertain the possibility that God was calling me for some kind of ministry, so I figured I should check the door to see if it was truly him knocking. The Bible told me one of the ways I could do this was to seek a multitude of godly counsel.[221]

The church had planned a garage sale in early spring at the head elder's home, and several of the other men were going to be there, so I decided it might be the perfect opportunity to talk with these experienced men of the church. After being there a while, I took one of the elders aside and asked, "How would you know if God wanted you to do something?"

He did not answer immediately, but after a thoughtful pause, he needed clarification and responded, "Do you mean if God wanted you to do something? That is, if God had a specific task for you to do, how would you know?"

"Yes. If you felt led to do something," I asked, "how would you know it was God and not the devil or your own imagination?"

He answered, "I believe God communicates his will for us in different ways, just like what we read in the Bible. We see he uses a variety of methods, depending on the person and that person's circumstances. I would also keep in mind that all the Lord's communications will always be in harmony with his written Word and never contradictory to it. We should also remember the Lord is not trying to play tricks on us. Jesus wants us to understand him correctly. Keeping these things in mind, I would pray and ask him for confirmation because of my lack of understanding. And one more thing, sometimes our confusion may be from not having the desire to do what God may be asking us to do! If that were the case, I would confess that to him and ask him to create that desire in me, to do His will. The same would go for our abilities. If we do not have the abilities to do what he is asking us to do, then ask him to give you those abilities. If he does, then you know for sure that your understanding is correct, remembering, of course, this may not be instantaneous but a process over time."

The elder's answer certainly struck home with me! I have never forgotten it. It is about as fresh in my mind today as the day he uttered those words. It was difficult for me to accept his answer at first! And the amazing thing was, he would not have known what I was asking him about unless God told him, and if the Lord did tell him, the elder never revealed it to me, and he did not ask what it was I thought God wanted me to do, yet he answered my question in every detail that I had wondered about!

In the days after the sale, I managed to seek counsel from a few more godly members of the church. In one way or another, each one gave me similar answers. Yet it was the first answer that meant so much because I did not have a desire to be a pastor, minister, or preacher of the gospel! Sure, I wanted to be actively involved in sharing the gospel, but I was not looking to become a pastor! For the life of me, I could never imagine in my wildest dreams God could want someone like me with my past. I simply could not fathom it! I thought about it and prayed about the elder's answer, and the more I thought and prayed about what he had said, the more I realized his answer was from God!

In the early part of that year, someone told me about a job opening in Mt. Vernon, the county seat. A builder was to remodel one of the banks, and the Job Foreman was looking for a carpenter's helper for forty hours a week. I hurriedly made my way there to apply for the job. After filling out the application, the foreman talked with me about my building experience and then sent me to speak with the lead carpenter, who was a lay pastor at one of the Baptist Churches in Vidalia. He worked with their youth department and was on the church's schedule to help with the preaching. After talking with him and the foreman again, I was hired.

At first, the lead carpenter and I got along great, and we talked about the Lord throughout the day when it did not hinder the job. One day at lunch, he asked several doctrinal questions, and before answering his questions, I explained that I had no problems talking about the Lord and his Word, but I certainly did not want to make anyone angry since I might understand the Scriptures differently. He spoke right up, assuring me that would not happen with him. If he did not agree with me, he would tell me what he understood, and we would leave it at that. I agreed and answered his questions. A few days later, he asked me what I believed about death. I said, "You mean the state of the dead?"

He replied, "Yes, the state of the dead."

Opening my Bible (we both read our Bibles at lunch), I began reading several verses. Then I read one of the many verses that say when a Bible character would die, such as King David, "he slept with his fathers and was buried" (KJV).[222] Moving on to the book of John, I read where a messenger came and told Jesus that his good friend Lazarus was near death and his sisters were calling for Jesus to come and heal him. His disciples wanted to go straight to Lazarus's home, yet Jesus declined, but the disciples urged the Lord on saying if they did not hurry, Lazarus would die. Jesus told them Lazarus's illness was not unto death. A bit later, Jesus told them, "*Lazarus sleeps.*"[223] So they said, if he is sleeping, they should not wake him up. The Lord responded by telling them, "*Lazarus is dead.*"[224] I told the carpenter I believed what the Scripture says. Throughout the Bible, when people died, just as Jesus did, it was equated with being asleep, in the grave, waiting for the Resurrection Day or, in the case of the wicked, the Second Resurrection.

All of a sudden, he blurted out, "Oh no! I do not believe in soul sleep! That is not true! My Bible says, 'absent from the body, present with the Lord.' [Please read this endnote.][225] All I believe is what comes out of my Bible!"

I decided to hush and let him calm down. We went back to work, but he only spoke to me the rest of the day when he had to. The next day was Friday, and at lunch, he ate by himself in his truck, and at 5:00 p.m., he wasted no words or time leaving.

Here I was in another altercation about what the Bible said, and it really bothered me because of the agreement we had before our discussion. I prayed about what the Lord would have me do come the next Monday. I did not want him to be upset, but I could not understand him getting so worked up over something that was so simply put in the Bible by Jesus himself! The Lord reminded me of the man's own words: "he would not believe anything unless it came out of his Bible." Sunday night, I sat down with my Bible and two sheets of notebook paper at the kitchen table and wrote down about forty Scripture references that dealt with the state of the dead and a second copy for me.

The next day, he talked a little more during the morning but at lunch went back to his truck to eat. As lunch was ending, I walked to his truck and handed him one of the lists of Bible references. I reminded him friendly what he said last week at lunch; you "would only believe what came out of your Bible, so I wrote down some Bible references for you to read in your Bible and pray over what they tell you about death. I hope you will forgive me because I thought we had an agreement to not get angry over what we shared with each other. I certainly did not mean to make you angry."

Taking the list, he glanced at it, then folded it, and put it in his Bible, saying, "Sure, I'll read them, but if they tell me the dead are in soul sleep, I will not believe it!" Nothing else was ever said about that subject or any other Bible subject while I worked there. The job ended in the first part of April.

The next Sunday, my pastor came for an unexpected visit because he wanted to have a heart-to-heart talk with me. He mentioned he had been trying hard not to push me, but in case I did not realize it yet, he had been trying to groom and lead me toward this moment when he would tell me that he truly believed I should enter the ministry. "We have not talked about this, but I believe the Lord has been speaking to you about this very thing," he said.

I was absolutely stunned! We had not talked about that. He had only given me some instruction about preparing my sermons but nothing to make me think he was sensing the Lord's prompts and tugs on my heart about entering the ministry.

He said every spring Southern College (now Southern Adventist University) hosted what they called College Days. It was an open house event for prospective students to come for a visit. They will be taken on group tours of the campus and community, meet various staff members and current students. All their questions about school life and the curriculum of their prospective career will be answered. They will eat in the cafeteria, sleep in the dorm rooms, worship at the campus church, and attend a Saturday night Vespers and a social. He was recommending I go for the visit, especially since it was free and he had some business up there to attend to, so he could provide my transportation.

Hesitantly, I replied, "Pastor...I do not know! I would be lying if I told you that I have not heard the Lord speaking to me about ministry, but I really do not want to be a pastor! Besides, I have no money to pay for the move or college education. My wife is still far from accepting this message, being baptized, and joining the church! I doubt her family would go along with such a move. I simply do not see that it is possible!"

He was well-prepared with answers for each of the reasons I gave for not being able to go. He said, "Listen, you don't know for sure what area of ministry the Lord wants you in yet. If you are totally closed to being a pastor, there are many other ministerial positions! College gives you the time for God to prepare and lead you where he wants you to serve while giving you and Becky the time to spiritually mature and her to join the church. You both will make many new married friends that will be a great support. As for the money, there is certainly no problem there. The school helps each student to find a job, most of which are right there on campus. You work around your class schedule. Or you can get a job across the street at Little Debbie's Bakery. The McKee family are members of our church, and several of them sit on the board of directors of the college. They hire a lot of students! But if you want to, you can find a job off campus in town.

"The school financial office helps everyone obtain government grants you do not have to pay back and scholarships, if you qualify. Once you are there a while and people get to know you, there are people who live around there or work at the school who are always looking to help young couples with their school and family needs. The possibilities for assistance are endless! As for the cost of moving, I'm sure we can find several men at our church who have trucks that would be glad to help move you and Becky to Collegedale. They love you both and want to help you. If Becky and her family are not comfortable with her suddenly moving way up there, maybe it would be better for you to go first, get setup in campus housing and get a job, and she can come before school starts." He said, "Oh, and one more thing. I want you to go to College Days like I have explained, but I would like us to go a day early so we can sit in several religion department classes and you can meet several of the professors in between classes. This will help you see what it is like in the actual classes you will take if you decide to enroll."

The pastor finished his recruitment speech by saying, "I promise you will receive no pressure from me or anyone else at the school to enroll. I know you love the Lord and want to do his will. All I am suggesting is to give him the opportunity to make things clear for you and Becky by going with me to College Days and see how the

Lord leads you from there. If you go and decide not to enroll, no one will be mad or upset. That will be between you and the Lord."

Based on those conditions, I said, "Okay, I am willing to go for the visit."

After Pastor Williams left, I shared with Becky everything we talked about. She did not seem interested, but she agreed for us to think and pray about it since it was another two weeks before College Days.

After College Days

The visit was amazing! Pastor Williams knew most of the professors, and several invited us to sit in classes on Friday. I had never been to a Christian school, and I could not get over the idea of earning a college degree with Christians all around me! Christians were in the dormitories and library. Christians would be teaching me and beginning every class with prayer, and it was so easy to see these professors truly cared for their students! I had attended several other colleges where the students were simply numbers on the rolls, and most professors could care less whether you passed or failed.

We also visited administrators, staff, and friends of his in the community who loved to help students and had helped him financially. Listening to them reminisce about old times and experiences their families shared together was a treat! And of course, we attended the planned items on the College Days agenda.

I made up my mind on that trip that the Lord Jesus was calling me to ministry, and I could not fight it anymore. It seemed that everywhere I went and everyone I talked to was speaking to me about ministry! I was at the point in my conviction if I did not follow this calling, I might very well walk away from my faith!

The pastor and I talked quite a lot on the way home from Tennessee, and I laid it all out to him about what I was facing with my wife. She was spiritually up and down. One week, she was interested in the Lord, and the next week, she had very little interest. I never knew from day to day how she felt about her relationship with

Jesus and me becoming a pastor. She always said she believed but was not committed to any church, and I had no real idea how to move forward like that.

As we talked he advised, "I don't think you can move yet. I don't think God really expects you to, and it may be you have to be very careful and methodical and commit yourself to even more prayer for Becky than what you have already done. But I do believe God will do everything he can, short of forcing her, to convert her. Our time-table is about getting you to college this summer if at all possible. For financial reasons, we will find you work through the summer so you can save a down payment to enter classes in the fall. However, our timetable may not be God's timetable, so we need to pray about this and place it all before the Lord and believe that he is going to give you an answer. If our timetable turns out to be different from the Lord's, so be it. We will adjust ours to meet his." He suggested we pull over and pray for Becky before we reached my home. We did and began what turned out to be a wonderful season of prayer! We poured out our hearts; the pastor first and then me, asking God for the conversion of my wife.

Getting back on the road, the last few miles of our trip was so joyful, and when we arrived at home, I will never forget what happened because it was one of the highest moments ever in my life! As we pulled into the driveway, Becky came running out of the house to greet us. Tears were streaming down her face! She was not wearing any jewelry or heavy makeup, and she was not smoking. Crying like a baby, yet smiling as she was telling us that a few minutes before she had felt the leading of the Lord and had turned her life over to Jesus! She had invited him into her heart and laid aside all her doubts about joining the church and moving away so I could enter college. She laid it all at Jesus's feet, and he had given her perfect peace!

At that moment, the pastor and I began giving God praises for my wife's miraculous conversion and his powerful answer to our prayers! It was almost too good to be true, and we just bathed in the joy from God that was flooding our souls! It was another refreshing drink of his *living water*!

Over the next two weeks, Pastor Williams and I finished giving Becky a series of Bible studies, and she was baptized into the Baxley church. Now with the confidence we were doing God's will, we were busy making plans to move to Tennessee in late May or early June.

Chapter 30

The Lord's Eyes, Ears, and Hands

The eyes of the Lord are on the righteous, and his ears are open to their cry…and [he] *delivers them out of all their troubles.*

—Psalm 34:15, 17

As things typically go when there is a big victory through the Lord, Satan does not want you to enjoy that victory very long. A week passed after Becky's baptism and arriving at church that Sabbath, we exited the car and made our way into the sanctuary, greeting people while making our way to where we usually sat before Sabbath School started. I made my way over to Sister Noel Bennet who sat in the third pew on the left side of the sanctuary every Sabbath she was there. In her eighties, she was an outspoken African American lady who was an extremely caring, loving individual whose husband, James, had not long ago died. As she sat patiently waiting for the class to begin, she was always reading her Bible.

As I approached, Sister Bennet looked up from her Bible straight into my eyes with a cold dark piercing look as if she was trying to see through me rather than look at me. In that same moment, our hands met, and instead of the normal, gentle, brief clasp, this little woman grabbed my hand with a strongman's grip and would not let go. I attempted to shake her hand, but her arm strength was overwhelming! She spoke almost immediately and said, "I hope you can forgive me for not delivering the Lord's message to you in the past. I have repented of this, and I must deliver His message today."

Without pausing for me to say anything, she went right on speaking as she seemed to continue looking through me, tightly gripping my hand, and speaking in a low, monotone voice. "The Lord wants you to be warned. The devil does not want you in the pulpit, and the Lord wants you to know that the devil is going to come at you hard!" With her message delivered, she let go of my hand, broke our line of sight, and immediately went back to reading her Bible as if I was not standing there.

I had never witnessed anything like that in my life, and it was terribly difficult for me to concentrate on the lesson during class. However, by the time the church service started, I had momentarily put aside the thought of our encounter, and when the service was over, we went through our regular routine, shaking hands and telling people goodbye as we left the sanctuary. On the way to our car, we passed the children's classrooms, and I noticed another senior member, Sister Cletia Seebeck, standing in an open doorway. Becky had walked on toward the car, but I stopped to speak. Like Sister Bennet, this lady was also in her eighties, and I had always thought of her as a saint of God.

Stepping toward her, I extended my hand, when all at once with the same piercing look of the previous sister, our eyes were locked. Our hands grasped each other's, and it was obvious she would not let go until she finished speaking to me! As I started to speak, she said, "Just keep your eyes on Jesus. Just keep your eyes on Jesus." She then said it a third time, "Just keep your eyes on Jesus." With that, she dropped my hand, turned, and walked away as if I was not standing there.

When I got into the car, Becky had it running and was a little irritated that I stopped to talk because it was hot. Asking what I was doing, I simply told her that Sister Seebeck was telling me goodbye. She knew, however, there was more to it than I had said and tried to get me to say more, but I told her that nothing was wrong, and we rode quietly home.

I thought about what had happened most of the night, not sleeping very well, and early the next day, I went outside to think in the fresh morning air before Becky woke up. I strolled across the yard and sat down in the car. After running everything that happened through my mind again and praying, the only conclusion I could reach was the Lord was speaking to me, and whatever his reason was, it was extremely important for him to get my attention!

Going back inside, I pondered some more, prayed again, then began digging into his Word, which is what I usually did when I was not coming up with any answers to my questions. In a while, something I read put a thought in my mind. Perhaps something so unexpected and tragic was going to take place that the Lord saw fit to warn me in advance! According to Sister Bennet, the devil was going to attack soon, and Jesus wanted me to know in advance that he was not going to leave me to face the situation alone, and I could be encouraged by the fact that he had warned me!

On Monday, I was in the process of preparing to go to the Georgia Cumberland Conference Camp Meeting to be held at Southern College. Pastor Williams had talked with the conference president when we were at College Days and told him how I came to find the church through the Three Angels Broadcasting Network, so he extended an invitation for me to come and share my testimony during Sabbath afternoon Evangelism Hour.

By Tuesday, I noticed that since the last Sabbath, Becky had not regained her usual jovial attitude; in fact, she was strangely quiet with little conversation. I thought it was because of getting used to the new job working all day. However, Wednesday evening, she informed me she was not going to Camp Meeting as we had planned. I was stunned! I questioned her, but she did not want to talk about it, and that confused me even more. Then she told me that she could not go because of work.

As she was leaving for work the next morning, I asked her if she wanted me to call or visit her boss and explain the situation; he might let her off then. But she made it very plain that she did not want to go because her boss liked her work so much he had already given her a big promotion, and she did not want to mess that up. Then she told me because our car had been put into her grandfather's name, I could not drive it to camp meeting. If I was still going, I would have to find another way to go! She left for work, and I spent the day totally confused!

I was sitting on the front steps that evening when she drove up and getting out of the car, she was smoking again. As she approached, I asked why she was smoking, and she curtly said, "Because I want to!"

I sat there a few minutes to let the situation calm and then went inside to find her in the bedroom packing a suitcase, and I asked, "What are you doing that for?" She informed me she was going to spend the night at her girlfriend's home and would go to work from there, probably not getting home until late the next night.

Needless to say, her bizarre behavior since last Sabbath was weighing heavily on me, and I did not know what to do next! I did try to talk with her a little bit, but she walked out of the house, putting her suitcase in the car and abruptly took off down the dirt road! That was the last I saw her before the camp meeting.

When she was out of sight, I stepped across the road to her grandparents' home and told them what had happened while expressing my deep concern and confusion, hoping they would give me some answers. I knew it was common for Becky to talk with her people when she was keeping something from me. But they just listened and were pretty tight-lipped, except telling me what they always said when they did not want to say anything. "Well, you know how she is."

I walked down to Louise's, and while finding her to be just as tight-lipped as her parents, I sensed she wanted to say more. I pleaded with her, but she would not give in, so I walked back home and had another long night with very little sleep and lots of confusion and prayer. The psalmist described my feelings exactly, "*Let me be delivered from those who hate me, and out of the deep waters. Let not the floodwater overflow me, nor let the deep swallow me up...*"[226]

In the morning, I turned my thoughts toward finding a way to get to Tennessee and share my testimony. I would simply have to leave mine and Becky's problem until I returned, and I told the Lord, "Father, you see my circumstances, and if this is something you truly want me to do, you need to provide the transportation I need. It is all up to you, my Lord, so please show me what to do."

After sitting around the house all day, about suppertime, the thought came to me to walk a couple of miles up the road to my aunt's home. I did, and when I arrived, Aunt Martha was driving up from work, so we talked and I shared with her what had happened and my total confusion with how I was supposed to keep my appointment at the camp meeting. She could tell I was extremely low and asked me to stay and eat supper. After supper, her eldest daughter, my cousin Pam, called. Her mother invited her to stop by, and when Pam got there, she asked me about the camp meeting. I informed her that with the last-minute situation at home, I had no transportation, so it looked as if I would not be going.

Pam said she was so sorry to hear of these troubles because she, and the rest of the family, was quite proud of me. They had seen the tremendous change in my life and were very happy for me. She said, "I think this is a great opportunity for you to go and share how your life has changed! I don't want you to miss this opportunity! You are welcome to take my car and use my credit card for the trip. If you need anything else, let me know."

I was dumbfounded! And yet I knew this was another direct answer to my prayer and out of the most unexpected place!

The next morning, I got up early, finished packing my clothes, and took off for Collegedale, Tennessee. That evening, just about sundown, I checked into the boys' dorm, found my pastor, and got ready for and attended the opening meeting. I do not remember the subject matter of the meeting because all I could think about was that my Lord had literally brought me to the camp meeting! Jesus was continuing to confirm what he wanted me to do in spite of my problems, and I simply needed to "keep my eyes on Jesus."

Sabbath afternoon, before coming out on the stage, I was very nervous, but the pastor pulled me aside and had prayer for me. He told me to just relax and answer his questions because he would be interviewing me, leading me from point to point, and all I should do was follow his lead. I followed his instructions, and it all went well and was a wonderful experience for me.

Sunday morning, as I was leaving Collegedale, my mind was brought back to the trouble between Becky and me. I did not feel right going home yet. I needed a little more time to think and pray, so I decided to head for my parents' home in South Carolina. I stopped and gave them a call to make sure I could come on the spur of the moment, and Mama told me to come on. After visiting with my parents for a couple of days, I felt better and headed back to Georgia to work on the situation there.

Chapter 31

The Crossroad

*With whom did he take counsel, and who instructed him,
and taught him in the path of justice? Who taught him
knowledge, and showed him the way of understanding?*

—Isaiah 40:14

It was midafternoon when I drove into our driveway, and though Becky was not yet home, I knew she was scheduled to arrive around 6:00 p.m. I went inside and looked around for any evidence she might have come home while I was gone, and I could see that she had been there for at least one night. So I unpacked my travel bag, got something to drink, and resigned myself to enjoy the fresh air and nice weather sitting on the front steps, reading my Bible.

My wife drove up at about 6:30 p.m., and looking at her as she closed the car door, I thought to myself, "She must be wearing every piece of jewelry she ever owned, along with an extremely short skirt." Approaching me, she acted as if she did not care whether I was back home or not, but she looked at me and said, "Come on in, there is something I need to talk with you about." I could tell by her tone of voice and cold look, this was not going to be good at all.

We sat down in the front room, and she proceeded to tell me "she didn't love me anymore and had made up her mind she was not going to be a preacher's wife!" She continued, "I'm in love with my boss, and while you were at the camp meeting, I talked with the county sheriff. I'm giving you one week to pack and get out, and if you are not gone by then, the sheriff will be here to serve you with papers and put you out! My mind is made up, and there is nothing you can say to change it. I don't want to talk about it, and I don't want you bothering Mama, Papa, or Granny! It's my life to live as I choose, and they can't make me do what I don't want to do. We are finished!"

With all that had happened over the last two weeks, good and bad, I could not believe what I was hearing! As her words rolled out over her lips and penetrated my mind, my heart began to throb like never before! My chest tightened, and I could not seem to get enough air! Tears were flooding down my cheeks, and confusion like I had never experienced was capturing my mind!

Though I continued trying to reason with her, she still would not talk. Throwing some more things into an overnight bag, she paused and said, "I will be gone the rest of the week. I won't be here while you're here, but I'm coming back next week, and if you're not gone, I'm going to the nearest telephone to call the sheriff, and he'll come to forcibly put you out! Do you understand?"

I answered, "Yes, I'll be gone." I knew there was no use saying anymore. She walked out the door and briefly over to her grandparents' house then got in the car and left.

It was now June 1989, and I had not taken a drink, or desired one, since August 1986, but now I was literally falling apart! I was shaking uncontrollably just as I used to shake in some of my worst hangovers; in fact, I think it was worse. Standing there, looking out of the kitchen window as she drove down the road, I felt like there was a huge hole in my chest where my heart had been totally ripped out! The pain was indescribable! So much so, the only thing I could think about was getting a drink!

In the terrible shape I was in, I had no idea from moment to moment how to function, and the carnal flesh I lived in needed a bottle of booze to stop the pain! The more I thought about a drink of alcohol, the more it moved me toward reality. I was going to town and buy me a bottle! There was no doubt about it, and I did not know if I would ever be sober again!

Suddenly, the thought came to mind about praying, and I looked up into the ceiling, trying to see through the roof into heaven, and blurted out, "Lord! As your child, I don't want to do this, but as a sinner, I need this! And if you do not help me now, I am going to fall!"

The Lord's response was instantaneous; the grace of Almighty God flooded my body and mind! It happened just like when you walk into a dark room and flip the light switch on. Instantly, there is light! It was that fast that I had the power to overcome! The moment before, I knew I was going to fall, and the next moment, I knew victory was mine! Praise God! It still hits me today as I am telling you! God's amazing grace to needy sinners is always available to us! He can take us when we are flat on our face in our wretched lives, picking us up with his strong arms of mercy and healing, and take us to his well of *living water* for the victory and peace we need! Amen!

The next few days were pretty much a blur. I remember hanging around the house, occasionally walking up and down the dirt road beside the river, thinking, praying, and wondering what I should do next. As good as the Lord had been to me, my mind was like "a reed shaken with the wind."[227] Sometimes I felt like I was high on the mountain of God and full of courage, other times wondering how I could even think about going forward with my plans to enter school when my marriage had fallen apart. Each day, I was on an emotional roller coaster with periods of being down and out, then up and soaring, weeping, then peace, confusion, and then concord. But with my Bible at my side, the Holy Spirit would lead me to the still waters of Jesus, and I finally found myself in the middle of the week when I knew I had to make my decision about what I was going to do. I could not call the pastor because he told me coming home from the camp meeting that he would be out of town for the next two weeks, so I prayed and these words came to mind, *Why not call Gus Nichols?*

Gus was the head elder of the Baxley church, a man in his seventies at the time. He tried to befriend Becky and me since we began attending church, but I had always been fairly skeptical of Gus because of listening to some gossip and consequently had not been open to receiving his friendship for most of the two years we were at the church. We spoke coming and going and at fellowship dinners, but that was basically it. A number of times, he invited us to lunch at his home following church, but we always politely declined the invitation.

Julia was Gus's wife, and together, they owned and operated a trailer park in Baxley, renting out a number of used mobile homes he bought and remodeled. In some cases, tenants wanted to buy a home, and he would finance it for them, usually because they were lower-income families, unable to obtain financing anywhere else. This was a method that Gus and Julia used to reach out to others and witness. In former years, Gus worked as a dairy farmer, a store owner, a mechanic, and various other jobs to make a living, and he was always using his work situation to witness to people, sharing the good news of Jesus and his soon return. I came to learn they tried to use almost every opportunity they encountered with their tenants or customers to share their faith. In fact, like my Granny Keene, Gus and Julia lived their faith!

I went to town to fill up Pam's car and used the telephone to call Gus. I briefly told him what happened, and he asked if he might come to the house and us talk some more. I told him that would be fine. A little later, Gus drove up; I invited him in, and we sat and talked for quite a while. I shared more of the personal details about what had been going on for several weeks, and as we came to the end of our conversation, he began to encourage me to press forward. He told me that he was not telling me to forget about my marriage, but he said, "Tommy, there have been so many indications that God has been leading you. The devil is desperately trying to turn you away from the path that God wants you to follow. I believe that if there is any hope for your marriage, God will open the door for it to develop further. You are at a crossroad, and you already know what God wants you to do! I believe you need to go forward in faith. I do realize your faith is weak right now as you struggle with so much going on in your life, but I encourage you to move forward in going to Southern College. I am so convinced this is the way you need to go, that I am willing to load the few things you have into my old pickup truck and take you to Southern myself and get you set up there! Like I said a moment ago, the devil is truly trying to stop you from following this road, and I sure don't want to see you let him win."

Gus was definitely not trying to push me. I never got that feeling from our conversation at all. It was from a heart full of Christian love that he was encouraging me not to give up following the Lord's leading. I will admit at first it seemed like with this decision another load of concerns would be dropped on my shoulders to bear with all the other because I could not understand how I could move forward, leaving my wife behind, even though she wanted me to. Unlike my previous marriages, I had put so much into this marriage, and in one way, I felt that if I were to leave now, I would be utterly giving up—totally throwing away any chance I might have of reconciling with my wife! So I did not give Gus an answer then but promised to pray and sleep on the decision, and I would definitely call him the next morning.

He agreed with that approach, prayed for me, and then left for Baxley. After eating something, I read my Bible and tried to get some sleep, but lying there a good hour or so, sleep would not come, so I prayed again. However, my mind would not shut down to rest, so I got up and walked around until I was tired. Stretching out on the bed again, tears began to come, and I called out to the Lord asking for peace, some rest, and a clear mind in the morning for my decision.

Chapter 32

God and His Friends

And the Scripture was fulfilled which says, "Abraham believed God, and it was accounted to him for righteousness." And he was called the friend of God.

—James 2:23

The next thing I knew, it was about an hour after sunup. The Lord had again answered my prayer because I felt rested and seemed to have a clear mind. As I ate some breakfast, I considered the decision before me. Gus had aided me in realizing that staying there for a few more days to let the sheriff put me out of the house would certainly not help my relationship with Becky. And where would I go? How would I get around and support myself? Some of my relatives or church members might help me for a few days, but that would only put them in a difficult position and probably hurt my relationships with them! The only open door I could clearly see was leading to Southern College. I decided to go forward in faith.

I walked to the next-door neighbor's house to use the phone. Calling Gus, I told him my decision was made, and I was going to Tennessee if he was sure that he could take me. He said he would be glad to take me and would leave his home right away to come load my belongings and hit the road.

It was one of the longest trips I have ever taken in my life. In one way, I thought I knew what I was going to do, but in another, I knew when I arrived, everyone would be a stranger and my whole world would be different! School would not start for another two and a half months. I only had about $20 in my pocket and hardly any decent clothes to wear to school. I needed a place to live and a job too. Deciding not to worry and keep trusting the Lord, I silently prayed, "Lord, you have been clearly leading me up to now, and I guess each day will put new questions on my list, so I am putting my total faith in you. I am asking you to please, please help me stay on the right path."

During that trip, there were large segments of quietness, and then we would talk for a while about my feelings, concerns, and fears. Gus would listen and then encourage me. Periodically, he would pull over, and we would have a prayer. I would feel a little better, and we would push on. By the time we made it to Collegedale, the Lord had used him to answer most of the questions I had on my mental list. It was like Jesus was feeding my friend, Gus, the answers to whatever questions came to my mind.

What I did not know is that Gus and Julia had a daughter, Jan, who worked at Southern College in the accounting department. Jan's husband, Merlin, also worked for the college as an associate recruiter. They had a house just down the road from the school, and they were actively involved in reaching out and helping young people who needed assistance and encouragement to get a Christian education.

When we arrived at the school, Gus took me inside and introduced me to Jan. He told her briefly what was going on and then took me to their home. We cleaned up shortly before Jan and Merlin got home from work and after changing clothes, she busied herself in the kitchen putting supper together. She and Merlin welcomed me with open arms and assured me they would assist in helping me to get settled into school and community life. I could not help but think, "Here I was worrying about what God was going to do and how he was going to take care of me when I reached Collegedale and he already had it worked out!

We stayed at Jan and Merlin's house for a couple of days, and during that time, behind the scenes, Jan was working with a friend of hers, Mary Morford, who was in charge of student housing. There were some older apartments up on the hill, across the road, behind the college library. There were two strips of multiple apartments facing each other, and each unit had two rooms with a full bath and a kitchenette. While they still used them, the school was trying to phase them out and replace them. They were mainly used for older single students, such as myself, or couples with no children. While these arrangements were being handled behind the scenes, I had been directed to fill out all my student paperwork, enrollment forms, and send for my previous college and high school records. I was then given a list of departments on campus that hired students so I could apply for a job.

I decided to go to the grounds department first. As I walked in, there was a young man walking out the door. I told the lady at the desk who I was and what I was there for, and she smiled and said, "Well, as a matter of fact, a moment ago, a job just opened up! That young man you passed coming in just graduated and received a call to pastor a church." Handing me a form, she instructed me to fill out the application, and then I could talk with the boss. I filled out the application, and she explained briefly what I would be doing and then led me into an inner office, introducing me to her husband, Mr. Lacey, who was head of the department. He talked with me for a few minutes as he looked over my application and then took me into the shop to meet the supervisor with whom I would be working and explained I was to start the very next day at 8:30 a.m.

I could not help but think, "Here was more evidence the Lord was working on my behalf! I was amazed how Jesus was working to provide for all my needs, often before I would even ask for his help! Just like Jesus said, *"For your Father knows the things you have need of before you ask Him."*[228]

Back at the administration building, I turned in the paperwork for my job at the student finance office and then stepped over to accounting where I was to meet Gus. That was when they informed me I was to move into the little apartment with all the utilities turned on. They had opened a student account for me as they knew I had no money and could not pay any rent or deposits up front.

Wow! God's river system is perfect, and the water that flows through it is cool, refreshing, and lifegiving! Whether its flow is silent or roaring, still or turbulent, genteelly rippling or rushing, the transportation of its liquid is always moving forward. His nautical chart, the Bible, clearly marks the safe course around each of the devil's treacherous elbows he places in this river. To repeat myself, it was simply amazing how God was working through his people to erase each one of my fears about whether or not I should be there! Immediately, Ephesians 3:20 came to mind: *"Now to him who is able to do exceedingly abundantly above all that we ask or think…"*

Gus then took me over to the apartment, and sitting in front of the door was a stack of groceries, house cleaning supplies, some bedclothes, bathroom items, and several pieces of furniture that Jan, Merlin, and Gus had bought or gathered to get me started. After putting everything inside, Gus gave me the apartment key, and I walked him back to his truck. He said he needed to go so he could get to bed early because he was leaving for Baxley early the next morning.

I was suddenly afraid for him to leave me! With all that God and his friends had done, I was still afraid of this new place, the people, the job, and this new life. I am sure that Gus could tell because as I stood beside his truck, he put his hand on my shoulder and said, "I know God is calling you to the ministry. I know that if you hang on in faith and keep going forward, God will see you through just the way he has been seeing you through up till now! Everyone here is going to help you if you will just stay here and give them a chance." He encouraged me a little more, and then he pulled $75 cash out of his pocket and put it in my hand. He said, "I wish I could give you more, but I don't have it to give right now. With the groceries, a place to stay now, and a job, I have no doubt that you can make it from here. You know my phone number, and you can call me anytime. I'll be phoning Jan and checking on you from time to time. We'll write, and when we come up here to visit, we'll stop in and visit with you too." He had a prayer for me, and I watched him get in his truck and drive off down the road to Jan and Merlin's.

At that moment, I realized a brand-new chapter of my life had just begun, and I was so grateful, so appreciative of how Gus had never given up trying to be my friend. I also felt ashamed for how I had pushed away from that friendship. The one thing I was sure of though, if there was nobody else in the world praying for me to make it, my friend Gus Nichols surely was, and I have thanked the Lord for he and Julia many times over the years that were still to come.

175

Chapter 33

Seeking God

Oh God, you are my God; early will I seek you; my soul thirsts for you...

—Psalm 63:1

The first morning in my new Tennessee home, in the midst of my morning devotional, I began to cry and plead with God to reconcile my marriage. I closed my prayer, went down the street to work at my new job, and at lunchtime came back to the apartment. I prepared my lunch, and as I was trying to eat my sandwich, I found myself going back into prayer, weeping again, pleading with God for my wife and me to be reconciled. After praying most of the lunchtime, I went back to work and came home again that evening, sat down to eat supper, and again, my mind went back to the problems within my marriage! It was a never-ending cycle, day in and day out, seven days a week, for the next few months! I would go to bed at night after kneeling for a long while before my rear window, looking up into the stars of heaven and pouring my heart out to God. In the mornings, I would wake up, and the first thing to come before my mind was to talk with the Lord and plead with Him some more. Three times a day, every day for months, my petitions were pressed to the throne of God!

I then came to the conclusion I needed to do more than pray. I felt like I needed to give the Lord every opportunity to give me answers, to teach me and spiritually fill me, so I began going to the library. I only had my Bible and two or three books, so I would go to the library, across the street from my apartment. I would make my way down to the lower level to the E. G. White room. There, I would scan the index to her writings where I was drawn to study the lives of Joseph and Jacob.

As I studied my Bible, along with what this wonderful Christian author wrote about these two patriarchs and the trials and struggles they went through, I began to realize that God was using their stories to keep me afloat. The more I studied, the more I prayed. The more I prayed, the more the pain in my heart found its way out through my tear ducts. Most of the time, it was as if God was using these stories and my prayer time to surgically remove the poison out of my heart and mind. He was replacing it with the truths of his Word, and the experience I was gaining showed me what it really takes for Christians to overcome in this world. It is not easy, but I learned early on that it is possible, by God's grace and by following his Word and plan for your life. In spite of all the pain I experienced during that time, I can look back now and see they were some of the most remarkable months I have ever lived. Jesus was busily working in and around my life in ways that so often would completely shock me when I realized it! The Lord truly never left me alone. He would constantly encourage me!

On the grounds crew, we cut grass, pulled weeds, planted flowers and shrubs, raked leaves and pine straw, and replaced mulch. God used us to make Southern College beautiful while through his Holy Spirit, he made us more beautiful in character. My supervisor, Mark Antone, was a young man, younger than I. He was a Californian and knew the horticulture field well. He was one of the kindest, sincere, and conscientious Christians that I have ever met in my entire life. Mark was not just my supervisor, but he became my good friend, a spiritual friend. Jesus used him on many an occasion over the next two and a half years of school to encourage me. He would often give me additional points to consider when I had decisions pending.

I remember one occasion while I was going through my marriage turmoil. In addition to my intense prayer time at my apartment, I looked for duties at work where I could be alone and have more time to pray and focus on the Lord. One day, I was working alone, and I became very depressed. Weeks had gone by, and I had not had a response from Becky. I had written letters and made telephone calls to her grandparents, but nothing seemed to be able to bring me a response from her.

Mark's routine was to periodically make his way around the campus to the various crews to see how their duties were progressing. This particular day, he came up to me rather suddenly. I did not realize he was there, and before I knew it, he asked me to get in his truck and take a ride. He said, "I want you to help me do something that I cannot do by myself." I later came to understand this was only an excuse. As Mark had approached me, he discerned I was deeply depressed even though I was doing my job. Being the caring, loving individual he was, he found an excuse to speak with me.

During our ride, he inquired as to why I seemed so down. When we came to the place where he wanted me to assist him with a task, he pulled the truck over and parked in some shade, and we sat there for almost an hour. Mark listened to me, and then he talked some, sharing from his heart. He shared some scripture with me, and I began to cry and pour out my heart to him. When I paused, he prayed for me, which always gave me great peace and comfort. We then took care of the little job that had to be done, and he drove me back to my site. It was constant efforts like this that Mark and his assistant supervisor, Jeannie, would make to see me through some difficult days. Between Mark, Jeannie, and Mr. and Mrs. Lacey, there was always someone at work that the Lord would use to raise my spirits and keep me going.

It did not stop there. Even my fellow students, some of the more mature ones, realizing what I was going through, would come to me at just the right time, say just the right words, or offer just the right prayer. Jesus was constantly looking out for me and encouraging me, not letting me slip underneath the surface of this life's dead river.

Another time, I was on the back side of the administration building, working, yet deep in my low feelings when Jeannie came out of the side door and seeing me asked how things were going and if I needed any assistance. I said, "No thanks. I am doing fine and do not need any help with this project."

As she was about to walk off and check on the next worker, she stopped, turned around, and came back to me, saying, "You know, I've been meaning to thank you for a little while now, but it kept slipping my mind."

I said, "Thank me? Thank me for what?" I could not imagine what in the world she wanted to thank me for.

She responded, "Well, you have been sharing with us the trials you have been going through these last few months. Whether you realize it or not, I have listened and watched you closely, and I wanted to thank you for allowing God to use you. It has been such a blessing, a real blessing." She began to cry as she continued, "It has been such a blessing to me with all you have been going through, I have seen how God could still use you to be kind, compassionate, and caring, always having a friendly, encouraging word to say, even to your supervisors." She said, "It's made a lot of difference in my life because I've been going through some very difficult times in my family lately. So I just wanted you to know that."

I was truly shocked but managed to say, "Jeannie, I had no idea that the Lord was using me. But if he did, thank Him, not me."

Chapter 34

Needs and Temptations

*And my God shall supply all your need according
to his riches in glory by Christ Jesus.*

—Philippians 4:19

The Lord knows how to deliver the godly out of temptations…

—2 Peter 2:9

At that time, some of the many spiritual pleasures on campus were these beautiful hand-painted signs. Each had a verse of Scripture or a profoundly meaningful commentary on them. These signs were usually placed in unexpected areas so that you would suddenly come upon them. Many of these locations were at corners or in coves of solitude where, in passing them, one might catch a moment or two to stop and read the sign and meditate on its message. Their messages always seemed relevant to my needs at the time.

I did not know, but Jeannie made most of these signs as one of her pet projects. One day, the sign I found confronting me was like God himself was speaking to me in the midst of my depression. It was a strong reminder that Jesus was walking with me and understood everything I was going through. He comprehended all the doubts and confusion I was feeling. Time and again, that is the kind of powerful message that was conveyed to me from those little signs!

In a conversation with Jeannie, not knowing that she was the main person who created them, I expressed how much they meant to me, and her tears began to flow. That is when she revealed that she had placed the signs in their specific locations. She knew that what happened to me so many times already happened and would continue to happen to others many more times as they walked around the campus. It was her prayerful purpose that through the power of God, these verses of Scripture and commentaries she had put on the signs would have a comforting and encouraging effect on people's lives!

Another tremendous blessing that was available to me by working with the grounds crew was that we started every day, punching in on the clock and then going upstairs to a little room, which we affectionately referred to as the Upper Room for morning devotions. These devotionals went for thirty to forty minutes. We were on the clock and having a corporate worship period to begin our day! A list was always posted on the bulletin board where anyone could sign up for any date/s if they wanted to lead out in a devotional. This privilege made our work experience on the grounds crew extra special! Of the twelve to fifteen students who worked there most of the time, 75 percent of them were religion or theology majors, and quite a few of them were preachers who gave us a wide variety of thought-provoking, heart-tugging devotionals, and thus, we came to look forward to starting each day there.

After a few weeks, I finally made contact with Becky, and it seemed to me that she missed me very much and had been seriously thinking about getting back together. Obviously, this rapidly built my hopes up. I wrote her several letters and talked with her again on the telephone, and she indicated she had made a bad mistake and wanted us to renew our relationship. However, she wanted me to return to Georgia for us to accomplish this.

All this time, I had been diligently praying, sometimes for hours. In my personal studies, I read in the Bible and other Christian books, where oftentimes a person who was seeking God for answers or miracles would enter into periods of fasting along with their prayers. So I began to fast, and after I had fasted for a day, I found it difficult due to the hot weather and the demanding physical work I was doing. I finally came to understand that I could do without food, but I could not do without drink at the same time, so I would try to fast one day per week, and as I began to hear from Becky more often, I fasted more. Sometimes I would fast for two or three days running and felt I could hear the Lord's voice much clearer! Certain things in the Scriptures now made so much more sense to me whereas before I had not noticed them as I studied. I began to think if I fasted and prayed enough, I could convince the Lord to make Becky come back to me! (I later learned this was the wrong attitude to have about fasting and relating to the Lord.)

For another week, I fasted four days straight, and I began to have dreams at night or see things in the daytime that would be an explanation of some Scripture or situation in my life. More and more, the relationship with Becky appeared to be reforming.

One day, as I was mowing the lawn, I constantly talked with the Lord. My thoughts were to and fro as to whether I should pack up and go back to Georgia or stay at school. It was getting close to registration day, and a decision would have to be made soon. I was overjoyed to think our marriage could be mended, and it was pulling strong at my heart. It was all I could do to keep myself from leaving immediately, so I persisted in prayer with Jesus for an answer as I mowed, asking him, "Lord, should I stay here, or should I go back to Georgia"?

God suddenly spoke just as clearly as if he was standing next to me, saying, *Stay here*!

I began to argue with him. "But I thought it was your will for marriages to be reconciled! It is in your Word that divorce is not your will! How can my marriage be mended if I stay here?"

Yet all the Lord would say was, *Stay here*!

Frustrated because I could not get anything else from him, I shouted back, "Do you just want her to die and go to hell?"

Immediately, the Holy Spirit spoke, instructing me to read Ezekiel 18:23. I asked, "Read Ezekiel 18:23? What are you talking about, Lord?" For the rest of the afternoon when I pressed him to explain, the Spirit always gave me the same answer.

I could hardly wait to return to my apartment, so I did not stay around to chat with anyone after work and hurried down the street to my home.

Walking in and picking up my Bible, I turned to Ezekiel 18:23 and read these words, *"'Do I have any pleasure at all that the wicked should die?' says the Lord."*

Rebuked by the loving Creator of the Universe, it was clear Jesus wanted me to understand that he loved Becky and wanted her saved as much as anyone else, and I should never again think that he did not care about another human being! He wanted all to repent and be saved!

As I sat there in my chair, I went back to my previous question from earlier in the afternoon. "Lord, how am I going to help put my marriage back together if my wife wants me to come home and you want me to stay here? How am I going to do this? Why do you want me to stay here?"

The Lord tenderly spoke these words that I will never forget, *Don't trust your heart.* I asked him over and over again to be sure I was hearing God correctly, and every time, he answered in the same way, *Don't trust your heart. Stay here. Don't trust your heart.*

Over the next few days, I came to understand what Jesus was doing. Though I did not want to hear it, Jesus was telling me my heart was too wounded, too tender, and could too easily be taken advantage of. He was protecting me. He wanted our marriage to be healed, yet he did not want to put me back into a situation where I would be less likely to follow him rather than my aching heart. Jesus knew my heart and Becky's too.

I consulted with several of my closest friends, and they all believed I needed to call her and try to convince her to come to Collegedale, and we could be reunited there. So the next evening, I telephoned and told Becky that God had specifically told me not to leave Collegedale and I thought it best for her to come to Tennessee. She instantly went into a rage and began cursing and condemning me like the same Becky who had booted me out months before! She went on to say that our marriage was over for good! She had made up her mind, and I would be getting divorce papers in the mail very soon. If I did not care about our marriage enough to return to Georgia, then it was over!

Needless to say, for the next couple of days, I was an emotional wreck, and though I went to work and fulfilled my duties, I could not get our situation out of my mind. I was so surprised about Jesus speaking to me the way he had and how the encouragement and counsel from my friends had turned out when I accepted it, yet it was still all I could do to stop myself from going back home!

By this time, it was the middle of August, and registration day for the fall semester was about ten days away. Like most of the summer had been, each day was an emotional roller coaster about leaving or staying. The struggle was terrible! I truly wanted to obey the Lord, but my heart longed to go home to Becky! Finally, I decided to go talk with my student adviser, Dr. Derek Morris. Before I did, I refigured everything about my financial circumstances discovering I would still be considerably short of funds to start the semester and would need to borrow quite a lot of money.

I told Dr. Morris my financial picture was still very bleak, and since I had taken a stand against going into debt before ever coming to Collegedale, I could not believe it was God's will for me to stay, enroll, and run up a huge debt to obtain a degree to be a pastor. Truthfully, I was using my financial standing as an excuse to go home, adding that once I had my personal life in order, I would return.

He listened to me but did not try to advise me, instead, inviting me to kneel and pray with him. As we did, he pleaded with God to make known his will for my life, especially the decision whether to leave school or not, to make his will known beyond a shadow of a doubt. Dr. Morris told the Lord I needed this kind of encouragement. He said, "Lord, if it is your will that Tommy stay here for school, we are asking you to help him recognize it by coming up with all or most of the money so he won't have to go into a great amount of debt. He needs to be sure about which way to go." When he finished his prayer, he gave me a big hug and shook my hand, telling me to get back in touch with him in a couple of days and to be sure and not leave until I had told him goodbye.

From there, I went to work and turned in my notice because the Laceys had been so good to me, I felt I should give them more than a week's notice, so I gave them two weeks. I told Mrs. Lacey I was putting my education on hold and heading back to Georgia, and of course, I used the same financial excuse I gave Dr. Morris. She seemed terribly shocked, but all she said was, "Okay. Sorry to hear this, and I'll tell Mr. Lacey," and she wrote down the date that was to be my last workday.

On Monday, I went to work as normal, and several people tried to talk with me and inquire whether it was true that I had given my notice and was leaving school. Each time, I explained my circumstances of what I felt was best for me, no one tried to change my mind. They just lovingly listened and supported me. I came to understand, after the fact, they were doing a lot of praying for me.

That Thursday, I came into work, and clocking in, Mrs. Lacey called me into the office and said, "You know that registration and classes are next week. I was wondering if you were still continuing your two-week notice and would leave at the end of the week?"

I answered her, "Yes, ma'am, those are still my plans."

She tried to talk with me a little bit and encouraged me to stay, but she quickly grasped that my mind was made up. As I was walking out of her office, she asked me a question that stopped me dead in my tracks. "Tommy, if I could get you in to see Dr. Sahly, the college president, would you be willing to give him your testimony and tell him you are leaving school before it starts?"

I was truly touched that one of my bosses was willing to go to such an extent to try to change my mind about leaving. I could not help but give her a grateful smile (and I wanted to run over to her and give her a great big hug) and thank her, saying, "I really do not know what good it will do, but sure, I would be willing to share my testimony with him."

She said, "Let me see what I can do. There is a college staff picnic this afternoon, and I'll see Dr. Sahly then. Let me see if I can get an appointment for you, and I will let you know something tomorrow."

That evening after work, I went home and continued to pack up the few belongings I had and made some notes about things I would be giving to my friends. When I finished packing and writing my notes, I stretched out on my bed and began to think about the situation. As I thought about my decision and how I was making that decision, I had to be honest with the Lord. He knew, and I knew that he knew, my reasoning was nothing more than me giving in to my weak heart, which he had warned me not to do. Just like Jonah, I had been clearly instructed, and here I was, trying my best to justify going the other way. This was how I lived most of my life, following a dead river that had no future. I knew that was wrong for if I went back home to Georgia, I might very well lose everything again, and most importantly, I might jump back into the dead river, losing my relationship with Jesus and drown! But the hope of repairing our marriage was a terribly strong current to fight, and I thought I had to go with it!

Chapter 35

Living Fountains of Waters

For the Lamb who is in the midst of the throne will shepherd them and lead them to living fountains of waters.

—Revelation 7:17

The next day, being Friday, we usually only worked a half day. As I came in to work, Mrs. Lacey looked at me and said, "Tommy, you do not have to work today because you have an 11:00 a.m. appointment with Dr. Sahly. Go back to your apartment, get your thoughts together, put on your Sabbath suit, and be at Dr. Sahly's office at eleven o'clock sharp! And when you get there, I want you to tell him how you came to be at Southern College and everything that happened in your marriage prior to that and then answer his questions,"

I said, "Okay!" After thanking her, I took off for my apartment and prepared for my appointment, taking a few minutes for prayer and to change my clothes, and then heading for the administration building. As I walked, I remembered Dr. Morris's prayer, "Lord, if it is your will that Tommy stay here for school, we are asking you to help him recognize it by coming up with all or most of the money so he won't have to go into a great amount of debt."

Reaching Dr. Sahly's office, I was wondering, "What is going to happen next?"

When I entered his office, he was standing at his secretary's desk. He looked at me and smiled, asking, "I guess you are Tommy Poole, right?" Inviting me into his office, he started the conversation by mentioning his conversation with Mrs. Lacey and then told me that he would like to hear my testimony and how it brought me to Southern College. He closed his office door and sitting down, I began my story. Occasionally, he would ask a question or two for clarification, but most of that next hour, he listened, and I spoke.

When my story reached the present time, he said, "I understand you are planning to leave Southern next week. You are working out a two-week notice and want to return to your home in Georgia to work out some pending personal problems." I acknowledged, and he went on, "I also understand you are worried about accumulating a large amount of indebtedness to obtain your college degree, and I completely understand your concern, but is there anything I can say or do to convince you to change your mind and give God a chance to work things out as you stay at school?"

I answered, "I really do not know, Dr. Sahly. With all the problems that are currently in my life, I am not sure they can be resolved without going home, and I certainly do not believe I should compound them with indebtedness!"

He expressed that he had a special fund (the President's Fund), but there was only $300 left for the semester and wished I had come to him sooner because he would have been able to help me more financially. "I will give you the $300, but I'm not going to stop there! If you will stay this semester and give the Lord an opportunity to work for you as he has obviously been doing all along, I will send you to the Student Finance Office, after calling the director and instructing him to do whatever it takes to find as much money as possible for you to start school and not have to pay a dime of it back! Will you at least go down to his office and talk with him? Then you can make a more informed decision whether or not to stay and begin this semester."

I was thoroughly stunned and felt as though my heart would burst out of my chest with joy! But I did manage to say, "Yes, sir, I will be willing to do that!" At this point, I already felt like I owed him that much because he sat there for an hour or so listening to my story! I could tell he was genuinely concerned that I make the right decision. So I went downstairs to Student Finance and told them Dr. Sahly had sent me to see the director. In fact, Dr. Sahly was speaking to the director as I walked into his office. Introducing himself as Ken Norton, giving me a big welcome, he ushered me into his inner office, closed the door, and said, "Even though it is very late, I feel we can do some things to help you go to school without having to run up a large amount of debt."

The secretary brought in my file, and Ken began adding the information from Dr. Sahly to the file, and then he began figuring what I would need to start school. In a few minutes, he looked at me and said, "We came up quite a bit short, but if you are not in a hurry, I want to make a few telephone calls to see what else we might be able to find, okay?" He then asked me to wait in the outer office until he finished making the calls. From what little I could hear, it sounded like his contacts were people that he normally reached out to in special circumstances, but he was unable to find any funds from them. In a moment, Ken called me back into his office as he pulled a file out of his cabinet. He said, "Tommy, it looks like you qualify for a special fund, which is a scholarship/grant. It is a scholarship for those who can afford to pay it back but is a grant for those, such as yourself, who cannot afford to repay the funds. The reason it is a special fund is because there are certain stipulations about whether or not you pay the funds back." He then asked, "You will be a theology major, correct?"

I responded, "Yes, sir."

Again, he asked, "Are you looking to go to work for the denomination?"

I said, "Yes, sir."

He continued explaining, "This fund is known as the Ruff Family Fund and is for students who, after graduating, go to work for the denomination. The money they receive from this fund is dispersed to the student as if it is a grant. The balance due of these funds is amortized [written off] over the period that you work for the church. In other words, for every month you work for the church, it would be just as if a payment was made toward your balance due of those funds, only not by you. However, should your employment with the church cease, you would be responsible for paying back the remaining balance as if it were a student loan." Then he asked, "Does this sound like something you would be interested in using"?

I replied, "Well, yes, sir. How much are you talking about?"

Doing some quick figuring with his adding machine, Ken responded, "It looks like this semester, with grants, earnings at the grounds department, and the Ruff Family scholarship, you have all but $800 of the $6,000 needed to stay in school." And with a big smile on his face, he asked, "Do you think you can stay here and see what else God can do for you based on these terms?"

Needless to say, I was flabbergasted! I sat there a moment or so, astounded that again, in spite of my trying to disbelieve God and his call to ministry, Jesus was bending over backward, answering Dr. Morris' prayer to let me know what he wanted me to do! Finally, I just said, "Yes, I will stay. I have got to try it!"

Hurrying back to the grounds department to share the good news with Mrs. Lacey, I found it was already closed for the day, to prepare for Sabbath. I managed to find her home telephone number and gave her a call and thanked her for all she and Mr. Lacey had done to intercede on my behalf. I told her, "I am not going back home, at least not this semester. I will stay and see what else God will do. As far as my marriage is concerned, I am going to call my wife this weekend and let her know what has happened, and while I definitely want to heal our marriage, at this time, there is no way that I could leave and come home in the face of how the Lord is working in my behalf. He has already revealed that he does not want me to do that."

I told Mrs. Lacey that I would try my best to encourage Becky to come to Collegedale and see what the Lord will do for our marriage here. "If we are here, we can benefit from counseling with many qualified leaders in the church." Mrs. Lacey agreed.

Of course, the next day at church, I was so overjoyed and looked for every opportunity to share with my fellow students in Sabbath School discussion about what God was now doing in my life. I wanted others to see how God was working! He had faithfully taken me from the depths of my dead river experience and was leading me into a life that was flowing from his *living fountains of waters*![229]

Chapter 36

River of Your Pleasures

You give them drink from the river of your pleasures.
For with you is the fountain of life.

—Psalm 36:8–9

The next week was registration, and like most students, I had been looking through the course catalog and the evaluation the academic department had done on my college credits to see what would transfer and the list of courses I would need to complete to receive my bachelor's degree in religion. It appeared I needed three and a half more years of college! I had already studied for six years because of changing majors several times. Yet my fundamental courses were completed with a good grade point ratio that assured my acceptance.

Registration day arrived, and I made my way to the gymnasium. Just before entering, the Holy Spirit spoke clearly and told me to *ask them if there is any way to cut the number of courses you need for graduation.*

Caught off guard, I asked the Lord, "What did you say, Lord?"

The Holy Spirit spoke again, *Ask them if there is any way they can cut the number of courses you need to graduate.*

I responded, "All right, Lord. I hope I am hearing you correctly. You have been working so powerfully in my life, and I trust you, so that is exactly what I am going to do."

Walking through the front door of the gymnasium, I momentarily stopped to see where the religion department was set up, and locating them, I made my way to their tables. Dr. Morris was my student adviser, so I took my schedule card and list of courses I needed to complete for my degree and handed them to him. He looked very shocked to see me but said, "Well, Tommy, I am very glad to see you here. Have your circumstances changed any?"

Of course, for the next few minutes, I shared with him what God had been doing in answer to his prayer just a little over a week ago. As I shared, his face lit up, and it was then I asked, "Dr. Morris, I have an important question for you. Is there any way the religion department can cut some of the courses off my list to get me out into the field quicker?"

He looked at me with the strangest look. It was as if he was shocked that I would ask something like that. He stood there for a moment, silently looking back at me, and then spoke, "Well, Tommy, just have a seat right here and let me go over and talk with my colleagues and see what we can do."

I sat down, and he called the other professors into a huddle at the other end of the table. Dr. Morris did most of the talking, and undoubtedly, he was sharing with them some of the background of my situation and how the Lord had responded to his prayer in meeting my financial needs. In just a few minutes, I saw this amazingly happy look on his face as he left their huddle and came back to where I was sitting. He then said, "It is just amazing! It is absolutely amazing!"

I asked, "What is amazing, Dr. Morris?"

He said, "It is amazing how God is working for you! I've seen the Lord work like this before, but every time I see it happen, it simply amazes me more!" He went on, "I've shared a little bit of your background and your testimony with my colleagues, and I asked them the question you asked me. I hope you are not in a hurry today because we'll have to do this in between assisting the other students, but the consensus is that we will sit down and design you a curriculum that will allow you to get out of here in two or two and a half years." Then he asked, "You've been in the military, haven't you?"

I replied, "Yes, sir, I was in the US Marine Corps for two years."

He said, "That's what I thought, and obviously, you are much older than the average student here. So sit here and relax. We're going to design you a program to get you out of here and working in the Lord's vineyard as soon as we can."

It was all I could do to sit there! I felt like I wanted to jump up and run and shout as some of the brethren from the charismatic churches do! I was so elated, and Dr. Morris continued shaking his head and smiling in amazement as he went back to help some students who were waiting for him at the table. Mentally, I joined him in thinking it surely is amazing!

When I left the gymnasium that afternoon, I was registered for all my first semester courses, and they were approved by each professor. The plan was laid out for exactly what they would require of me to receive a slightly different degree. My degree would not be in theology but religion with a minor in practical theology, and I would be working for the Lord in two and a half years!

When I called Becky the weekend prior to registration, I had difficulty reaching her but did talk with some of her family. I left messages for her, but she did not call back. The next weekend, after registration, I was able to reach her, and I shared exactly how the Lord had been working for me. At the beginning of the conversation, she was very anxious for me to say that I was coming home, and she sounded as if she could hardly wait until I returned. However, when I told her how I had come to understand that God did not want me to leave school, I could tell immediately her mood changed. I tried extremely hard to not let that happen by encouraging her that we now had a clear picture of what the Lord's will is for us, and if she really wanted us to be together since we both knew that divorce was not his will, the obvious thing for her to do was to get on the bus and come to Collegedale.

However, no matter how much I tried to encourage her with all the positive leadings of the Lord, before the end of the conversation, she grew terribly upset! She was not only argumentative but virtually explosive again, and the conversation was a total loss! I knew by what she said and the way she said it that she was not going to come. She tried to make it appear that if I was not willing to leave school immediately and come home to spend a little time with her and then we would return to Tennessee, it would prove that I did not love her and I really did not care about healing our marriage. This truly hit me hard, but I was absolutely convinced as to what God wanted me to do. I knew what he wanted her to do as well, but it was her choice not to follow His will. I could not agree to come back to Georgia, and the conversation ended rather abruptly! She told me not to call her anymore!

Registration day and the call to Becky took place during the last week of August 1989. Classes began three days later. I bought my books and started classes but was still carrying the tremendous burden about my marriage possibly ending, my wife's attitude, and what I was going to do if she did divorce me. How was I going to enter the ministry as a single divorcée? It was my understanding that the church usually did not give a call to single men, especially divorced ones!

While these things weighed heavily on my mind, all that God had done in the last few months provided an emotional buffer to help me out, giving me a temporary boost. Therefore all the negative development with Becky did not pull me down into the depths of depression like before. It did take a little while for me to cope with it, but I felt that I had hope and God had not tossed me aside. I knew that Jesus truly wanted me there in school, doing everything he needed to do to show me his will for my life.

I had all the funds required to attend school and pay my entire bill for the semester, except $800. Just before classes started, I came to work one day, and Mr. Lacey called me into his office. He told me he had been working at the college for many years and served, not only as part of the staff but also worked on a number of church and community projects. He said that he had worked very closely with members of the McKee family who owned and operated McKee Baking Company, the bakers of Little Debbie snack cakes. They operated two plants next to the college, and they supported the school, as well as the church, on a faithful basis. He explained that a number of students were employed there, and the plants ran three shifts. The two McKee brothers were on the board of trustees at the college, and Mr. Lacey said he had a very close working relationship with them.

The family had approached him about recommending a pastoral student who worked for him to fill a special family need. Their father, O. D. McKee, was up in age, and since their mother had passed away earlier that year, Mr. McKee had suffered several falls. As a result, the family felt that it was best for him to have a live-in nurse. They previously had a live-in nurse attending Mrs. McKee, and the family had established a good relationship with her, so they asked her to stay on and look after their father.

When the brothers approached Mr. Lacey, they were looking for a mature male, preferably one older than the average theology student who would pass a thorough background investigation. Mr. Lacey said that he thought of me. If I was interested, I would move into the McKee home, having my own bedroom and bath, next to the nurses' quarters, in a far wing of the house. I would assist Mr. McKee with his nightly preparation for bed and his getting up and dressing in the mornings. I was to sleep in a bedroom directly across the hall from his with radio monitors beside our beds. This would allow me to be aware of any needs he would have during the night so I could assist him. Hopefully, this arrangement would head off any further falls.

Mr. Lacey explained I would have to go through a multilevel interview process with the family, and they would complete a background check on me. He said if I was selected for the job, the McKee family would furnish me with a free room, bath, and a private place to do my cooking. I would provide my own food. They would also add a small hourly compensation to assist with the extra transportation expense to and from school and my meals.

I told Mr. Lacey I would be more than happy to go through the interview process, which was to begin the next day. He said that one of Mr. McKee's sons would be coming by my campus apartment to have the preliminary interview at 3:00 p.m. During that interview, the son would be explaining in more detail what would be expected of me.

That night, I prayed and decided that I would not try to cover up even the smallest detail about my "colorful past."[230] (As it turned out, this was probably one of the main reasons I was hired for the job.) I shared with him my past drinking issues and the number of my divorces; he seemed less and less interested, but he did take notes of the information and assured me that he would look into my past. When leaving, he paused and said, "I realize you have told me quite a bit, but I want to say this before I leave. If there is anything that you may have just now thought of or anything that you may have been holding back, I know how to investigate someone's background, so if there is anything in your past you haven't told me about because you think it may be too negative, I want to give you this last opportunity to speak up now because this is going to weigh heavily as we decide who we choose to hire for this position."

I assured him I had given him my entire testimony and I was being absolutely truthful with him. I told him that I would be happy to provide names, addresses, and phone numbers of those whom I had been involved with and whom I had mentioned in my testimony.

He said that would not be necessary and I would hear from him in about a week. Tentatively, the job was to last for three and a half months until January 1, 1990, when there would be an evaluation as to whether the services were still needed, and if so, they would consider if they wanted to continue my employment or find someone else.

With the meeting over, he left. I sat down to figure up the financial effect of such employment. I reasoned that since I would not have to pay rent or electricity to the college, at least until January 1 of the new year, or possibly longer, I was going to be ahead in my finances almost $900, for that period. This meant I would have enough income to buy groceries and pay the remainder of my school bill—$800.00—giving me a zero balance at the end of my first semester!

After another interview with the McKee brothers, a sister, and their father's nurse, I was offered the job and accepted it. I had a friend who lived and worked on campus and did not need his vehicle, and he agreed to lend me his car for a few weeks until I could obtain one. I then moved out of college housing and into my apartment at the McKee home.

Again, I could not deny the fact that the God of heaven was working for me, having a solution for every need that arose! Whatever my need was, it was covered with some leftover! Like Dr. Morris, I was constantly amazed at how Jesus was working on my behalf, and now I needed to find and buy a car with no money!

Chapter 37

Letters from Family

As cold water to a weary soul, so is good news from a far country.

—Proverbs 25:25

It was now early September when a letter arrived from Becky wanting me to call her. I called, and she informed me she was pursuing the divorce and would be sending the papers soon, and all I had to do was to sign and return them. However, I was still very interested in saving our marriage, but the only way she would consider that was for me to leave school and return to Georgia. Yet the Lord had already made it abundantly clear that I stay in school, not trusting my heart but trusting his wisdom, Word, and actions. I was to continue following his leading. If Becky truly wanted to mend our relationship, she would come to Collegedale, accepting God's will for our lives.

I restated my position to her in a kind but firm manner, positively making my plea based on how God had been working for us and telling me for her to come to Collegedale. She exploded again and would not hear anything further! She said, "The papers will soon be in the mail! Sign them and send them back," and she abruptly slammed the receiver down in my ear!

A few days later, the papers arrived, and after reading them through several times, I was still very concerned, wanting to save our marriage! I felt obligated to make another attempt, so I began to pour my heart out to the Lord! With many tears, I even tried bargaining with the Lord, but after realizing that was futile, I decided to talk with several older married students I had come to know and trust. Their counsel made it all clear again that I had to follow the Lord's leading, and Becky did too! Like me, or anyone, she had a choice to make, and I could not make it for her.

I decided to call one more time, but she would not talk directly with me, allowing her mother, Louise, to relay her small part of the conversation. And it did not take long for some extremely vulgar language to come from her that Louise would not repeat! She yelled in the background, "Sign the papers and return them now! I don't want to have anything more to do with you or our marriage!"

With that decision, I knew I had done everything possible to remedy the situation, short of turning away from the Lord! I walked over to the shopping center mailbox and then paused to send a silent prayer. I asked Jesus to please give me total peace when I signed the papers and dropped them in the box. The Lord answered my prayer, and I felt immediate peace and have never had another moment's doubt about if I had done the right thing! Not about saying yes to a divorce that God hates but to letting Becky decide for herself, which way she would go. She made her final decision about our marriage and would not partake of the Lord's *living water*.

Divorce is not the will of God, and now after causing this terribly painful experience three times for others, it was being heaped on me, and it surely hurt more than I had ever dreamed! But what I needed to do now was keep floating down this new river of life, in faith, following my Lord's plan.

It was around this time that my friend told me he would need his car in another week because his wife was starting a new job off campus. This was going to put me in a really bad situation since my apartment at the McKee home was about a mile and a half from campus. I needed a car and the money to buy it!

In my next homiletics class (preaching), Dr. Douglas Bennett passed around a sign-up sheet for any students interested in volunteering to speak during the semester. These appointments were at smaller area churches that were part of multichurch districts, and their pastors could not be at each church every Sabbath, so guest speakers were recruited to fill in when the pastor was not present.

It was a great opportunity for inexperienced speakers such as me to obtain some on-the-job training. The problem was, each student had to furnish his own transportation, which I would not have in a few more days. I signed up anyway, thinking if I could not hitch a ride with a friend, I would have to find someone to take my turn speaking. As we were leaving class, I mentally spoke to the Lord, saying, "Father, you know I will be losing my transportation in just a few days, so if you want me to fill these dates as a speaker, along with having a ride to and from the McKee's home to campus, I am asking you to provide a means of reliable transportation that I can somehow finance to fit my situation. Please meet my needs once again."

Two days later, I walked into the grounds department to work my regular shift when a student who just graduated that summer was there in the process of checking out of school. As I walked to the time clock to punch in, he looked at me strangely and then asked, "You need a car, don't you?"

I was totally stunned because I did not know him, except by face, but I replied, "Well, yes, I do, but I do not have any money to buy a car."

He said, "That's no problem! I have a car for you!"

So in case he had not heard me clearly, I repeated, "I really do not have any money in my budget to buy a car!"

He said, "You don't need to worry about that. We'll work something out. Come with me and look at the car. It's right down the street." I told Mrs. Lacey I would be right back, and he drove me in his newer car to where the old car was parked. It was a beat-up orange Yugo, a foreign economy car that looked like a Volkswagen Rabbit. He unlocked the door and told me to get in the driver's side to see how it felt. He then told me it had been sitting for a good while and the battery needed to be charged, but we could jump it off. He opened his trunk and pulled out his jumper cables, hooked them to both vehicles' batteries, and said, "Get in and crank it up!"

After the engine turned over several times, it started, and he told me to keep it idling for a few minutes, and then we would drive it around the school. So we did, and the car drove great! When we parked it, he drove me back to grounds, and I reminded him that

I did not have any money. He said again, "Don't worry about that, we'll work something out! The question I have for you is, do you want the car?"

I replied, "Yes, but I am not kidding you! I do not have any money!"

He asked, "Can you get $25?"

I answered, "Probably so. I am sure someone will loan me that much."

He said, "Great! You get the $25 today, tomorrow, or whenever you can and I will sign the title over to you. Then you give me two more payments of $25 each over the next couple of months."

I reiterated, "But I do not know when I can get another $50! My budget is so tight I can barely buy groceries, much less coming up with the money for the car and gas, oil, and insurance."

He told me, "Just concentrate on getting the $25, and I'll pay for your title transfer and tag. I'll trust you for the rest. So have we got a deal?"

Telling him yes, we shook hands, and I went to work my shift.

Before going home that evening, I stopped by the post office to check my mail, and there was a letter from my daughter, Brenda, in South Carolina. Since classes started, I had been writing her, telling her how mightily the Lord had been working for me in my finances and registration. This letter arrived just after Hurricane Hugo hit South Carolina and made its way up to Charlotte, North Carolina, leaving devastation everywhere it traveled. At that time, my ex-wife Linda and our daughter were living in Columbia, South Carolina, and because of the storm, it took a few extra days for Brenda's letter to get to me.

As I pulled the letter out of my mailbox, little did I know what was inside, other than the typical communication from a daughter who missed her father. I decided to wait until arriving at the apartment before reading the letter, so I went straight home. When I opened the letter, there were two immediate surprises: first, there was a $50 check made out to me for my birthday (coming up on the twenty-first of September) and second, the letter was mainly written in Linda's handwriting.

I could hardly believe the tone of the letter. It was actually cordial, nice, and though I had talked briefly with Linda during the summer when calling to talk to Brenda, though Linda was polite, the conversations were never long enough for me to determine whether or not she was still angry with me. However, this letter was sufficiently long enough for me to understand that her attitude toward me was much different since our second divorce five years previously. This letter was so positive and upbeat, yet general in nature, telling me about the hurricane they had experienced. She said they had been talking about my birthday, and instead of buying a gift, they thought I could probably use some cash, so that is why they sent the check.

Once again, God had answered my prayer and provided for me in a totally unexpected way, so I was now able to buy the little car! The next day, I met with the vehicle owner, paid him the $50, and he signed the title over to me and said he would go ahead and take care of transferring the title and get me a tag. I only owed $25, and my car would be paid for. Checking the mail several days later, I found a letter from Mother and Dad, and they, too, sent me a check for $50 for my birthday, and that allowed me to pay the balance on the car, fill the tank with gas, and have a few dollars cash in my pocket! Jesus provided me with suitable transportation that would take me through my college experience, all for $75, and when I had no money whatsoever. He provided it all!

On the way back to the McKee's, I started thinking about the money and the letter from Brenda and Linda. I knew that Brenda did not have money herself to send me, so I reasoned that at least half of it must have come from her mother. In fact, both the money and the letter baffled me, weighing heavily on my mind. It was something that would not let go. The letter was trying to impress itself upon me, and my thoughts were constantly trying to analyze every word, every part of each sentence, and I began to wonder if maybe I was overreacting.

By the time I reached the McKee house, I was totally confused. I went into my room and began to read the letter again, and in a few moments, there was a knock on my door. Opening the door, I saw it was Thelma, Mr. McKee's nurse. She had the room next to mine and just wanted to say hello and see how I was doing, as we had not had much time to chat during the last week. I truly respected the woman and knew from previous conversations that she had been married to two Adventist pastors; both had died while working for the church. She seemed grounded, theologically, and was just a lovely, spiritual individual. She was very particular with her care for Mr. McKee and sought to make him as comfortable as possible.

Because of my respect for her, I decided to ask her to read my letter and give me her best honest assessment. She agreed, and after she finished reading it, I asked her, "What do you think about it?"

She looked at me with a big smile and said, "This woman is still very much in love with you."

Immediately, my heart began to race, and I could not tell if it was because of fear or joy or both! And just as quickly, a very uncomfortable feeling came over me, and I asked, "Do you really think so?"

She responded, "I know so! You may not be able to tell it, but I guarantee if you let most women read this, they will tell you the same thing! That is what I hear in this letter."

I was now faced with a difficult ethical situation. On one hand, I was a married man, and my desire was to put my marriage back together. On the other hand, I had been without the closeness, love, and comforts of a wife for four and a half months. I had no hope, no indication whatsoever that my marriage was going to be repaired! Now, out of nowhere, with me not making any pitch or effort that would encourage Linda toward a relationship, she obviously was beginning to dialogue with me on a very friendly, basis and that scared me because I did not want to let the Lord down in any way. I certainly did not want to do anything else that would hurt Linda anymore because, through the years, I had hurt her more than enough! My mind was now flooded with so many thoughts, pros and cons, about the situation. There was the wife that did not want me, and now there was the ex-wife who seemed to be saying that she might want me, and it suddenly looked like I was in for another emotional roller-coaster ride.

I decided that I was not going to do anything but pray, hunker down, and take no action whatsoever! I would not get involved with trying to write letters to Linda that could be construed at all as me encouraging a romantic relationship because, as far as I was concerned, I was a married man! I did not want to do or say anything that would cause someone to think I was acting in a sinful, unethical way. I wanted to glorify God, and after all that I had experienced with him, I could not see myself throwing it all away to bend toward something that could very easily be sinful and just a comfortable situation. My ex-wife was not a practicing Christian, and I had no idea what her thoughts were about the Lord, let alone about Adventism. My role was to be faithful to Jesus, no matter what. He is consistently faithful to me, and so I will pray, study my Bible, and wait for God to lead me further down this new river of life.

Chapter 38

Snares of Death

*The fear of the Lord is a fountain of life, to turn
one away from the snares of death.*

—Proverbs 14:27

October 6, 1989, was a Friday, and as my habit was, I was up early
with Mr. McKee, but for me to be ready to assist him and finish getting ready for school, I would get up extra early and have my devotional Bible reading. That morning, I was strongly impressed to look
into the Psalms. Initially, I could not understand why I was impressed
to do that, but I began leafing through the pages in that book and
periodically stopping to scan the verses on the page just to see if I
might gain anything the Holy Spirit would alert my attention to.

It did not take long for that to happen. It was Psalm 33, and as
I scanned down the column, suddenly, the verses at the end of the
Psalm (verses 18–22) seemed to light up as if on a neon sign! The
Lord seemed to be magnifying and highlighting these verses at the
same time because he obviously wanted my full attention!

This is what they say:

> *Behold, the eye of the Lord is on those who fear
> him, on those who hope in his mercy, to deliver their
> soul from death, and to keep them alive in famine.
> Our soul waits for the Lord; he is our help and our
> shield. For our heart shall rejoice in him, because*

we have trusted in his holy name. Let your mercy, O
Lord, Be upon us, just as we hope in you.

As I read these verses, I was certain Jesus did not want me to miss them; in fact, he was speaking to me in a most deliberate way. When I finished my devotions and helping Mr. McKee I left for school with a bookmark, marking the page where this passage was located, and the constant question on my mind was, "What is Jesus trying to tell me through this passage?"

Like usual, when I walked into the lower-level door of the religion department building, I stepped into the mail room to check my mailbox. This morning, several of my classmates and Dr. Bennett were there making copies for our homiletics class. We were greeting one another, and then I heard the voice of Bridget, the Religion Department secretary, coming down the hall calling my name. "Tommy, Tommy Poole!"

I answered as I was turning to face her, "That is me!"

She said, "I have a very important message for you! A call came for you just a few minutes ago, from Columbia, South Carolina. I'm not sure who was calling, but it was about your daughter being in the hospital." Handing me a note, she continued, "They left this number and said for you to call as soon as possible!"

I could not imagine why Brenda would be in the hospital. She had always been very healthy, playing Little League Baseball and tennis for a number of years, having no physical defects or illnesses that I knew of. Momentarily puzzled, I was briefly scanning the room, looking into the faces of my friends and professor when Dr. Bennett spoke up and told me to go ahead and call on the department's telephone and not worry about the bill. Bridget took me into her office, made the call, and handed me the phone before stepping out closing the door behind her.

My ex-wife Linda answered the telephone, and I said, "It is Tommy. What is wrong?"

She replied, "I'm at the Richland Memorial Hospital," and her voice started to break. Between sobs, she continued, "Brenda tried to take her life. She took an overdose of medication, and the doctors are working frantically, but they don't feel there is any more they can do, and they don't expect her to make it. They think she will go into a deep coma and then die within twenty-four hours. So if you want to see Brenda while she is alive, you need to come right now!"

In that moment, I thought my heart stopped! I paused and then told Linda that I would leave immediately and be there as soon as I could. I was so stunned and shocked I began trembling—trembling so bad it was like trying to quit drinking again. I hung the telephone up and walked back into the mail room where everyone stopped and looked at me to hear what I had to say. Dr. Bennett asked, "What is the matter, Tommy?"

I told him, "My daughter, Brenda, is dying, and the doctor is giving her about twenty-four hours to live. Her mother says if I want to see her alive, I have to come right away."

I will never forget how Dr. Bennett put his arm around me and held me firm as he said, "Let's pray for Brenda, you, and your family." When he finished praying, he said, "You go on right now. We're praying for you and Brenda. Don't worry about your classes or assignments. Just keep us informed, and you be careful out there on the highway."

Walking out the same door I came in, heading down the steps to my vehicle, I was shaking so bad I knew there was no way I would be able to drive the three hundred plus miles to Columbia in that condition. I knew that I had to have God's miraculous help! Pausing on the steps, I stood there, looking out over the parking lot and then up into the sky as a prayer rolled out of my heart and off my lips, "Lord, I'm not going to make it if you don't help me! Please help me now!" In that split second, Jesus flooded my being with his grace and power, and in the next instant, calm settled over me from head to toe! The shakes completely stopped! Yes, I was still very much concerned about Brenda, but God took total control and gave it back to me.

I made my way down to my car and drove to the McKees to gather a few things in my travel bag. I told Mr. McKee and his nurse, Thelma, what was happening. They insisted I leave immediately, telling me not to be concerned about my duties because they would have someone fill in for me until my return. As I was walking out the door, they began having special prayer for Brenda, me, and our family. Heading out of the driveway, I laid my Bible on the seat next to me, and after settling in on the interstate highway, I opened the Bible to Psalm 33 so I could periodically reread it. Every time I looked at the passage, it seemed to stand out more and more!

As I drove further down the road toward South Carolina, I began to understand why the Lord had given me those verses. In advance, Jesus had given me verses that would offer strength, courage, and assurance in what was going to be the most difficult part of my life to that point! Knowing what was in process, the Lord was preparing my heart and mind with the power of his holy Word to sustain me through that time! So I simply left the Bible open to that powerful passage, and every few minutes, I would drink more of its supernatural water of life. And with each drink, I became more assured that God was somehow, someway, going to see us through this assault of Satan!

Other than praying and pleading for my daughter's life, the only other thing I could think to pray for during the whole trip was that I rightly represent Christ. I arrived in Columbia just minutes before sundown and the beginning of the Sabbath. Parking my car, I walked across the parking lot to the hospital entrance, knowing that I was about to see people who had never known this Tommy Poole. Coming before all these people who would be there under these circumstances, I could not help but feel my inadequacy to rightly represent the Lord. I wanted to simply be the person that God had started recreating me to be, reflecting the love and truth of Jesus. I did not want to put on a false face or try to be some theological expert and draw others into discussions about the Bible. I was not there for that purpose. If any of that did come up, I only wanted it to be the natural leading of the Holy Spirit. I only wanted to be the new Tommy Poole, a concerned Christian father who feared losing his daughter and trusted the Lord with the outcome.

Making my way through the front door of the hospital, I came to the information desk and received directions to the ICU and to Brenda. A doctor stepped onto the elevator with me, and we both tried to push the same button. We then got off on the same floor and found ourselves walking down the same hall toward the same nurses' station. Stopping right in front of the family waiting room, he looked at me and said, "You must be Mr. Poole?"

I answered him back, "Yes, sir, and you must be Brenda's doctor."

After introducing himself, he continued, "I was just about to address the family with an update. I'm glad you made it here safely. Why don't we go in and I'll brief you all together?"

We stepped inside the waiting room, and there, for the first time since I had accepted Christ and was born again, I was seeing Linda, our families, and a number of our friends we grew up with. The room was full.

The doctor began to speak, "I just met Brenda's father in the hall. I assume everyone here knows Mr. Poole?" Looking at me, he said, "As I told Brenda's mother, previously, we are doing everything we can possibly think of to save your daughter's life. At times, we have had up to seven physicians working with your daughter, plus the ICU staff. The problem is that Brenda took a massive amount of an antidepressant that is unlike most medications, which can be flushed from the body, if caught in time. It literally attaches itself to the fat cells in the body, thereby making it almost impossible for us to flush it from the patient's system. Brenda has taken such a large amount of this medication, and the natural effect on her body is to take her into a deeper and deeper state of coma. Eventually, in the next twenty-four hours, her body organs will shut down, and she will pass away."

He proceeded with his report. "We are contacting every specialist we can find with experience dealing with this drug, hoping to find any possible remedy for this situation. We just haven't found anything that will make a difference. At the present, we are following the recommendations of the poison control center in Atlanta, and we are literally packing Brenda full of charcoal, hoping this will absorb the medication from her body. But thus far, we are not having any response." Going on, he said, "I realize this is not good news, but I don't believe in holding back from my patients and their families. I want you and Brenda's mother, the grandparents, and any siblings Brenda may have to feel free to go in and out of ICU as you desire.

The staff will allow you to do this so long as they are not trying to conduct a medical procedure where they have to have access to Brenda. We will endeavor to keep you up to date on any changes in Brenda's condition. But let me reiterate, at this point, we do not expect any good changes at all."

So with that report, we knew where we stood. Our daughter was dying. Her body was literally shutting down. We had no idea why she took the medicine. We were totally baffled.

Later that evening, most of the family and friends had already made what many of them expected to be their final visit beside Brenda's bed, giving her kisses and shedding tears and whispers of love and then going home. Our friends, Dale and Laura Cook, had gone to sleep in the waiting room while Linda and I decided to stroll for a bit up and down the halls. Periodically, we would check on Brenda, and in between, we walked around the hospital hallways, eventually winding up back in the family waiting room.

Chapter 39

More than I Can Handle!

Fear not, for I have redeemed you; I have called you by your name; you are mine. When you pass through the waters, I will be with you; and through the rivers, they shall not overflow you.

—Isaiah 43:1–2

It was not really late, but visitation hours were over, and there were very few people left in the hospital. I asked Linda if she would mind if I called the local Adventist pastor to come and have a prayer for Brenda. She told me that was certainly all right, and she welcomed anyone who was willing to come and pray. I found a telephone booth with a phone book and looked up the local Seventh-day Adventist Church. We were in Columbia, but the closest church was in West Columbia, so I called that one. An answering machine picked up my call, saying there were evangelistic meetings going on each night at seven thirty. The time on my watch indicated the meeting was probably still going on, so I left my name, phone number, and a brief explanation of the circumstances, and it was only a few minutes until a gentleman returned my call. He happened to be one of the elders of the Columbia First Church who was assisting the pastor with the meetings. His name was Les Pratt. Les assured me that he would deliver the message to the pastor as soon as the meeting was over, and both he and the pastor would come to the hospital right away to pray for our daughter.

As Linda and I waited for them to arrive, we talked about what each of us had been doing with our lives during the last four and a half years. Linda was very inquisitive as to how I came to be a Seventh-day Adventist Christian and how I then came to the decision to study for the ministry. It was the perfect time to share my testimony of how I had come to know Christ as my Savior and Lord. She wanted to hear the story, so I shared that experience and from there how the Lord led me to the Adventist church and then called me to the gospel ministry. Linda listened intently! She soaked it up, and I was happy to share the story with her! Periodically, she would ask questions, and I would fill in more details.

As I finished, there were a few minutes of silence, and after that lull, Linda spoke up and said, "I have been hearing God call me and Brenda to the Seventh-day Adventist Church for over a year." She looked into my eyes and continued, "And whether Brenda lives or dies, I've made up my mind that I am going to stop running from the Lord, and tonight, I'm giving my heart and life fully to Him. Could you help me out by giving me Bible studies?"

I was so shocked! Yet I was so elated! I had been praying for them—for Brenda and Linda to come to know Christ and to study, understand, and accept the Advent message for months! And now in the worst situation of our lives, God was powerfully working to answer my prayers! Brenda had already basically accepted the message after what I had been able to teach her when she would come and visit me, but now it was Linda who was turning her life over to Christ and asking me to help her study the Bible truths so that she could join the Adventist church! I was so shocked I did not know how to respond! It seemed like my breath had been taken away! For a minute or so, I could not find adequate words!

Then she looked me straight in the eyes again and asked, "And by the way, do you think there would ever be a possibility of us putting our marriage back together?"

Well, I could not stand anymore and came up out of my seat! My hands went up in the air, and the only thing I could say to her was, "Wait a minute! Wait just one minute! This is more than I can handle! I am still a married man! I cannot talk about this. I cannot even think about this! It is wrong for me to be getting involved in such a conversation! Besides, if I were not married, I do not know if we have biblical grounds to be remarried again! I do not know if it would be possible!"

Linda became very apologetic, and I did not want to hurt her feelings, especially in the midst of such an important decision that she was making for this life and her eternity!

I said, "No, no, you misunderstand. I'm very flattered that you would even have a desire for us to get back together, but you see, I must be very, very careful! I have given my life to the Lord, and I have been trying my best to follow his Word in every way that I know, as I have studied the Scriptures. I do not want to do anything that would tarnish the Lord's name or the reputation of his church. I am technically still married, and because of that, there are ethics involved that I must deal with in a proper biblical manner. It is the same for you. However, you did not know because you have not yet studied enough to understand. I'll be more than happy to assist you in any way that I can in teaching you the Bible truths so you can understand your ethical responsibilities to the Lord, but you will have to be patient in getting an answer to the question you just asked. For now, let it be enough for me to say this… Answers to such questions will have to come from God's Word and his experienced elders in the church. I cannot give you answers to such questions because I do not yet have the knowledge or experience to do so. Can you please accept this answer for now and patiently wait on God to give you a more complete answer from the Bible?"

She said that she could because she did not want herself or me to do anything against the Lord.

I went on to say, "I am so amazed to hear you say that God has been calling you and Brenda to the Adventist church! Why do you say that?"

She replied, "Well, during the last few years, the two most important people in my life, other than Brenda, who came from totally different lifestyles and circumstances, found their way into the Seventh-day Adventist Church. I have listened a little to what Brenda has tried to share with me, and even though I do not understand quite a bit of it, I can see the change that has come over you. When talking to you, not only tonight but in telephone conversations that we would have when you would call Brenda or the few times when we would meet when I would bring Brenda to stay with you, I have seen that you are a totally different person. That is the same way that Laura Cook is. Her life has also totally changed. I've been thinking that if you two, who have had a closer personal relationship with me than any other two people, have changed so dramatically, there is something there, and I want it! I want it to be in my life too! That's why," she said, "I want you to help me learn and change my life because I want what you and Laura have!"

We continued to talk, and eventually, Pastor Denver Cavins and local Elder Les Platt arrived. We sat in the family room for a little while and filled them in on our background and how we had come to be where we were. Then we all went to the ICU where Brenda was and surrounded the bed and Pastor Cavins prayed a wonderful, heartfelt prayer. We thanked them both for coming, and Les went on home, but the pastor stayed a while longer.

As he got ready to leave, I walked him to his car because I had some questions for him concerning my marital status since Becky forced me out of our home, took up with another man, and now had filed for divorce. And then there was Linda's decision to accept Christ and become a member of the church. I felt as if I needed somebody's personal counsel. Though I did not know this pastor, I needed help and called him, and he came. I thought I should at least talk with him, brother to brother. He was not much older than me, but he had been a pastor for quite a few years. We had not only age in common, but he also had been in the US Marine Corps like me, so I made my inquiries of him.

In our conversation, he gave me some good biblical advice, encouraged me, and prayed with me. He told me that if Linda was really serious, perhaps I could bring her to his baptismal classes. He had a complete series of the messages that he was currently giving, on tape, and he would be more than happy to loan Linda the set and give her a set of printed lessons to go with them so she could get caught up and then join the baptismal classes. If she needed additional materials, he would do what he could to supply them too. He then added, "Let's take first things first. Let's see how things go and what develops with your daughter's situation because, at this point, that is the most important part of her life." He gave me his contact information, I thanked him, and he left.

I had so much on my mind and heart, from my daughter's condition being near death, to the decisions made by Linda and the desire she shared of possibly putting our marriage together again. It was just as I told Linda earlier. It was all too much for me! I was overwhelmed! So much was happening at the same time it was like a flood, and it was truly more than I could handle without God's help! There was no way that I could now go back upstairs to that waiting room and go to sleep! No way!

Chapter 40

Praying for a Miracle

*One who turns away his ear from hearing the
law, even his prayer is an abomination.*

—Proverbs 28:9

I spent the better part of that night walking the hospital parking lot, praying as I walked. I racked my brain, trying to remember any unconfessed sin as I pleaded with God for both my daughter's life and eternal destiny. Being out there so long, I probably looked suspicious because the security guard came along just before daybreak, Sabbath morning, and told me that I could not continue walking around the parking lot. He said I would have to go inside or leave the property.

I made my way back into the hospital and up to the ICU floor where I looked into the family waiting room where Linda and the Cooks were still sleeping, so I went into the ICU to check on Brenda. The nurse gave me a very compassionate look as if to say, "I'm sorry. There's no change." So I walked the halls until I realized it was 6:00 a.m., and I decided it was time to wake up Linda and the Cooks. I had no idea how much longer Brenda would live, but I knew they wanted to see her one more time before she died.

Waking them, Linda wanted to see Brenda right away, and the Cooks said they would wait, so we walked down the hall, and when we walked in the door, we were stunned by what we saw! Several nurses were standing beside Brenda, and they were putting restraints on her arms and legs because she was waving them frantically, though not awake, as if she was trying to fight them! When we reached her bedside, the nurses wanted to make sure we did not gather any false hopes, and they assured us this was normal. They explained it as muscle spasms and completely involuntary. One of them described it as the natural way the muscular parts of the body react just prior to the person going into a deep coma. She said again that we must not get our hopes up at all!

Linda and I went back to the waiting room and found Laura and Dale fully awake, and we told them what we had seen. About that time, several family members began returning, as did the doctor who explained to all what the nurses had told us, saying any time now, Brenda would start submerging into a deep coma and more than likely not make it through the day. Linda and I walked back to Brenda's room with the doctor, and this time, when we walked in the door, the nurses were still attending to her and she was still responding with the same actions in her arms and legs. But now there was a huge difference!

Her eyes were wide open, and she was trying to make conversation, even with the respirator tube down her throat! She was actually trying to communicate with them! I then noticed the nurses' huge smiles, and the doctor stopped dead in his tracks! He was astonished! He looked at Brenda, then at us, and then back at her, not saying a word! Then he turned and looked me straight in the eye and said, "She is 300 percent better than we ever thought possible! I absolutely have no explanation for this!"

Immediately, I responded to him, "I do! There is still a God in heaven that hears and answers the prayers of his people! This is a bona fide miracle of the Lord God Almighty!"

With half of a smile, he simply shook his head in acknowledgment.

Nothing the hospital staff had tried helped, and they did their best to prepare us for the worst. But then Friday's sunset and the holy hours of God's Sabbath began and at various times throughout those holy hours, God's people prayed! A Sabbath-keeping pastor preached the gospel in his church and then came with his elder and prayed. In the hospital waiting room, two family friends were

Sabbath keepers, and they prayed. Before the pastor arrived, a repentant mother prayerfully made her decision for Jesus because she had witnessed the changed lives of two people she knew well since they had accepted and followed God's Word, including his true Sabbath! A father who had met Jesus several years before on a lonely Georgia highway and was now studying for the ministry in God's Sabbath-keeping church walked and talked to the Savior most of the night! While back in Tennessee, many Adventist Christians were keeping the Bible Sabbath and praying for a teenager who had made a decision in ignorance!

These folks prayed! The Creator of the Universe listened and sent his angel to the poison center in Atlanta to whisper a miraculous message in a person's ear, "Tell the hospital staff in South Carolina to fill the girl's stomach with activated charcoal!" So they did! It absorbed the medication in her body, and as that Sabbath morning was dawning, God opened the young girl's eyes, waking her up! And by noon, she was in her own private room, telling her parents what caused her to make the decision to end her life. Yes, our God in heaven still hears and answers prayer according to his perfect will!

We know why this miracle happened because the Bible tells us. *"The way of the wicked is an abomination to the Lord, but he loves him who follows righteousness."*[231] *"One who turns away his ear from hearing the law, even his prayer is an abomination."*[232]

After church services had ended, I telephoned Pastor Cavins and gave him the joyful report of God's miracle and Brenda's condition, and as well, I reminded him of Linda's decision and her desire to begin studies and attend his meetings, so he invited her to the baptismal classes as well.

Sabbath afternoon, Brenda explained why she made the decision to take her life. She had spent the night with a girl she met at school that seemed to have a lot in common with her. That evening, the girl's parents went out, so Brenda's new friend went into her parents' bar and made them a drink. Brenda did not want the drink, but when the girl told her it would make her feel better, Brenda agreed. After Brenda had returned home, still feeling guilty several days later, she awoke on that Friday morning, thinking that since she knew drinking the liquor was wrong, a sin, then God would not forgive her. She said, "If God was not going to forgive me, then I would be lost, and I did not want to go on living knowing I would miss out going to heaven with Jesus when he came to get us!" So that is when she went into her mother's medicine cabinet and took a handful of Linda's antidepressants. When the girlfriend and her father came to take Brenda to school, Brenda told them what she had done, and they called 911!

It was a clear case of Satan causing a teen, which did not know God the Father well enough, to believe a lie about him and choose to die! I've wondered so many times since hearing Brenda tell us that, how many people have believed the devil's lie about God and will be lost because of it?

As the three of us talked in Brenda's room, we told her about the decision her mother had made the night before, and she was overwhelmed with the joyful results of two miracles: first, God saving her life and knowing he had forgiven her, and second, her mother accepting Christ, desiring Bible studies and wishing to become a member of the Adventist church. Brenda was so thrilled, and we shed many happy tears together that Satan's plan was foiled, and God's desire for all of us was made true!

That next week, I accompanied Linda to several of Pastor Cavins's evangelistic meetings and a baptismal class to get her started. Even though the other attendees were well ahead of her, she fell right into place with the group. She began studying her Bible with the lessons from the meetings, reading the supplemental materials, and listening to the cassette tapes loaned to her by the pastor. In fact, she had consumed her studies for that week and was asking for more. I have often described Linda's experience as a barren, dry desert, when the rain comes, it soaks up every drop of water that it can! At times, it challenged me to keep up with her because of how fast she was learning her Bible!

After staying at my parents' home during that first week, Linda and I began meeting with a hospital family counselor on Friday, and I returned to school on Sunday to gather my assignments. By the time I returned to Columbia the next Friday, another miracle was taking place! I left Linda a brochure from our church's Stop Smoking Seminar. With the tips it provided and prayer, she had begun and was almost finished with the five-day process of giving up tobacco! This was so amazing because she had been smoking three packs of cigarettes per day for several years and was a smoker since we were sixteen! It had taken a toll on her too because she had a terrible hacking cough most of the time. She told me that she would even get up during the night to smoke. But the Lord was giving her the victory as she prayed and followed the tips in the brochure. She was completely off the tobacco by the following week and has been ever since.

After several weeks of meeting with the baptismal class, along with much prayer, Linda was ready and anxious to be baptized. She attended the last few evangelistic meetings by herself while I was back at school, and after coming back to Columbia the next Friday for our meeting with the family counselor, the next day, Sabbath, she was baptized with the group from Pastor Cavins's meetings on October 21, 1989, the day after turning thirty-seven years old. As it turned out for Brenda, she had been studying, off and on, for a good while, and she only had a few lessons to complete, which she did the week she came home from the hospital and was baptized the week after Linda on October 28, 1989, as a new member of the Columbia First Seventh-day Adventist Church.

Chapter 41

Together Again?

I will betroth you to me forever; yes, I will betroth you to me in righteousness and justice, in loving kindness and mercy; I will betroth you to me in faithfulness, and you shall know the Lord.

—Hosea 2:19–20

My weekly visits continued for family counseling until, on one occasion, when Linda sat me down and told me she had been doing a lot of serious praying and thinking. She felt it would be in all our best interest for her to quit her job and for her and Brenda to move to Tennessee. I was caught totally off guard by such a decision and certainly not comfortable with even discussing the subject since I had recently given into Becky's demand to sign our divorce papers and return them to her. I guess most people would go ahead and consider themselves divorced, but technically, I did not because I had not yet received my copy of the decree from the Georgia court.

Honestly, I could not deny thinking about the possibility of us remarrying, but I had no idea whether we were biblically able to remarry. Other than Pastor Cavins, I had inquired with several of my religion professors, but as yet, there had not been any decisive counsel given to me. Plus, the more I thought and prayed about it, the more I reasoned that at that time, such a decision (Linda and Brenda moving right away to Tennessee) was moving too fast. It seemed to me that Linda was making this decision based too much on her emotions, and I could easily fall into the same trap. As an older Christian, it was my place to try to slow her down until I had clear counsel from my elders.

In addition to understanding our marital status from the Bible, Linda had a great job! She started working for this well-known national insurance company out of high school as a rate clerk, and she had progressed to the position of an underwriter in the Columbia regional office. She did this with only in-house education. She and Brenda had a very nice patio home and cars. With her current standing, it seemed unwise to me for her to quit that job and move, especially if remarriage was scripturally impossible.

I explained to her it seemed as if we were trying to jump ahead of what we knew for certain and the required process to follow. I told her we needed to trust God more and let him lead, as I had told her the night at the hospital when she first asked about the situation. I carefully reminded her that my commitment was to Jesus first and his calling on my life and nothing, not even the strong desire of wanting my family back could interfere with God's will for me. I also reminded her of her expressed priority that same night. She had said that whether Brenda lived or died, she was turning her life over to Jesus totally! God had been calling her, and she was not going to run from him anymore. I said, "We are both going to have to trust the Lord and allow Jesus to open and close doors so that we could be sure it was his leading and not our own."

Linda agreed, and she backed off from quitting her job and moving until God gave us more answers. She encouraged me to go back and talk with my professors again. In fact, she offered to go to Collegedale and talk with them. She said, "Whatever they think would be in your best interest for serving the Lord, I'll accept and be happy with that because I want us both to be right with the Lord!"

Sunday, I went back to school with the purpose in mind of taking my situation back to my school elders. Monday, I made an appointment and went to see Dr. Jack Blanco, head of the Religion Department at the time. He was very encouraged when hearing how God had delivered our daughter from death's door and was now leading Linda through her conversion. He decided, after talking with some of the professors, he wanted an interview with Linda, telling me that while he did not mean to sound as if he was not concerned about Linda and Brenda's future, he was trying to look out for my best interest and God's calling on my life. In the long run, he wanted to do what was best for Linda and Brenda too. Then in a loving, fatherly manner, Dr. Blanco said, "I realize there's a lot of emotion involved in this, and you need to understand, we know you, Tommy. We understand who you are and what makes you tick, but we don't know Linda. And we feel it would be in your best interest if she is willing to come here and talk with us. Is this suitable for both of you?"

I told him it was and that Linda had suggested this herself. So we set up a visit during the next week, and Linda used several vacation days to make the trip. The interview was in Dr. Blanco's office, and he was the only professor present. However, as we arrived, Dr. Morris was discussing something with Dr. Blanco and was able to meet Linda before leaving.

The interview went very well, and after talking and praying with us, he was comfortable and convinced that Linda had experienced a genuine conversion, and it was God's leading. Dr. Blanco told us that he felt sure that through all which had taken place, the Lord was opening the door for us to be reunited as a family. He explained that he had already talked our situation over with the other professors and believed that because Linda had never remarried, even though she had not been a converted Christian, biblically, we were on sound ground as far as remarrying. Before leaving his office, we knelt, and he prayed for us and gave us his blessing, which meant so much to both of us! I never will forget what was said after Linda finished giving her testimony about coming to Christ. Dr. Blanco asked, "Do I understand correctly that you want to be remarried? Have you thought about a date?"

Linda immediately spoke up and answered him, "ASAP!"

He broke out with hardy laughter, getting a huge kick out of her response, and with a big hug for each of us, he said, "Take care of each other," and our visit ended. We returned to Columbia and gave Brenda the good news.

However, there was still one more major obstacle we needed to pray and plan for. That was regarding Linda leaving her job and her family. I was not one of her family's favorite people, and with the track record I had, they would think Linda was losing her mind by quitting her job and moving Brenda and herself to a strange new place with, what seemed to be, not a lot of thought given to it. I was very worried about the relationships that could be harmed between Linda and her family, and I truly tried to persuade Linda to postpone their move. After all, we were not married yet. We were now planning to get married, and certainly, we were not going to be living together, but I just felt that it might be best if she and Brenda stayed in Columbia a little while longer until we were very close to the time of our remarriage.

However, the more she thought about it, the more convinced Linda became, and she said, "No! If we are going to put this family back together, we need to be together, and even if we aren't living together right away, I want Brenda to get settled there in school as soon as possible."

So before I knew it, she had talked me into accepting their move to Collegedale around the middle to late November 1989. I would go back to Tennessee and begin making preparations for them to move. Linda was going to give her notice and begin packing.

Of course, her family did think she was losing her mind! They thought it was the wrong thing to do and especially considering the position she held at her workplace. They could not imagine her turning around and walking away from that! But she talked with them, and I guess she showed enough determination so that after a few weeks, they realized they could not talk her out of it. They may as well give her their blessing and pray that everything would go well. That is what they did and were very gracious and helpful during our time of transition.

I think seeing the great change in me helped them to accept it all. The fact I was attending college and obviously not fooling around with my life anymore helped them see that I was a changed man. I looked different, talked differently, and acted differently, and I was seriously pursuing the Lord's calling in the gospel ministry. I am sure the changes they could see and hear in me helped them to finally pitch in and assist Linda and Brenda with this great decision and change in their lives. Of course, I realized that time would be the major factor in my relationship with them changing for the better.

Returning to school, I began preparing for their move to Collegedale by going to my good friends, the Wittenbergs. Several days later, Jan sent me to see Mrs. Mary Morford, who was in charge of campus housing, and had been a tremendous help when I first came to Southern. She arranged for an apartment for my girls before they arrived. Since Linda and I were not getting married yet, I would continue living at Mr. McKee's until my agreement with him expired on New Year's Day in January. I called Linda that night and gave her the good news concerning the apartment, and she was amazed!

She turned in her notice at work the next day, and the people there were so sorry to lose her but wanted to help any way they could and began trying to make connections for her with other insurance companies in the Chattanooga/Collegedale area. They hoped to assist in finding her a position in a similar situation, so they called and wrote letters of recommendation, lining up interviews for her. Everything was working out in perfect timing, and we understood this because God's timing is always perfect!

By Thanksgiving, I had a truck hired and moved Brenda and Linda into their campus apartment, and after the holiday weekend was over, Linda was pounding the pavement, attending her interviews, trying to find a job. Of course, I had confirmed my agreement with the McKee family about working for them until the first of the year, and I fully intended to keep my word. There was even a possibility after the New Year for them to hire me further, and with finances being very tight, I wanted to keep all my options open.

One evening after I had been helping the girls get settled into their apartment, Linda asked me to sit and talk before leaving for the day. She asked about us going ahead and getting married instead of waiting until after the first of the year. She said, "You can still live up to your obligations with the McKees, but we will finally be reunited as a family, and I will feel much better about everything if we are."

At the McKee's that evening, I thought and prayed about her question. The next day, I went to Dr. Bennett and asked if he would be willing to perform a private ceremony for us in the

Religion Department Chapel. He hesitated in giving me an affirmative answer; I am sure, out of being the very conscientious Christian that he was and always striving to do the right thing. Refreshing his memory, he inquired as to our circumstances again, how Linda and I had come to be divorced, when that divorce took place, and when we were converted. For clarification, he then asked about how and when my marriage to Becky ended, and I told him, "The final decree was on December 4, 1989, a few days ago." After repeating all the information we gave Dr. Blanco, I told him we wanted the ceremony that Thursday because I had a day off from work on Friday, and we wondered if that would be convenient for him. He said he would like to have a day to think and pray about it and he would let us know by Wednesday evening, and I agreed.

It was Tuesday, and that afternoon, I went to Jan's office to let her know what our tentative plans were. I told her Dr. Bennett seemed hesitant and asked me for a day to think and pray about performing the ceremony and that it was fine with us. However, I was unable to speak with him on Wednesday evening, and when I spoke with him on Thursday morning, he wanted to postpone until Friday, so I headed to Jan's office to inform her of the change in schedule. I did not know it then but later found out after I left Jan's office Thursday, she consulted with Mrs. Bennett, who worked with her. Mrs. Bennett then got on the telephone and became a strong advocate for Linda and me with her husband! Meanwhile, I had stopped by the Religion Department to pick up some books on the way to Linda's apartment to share the news when Dr. Bennett came out of his office and seeing me called me aside. He told me that he decided for us to go ahead with the wedding! "Go get Linda, and I'll get the department secretary, Bridgett, as a witness, and we'll go upstairs this afternoon and tie the knot again!"

For sure, I was elated and went to tell Linda! I then drove to the McKee's, showered, put on my Sabbath suit, and returned to pick up Linda. At 4:30 p.m. we met Dr. Bennett and Bridgett in the Religion Department Chapel, and he remarried us, giving us a loving, gracious blessing.

Because of the circumstances with me living and working at the McKee's, we planned on not having a honeymoon right away, so I drove Linda back to the apartment and headed back to the McKee's for the evening. But when I walked into the house, O. D. and Thelma were sitting in the living room love seat, arm in arm, with great big smiles on their faces! They looked at me and together asked, "Who are you?"

A bit confused, I repeated their question, "Who am I?"

O. D. asked again, "Yes, who are you?"

They looked at each other, and Thelma said, "We don't know you! Who are you? What are you doing here?"

Still confused, I said, "Come on now, you know who I am, and you know what I am doing here."

They broke out into another smile, and O. D. asked, "Didn't you just get married?"

I said, "Yes, sir, I did!"

Thelma then asked, "Well, where is your bride?"

I answered her, "Oh, I just now dropped her off at the campus apartment."

And Thelma shamefully teased, "That's no way to treat a new bride! We think you need to turn right around and go move in with your family!"

I replied, "Oh no! I cannot do that because we agreed I would work here until the first of the New Year. Linda and I both want to fulfill my commitment to you and your family."

O. D. spoke up, saying, "Oh no, no, no! That will not work because you don't have a job here anymore! I have let you go! You're fired!"

But I said, "Come on now, really, I do not mind living up to the agreement! I truly appreciate what you are trying to do. Linda and I feel that finishing the agreement is the only right thing to do."

However, they insisted I needed to be with my family, and they assured me the McKee family knew about their decision and agreed, so it was perfectly all right for me to go. I could consider it a wedding gift and their way of saying "Congratulations on your happy occasion!"

Suddenly, it was very plain there was something different about their relationship, at least different in my eye, more than just being nurse and patient. I was told a few days later that my assumption was correct. Mr. McKee and Thelma had actually been planning for a few months to be married but were waiting until the New Year when my agreement with them would be fulfilled and my services were no longer needed. I then found out they had already made all the necessary arrangements and were not going to be left alone until their wedding. A family member was moving in temporarily that night and would be there until the first of the year. This is why they insisted I move in with my family right away. That was December 7, 1989.

The next day, Friday, I had my homiletics class with Dr. Bennett, and it was also my first turn to preach in class for a grade, not by the professor only but by my student peers too. Linda was also attending. I had been working on the message most of the semester, and I was one of the last students on the schedule to speak. The message was basically my testimony of coming to know Jesus and how he had put my family back together! There was a full class of about twenty students, all male and one female, in addition to Dr. Bennett, and before my message was over, it seemed there was not a dry eye in the same chapel where God had reunited Linda and me less than twenty-four hours before! Most of my fellow students had totally forgotten to give me an analytical grade because they were so touched by what God had done in our lives. When it came time for Dr. Bennett to give his analysis, he said that he was speechless! The message was such a blessing to everyone that as our class time ended, they all crowded around and hugged us while extending their personal congratulations and blessings for our family!

Everyone, including Dr. Bennett, gave me a perfect score and an A grade!

Chapter 42

Troubled Waters and More Blessings

*Save me, O God! For the waters have come up to my
neck... I have come into deep waters, where the floods over
flow me...let me not sink...nor let the deep swallow me
up... Let your salvation, O God, set me up on high.*

—Psalm 69:1–2, 14–15, and 29

It was so wonderful being back together even though at first we had
to live between the packed boxes. The New Year brought me a new
semester, and Brenda was enrolled in Collegedale Academy in the
eleventh grade. Of course, she was going through the process of making adjustments, but we all were adjusting. For a while, we rode a
spiritual high, produced by how Jesus had miraculously brought us
back together. But as the days turned into weeks, we started coming
back down to earth and to the reality of our circumstances. Linda
did not have a job yet, and she was quite concerned about that. Yet
after a number of interviews and with great letters of reference and
some telephone calls from her former employer, the Lord opened the
door with a large insurance agency that did a lot of business with her
former company!

However, Linda and Brenda's lifestyles had been very different
from mine. They were used to living in a larger home and having
plenty. Then all of a sudden, they were living in this little bitty apart-

ment, about five hundred square feet, and we still had boxes stacked up everywhere with nowhere to unpack or sort. As time went on, Linda began suffering from claustrophobia, causing her to sink into the depths of depression, and we had no idea she was claustrophobic.

There were also adjustments to make in her work situation. Even though she went to work for another insurance agency, she was put into a new situation producing extra stress. Of course, there was the fact that Linda and Brenda were very new Christians and we were trying to make friends and find the church where God wanted us to be actively involved.

Eventually, Linda's depression would get to the point where I thought she would have to see a doctor. I started considering this when one morning, the three of us were sitting at the breakfast table when Brenda said, "Dad, I had a really strange dream last night."

I replied, "You did? Do you remember what it was about?"

She answered, "Yes, Daddy, I do." She went on to tell me it was a dream about her mother.

By this time, Linda had finished her breakfast and had gone to finish getting ready for work. Brenda continued saying, "Mama was in a large body of water, deep water, and she was drowning! She kept going down because she could not swim." In reality, this was true. Linda could not swim, but Brenda had taken swimming lessons at an early age and could swim very well!

In the dream, Brenda was watching her Mom call out for help and she is drowning, and there is no one around to assist but Brenda, so she jumps into the water and rescues her Mom, bringing her safely to shore.

From the moment Brenda began telling me what her dream was about, it was as if the Lord was putting the interpretation into my mind, and by the time she had finished telling me the dream, I knew exactly what the dream meant!

We both knew Linda was depressed and going through quite a struggle, but we did not understand how stressful or how difficult this adjustment period was going for her until then. But as Brenda told me her dream, the Lord revealed to me that Linda was definitely going down; she was spiritually and emotionally drowning in her very own dead river! There had been so much, so fast, and what I got from the dream was that I could not rescue her! Brenda would have to rescue her mother!

With the depression, there seemed to be an invisible barrier erected where Linda's and my communication began to break down. I could not get her to talk with me because she would take everything I said the wrong way; she grew to be very irritable, and our communication basically shut down. Yet the Lord, through Brenda's dream, was revealing the true nature of Linda's situation, and I saw that because she and her mother were so close, Brenda was going to be the only one who could jump into the deep water and save her mother!

I told Brenda what I understood the dream to mean, and at first, I thought I might be putting too much on this high school student, who was also a brand-new Christian, trying to adjust to her new surroundings and make new friends. But the more I thought and prayed about it, there was no one else in the dream that could help with the situation. It was not that her mom wanted to leave or was unhappy with our marriage, nor did she want to leave the church. It was simply that everything had happened so fast, and the change in their lifestyle had come so quickly it was very difficult for Linda to hang on and stay afloat. The fact that she did not know how to literally swim was symbolic for not knowing how to float above the emotional and spiritual troubled waters.

Brenda set out immediately to rectify the situation. She and I started to have little chats about what to do or what to talk about or how she could approach her mom about various circumstances. It was wonderful how God blessed us! "*And it shall come to pass in the last days, says God, that I will pour out of my Spirit on all flesh; your sons and your daughters shall prophesy, your young men shall see visions, your old men shall dream dreams. And on my menservants and on my maidservants I will pour out my Spirit in those days; and they shall prophesy.*"[233] Brenda saved her mom's life, emotionally and spiritually, during those difficult months of transition! Linda made steady progress, and by spring, she had pulled out of the depression. She had adjusted well to her work, and her new role as a Christian mother and wife of a soon-to-be pastor. This was just another one of those miracles that God continued to work in my family's life to aid us during a very difficult time and to move us forward in his service!

Another situation, showing the Lord's leading soon followed. Due to the way the US tax laws are set up, if you are married on the last day of the tax year, December 31, you are considered married for the whole year. The classification of "married, filing jointly," is usually the lowest tax rate for couples. Linda and I, having remarried on December 7, were able to take advantage of that law. Being single for most of the same year, Linda had her payroll taxes deducted from her checks as "single," which is a much higher tax rate. Being married for most of that year, I had my payroll taxes deducted from my checks as "married, filing jointly," but I also had very little income, so what taxes were deducted was very little. Yet because we were married before the year's end, we were able to file as "married, filing jointly." This gave us a substantial refund!

Once again, the Lord had already worked things out so that my first semester (fall '89) and much of my second semester (spring '90) accounts were paid for. And as I looked further into the situation, I discovered another blessing! The school had a provision, whereby if you paid cash for all the semester's tuition, up front, they would give you a 5 percent discount. Adding the income tax refund together with the 5 percent discount, we wound up with enough money to finish paying for the second semester (spring '90), summer semester ('90), and my third semester (fall '90) too! What a tremendous blessing from God! Everything he does is always enough and on time!

To this point in time, ever since I have known her, Linda has always liked to wear a lot of jewelry. She did not buy cheap jewelry either! Through the years, she had accumulated a jewelry box full of diamonds, gold, and silver. Now following the teaching of the Scriptures, being a Seventh-day Adventist Christian, she possessed a lot of jewelry she no longer wore. One day, we were talking about finances and discussing how we were going to pay for my fourth, and final, semester without having to take out a loan. Linda immediately spoke up, "We can pawn my jewelry!"

I first hesitated to accept her offer. I knew that while she did not want to wear it, so much of it held sentimental value to her, and I hated to see her sell it for no more than a third of its market value. She insisted though, and the next day, we started shopping to see who would give us the best price.

Eventually, we sold most of her jewelry to one person. We certainly did not get what it was worth, but the Lord blessed us to receive a much better price than we would typically get in a pawnshop. We had to have the money, and the man that I dealt with knew all the jewelry was safe and not stolen. He understood I was a ministerial student, and because of our beliefs, my wife did not wear jewelry anymore. The Lord truly influenced our deal, so we obtained good prices! In fact, combined with the grant, scholarship, and my work income, her jewelry brought in enough cash to finish paying for the remainder of my school (spring '91)! We knew exactly why these blessings continued to come from God. Again, it was because out of love for the Lord, we continued to follow his Word. "*Bring all the tithes into the storehouse, that there may be food in my house, and try me now in this,' says the Lord of hosts, 'If I will not open for you the windows of heaven and pour out for you such blessing that there will not be room enough to receive it. And I will rebuke the devourer for your sakes...*"[234] Ever since I became a Christian, I have followed God's instruction of returning the tithe, which is his, and God has faithfully blessed me through his promise!

But there was more! The Lord also blessed us with enough income from Linda's new job and Brenda's part-time job, to pay the tuition for Brenda to attend and graduate from Collegedale Academy! Plus, a larger, more comfortable duplex apartment became available approximately a mile from both schools, and the rent was right on target with Linda's remaining income. "*Assuredly, I say to you, there is no one who has left house or parents or brothers or wife or children, for the sake of the kingdom of God, who shall not receive many times more in this present time, and in the age to come eternal life.*"[235] Once again, Jesus had brought us through troubled waters, only to continue fulfilling our needs.

Chapter 43

Whom Shall I Send?

Then I said, "Here am I! Send me."

—Isaiah 6:8

Every year, different geographical church conferences needing additional clergy have administrators come to interview prospective pastors at the various church colleges. Students are given several weeks' notice of who is coming and when. An appointment sheet is passed around, and students sign up for interviews based on their class schedule. Of course, I signed up to meet with every conference interviewer.

At the end of my junior year, May 1990, I interviewed with Pastor Don Shelton of (then) the Dakota Conference. Originally from Texas, he had been elected as conference president a year or so prior to my interview. Being a Southern boy, he had a special place in his heart for Southern College because of their biblically balanced, conservative theology, and he was looking for several new pastors. Linda and I interviewed with him and (he later told us that he was very impressed with us and wanted us to come to the Dakotas) he said he definitely wanted to talk with us in my senior year.

Then in January 1991, I was in a homiletics class when Dr. Maurice T. Bascom, PhD, from the General Conference world office in Silver Spring, Maryland, came to visit us. He had been selected by the General Conference to set up a brand-new mission program, placing English language teachers as missionaries in universities across Mainland China.

They would teach conversational English to interested students while building personal relationships with them. As time would go on, perhaps these Chinese students would begin to inquire about our Christian lifestyle and ask questions that would hopefully lead to Bible studies and eventually become new Christians. Dr. Bascom was recruiting primarily at colleges because he felt that most of his teachers needed to be college-age young adults. But he was also taking a few older, more mature folks like Linda and me to place in certain schools. He spoke to us in general about the program, and as I was sitting there listening to him, I heard the Holy Spirit speak to my mind saying, *At the end of the class, go and speak to him.*

At first, as I had done before when hearing God speak to me, I passed it off as my imagination. But when the voice came back again, I realized the Lord was speaking to me. Once more, I heard him say, *At the end of the class, go and speak to him.* So after class, I made my way up to Dr. Bascom and introduced myself. He asked a little about my background and if I was interested in going overseas.

I said, "Well, to be honest with you, I was not ready to entertain the possibility, but as you spoke, I felt impressed by the Lord that I needed to come up and speak with you." I told him the impression had occurred several times, and I felt as if it was really the Lord, and I needed to find out more.

Dr. Bascom explained how the selection process would work.

After listening for a few minutes, I said, "I have a brand-new Adventist Christian wife, and she has had very little scriptural training, except the fundamental beliefs while studying for baptism. We have a daughter graduating from high school this year, and she will be staying here for college, so I cannot see how the Lord would want us to go."

He asked, "Do you know for sure right now that the Lord doesn't want you to take this particular call?"

I responded, "No, but I am willing to pray about it."

He then suggested, "Why don't you do this? Why don't you take these applications home? You and your wife fill them out and pray about it. If you feel that you should send them in, then do so. If you don't, you haven't lost but a few minutes of time. We will be going through hundreds of applications. There will be a three- or four-month weeding out process, narrowing down to those we think are the best candidates for each particular location. We will be looking for fifty teachers, so the odds are very great against anyone getting the call. Just take the forms home and talk with your wife, pray together, and leave it in the hands of the Lord. Do whatever God tells you to do."

I told him that I was perfectly willing to do that.

So I took the applications home, but I kept them hidden for a few days because I was wondering how in the world I was going to bring up the possibility of becoming a teacher in China to my brand-new Christian wife who already had experienced lots of difficulties making the transition to Collegedale! After a few days of praying and thinking, I decided I would present it to Linda the same way Dr. Bascom presented it to me. I would not try to convince her; I would not try to sell her on the idea. I would simply give her the information and tell her what the options were. So I did. And just as I figured she would be, she was extremely negative about even the possibility! "No, no, no! I can't! No, no, no! I can't go to China! I know very little about the place. It's a communist country! They have a strange language!" And on and on she went. There was one excuse after another, so I sat there and patiently listened to this long list of excuses why she could not even consider going!

When she finally stopped talking, I said, "That's fine. That's fine. I am telling you just what Dr. Bascom told me. The Lord did not tell me to go to China. The Lord simply told me to go and talk to him and get some more information. So I got some more information. Dr. Bascom did not try to convince me to go, and I did not sign us up to do anything! He just gave me these applications and said to take them home and think and pray about it. If we felt impressed that we at least needed to give the Lord a chance to open or close the door, then we would submit our applications to the selection process. That's it! And I told him I was willing to do that."

A few weeks went by, and nothing more was said about China. Then, periodically, I would ask Linda, "Have you given any more thought to submitting the applications?"

She would reply, "No, I have not."

After a month, it seemed that she had mellowed a little bit, and she kept saying, "I don't see how... I don't want to say no to the Lord if he is trying to lead us in a certain direction. I just don't see how we could go. I don't see how we could do it." After a few more days, without me asking her again, out of her love for the Lord and not wanting to tell the Lord no on that possibility, she said, "Okay! We'll send in the applications, but if I feel that I cannot go at the end, don't get upset with me if I say, 'No, I'm not going.'"

I told her, "I will not get upset! I absolutely will not. I do not even know yet if we should go! I am just looking at the possibility as Dr. Bascom said. And I am praying regularly about it. I know that we have this call from the Dakota Conference, and there are several other conferences for us to interview with, so it is not as if we have no other place to go to work when I graduate."

The winter ended and spring came, and we began getting letters from the Teachers for China office. The first letter said something to the effect, "Congratulations, out of the hundreds of applications, you have made it through the first step of the process, and now we are entering the second phase. There are two hundred names still to be considered for this. We just wanted to keep you up to date and let you know that God is working and opening up doors of universities in which to place our people. Things are going well." A few weeks later, another letter arrived, telling us we had made it through another step in the selection process. This went on through the spring and to the end of school.

Just before graduation, we had a final interview with Pastor Shelton, and he told us that he wanted four Southern College Religion majors to come to the Dakota Conference, and he wanted me to be one of them. So we let him put our names on his list. At that point, we were not shutting any doors, but I believe Linda was thinking in the back of her mind, "We are not going to China. We are going to take the call to Dakota." But I never nagged her or pressured her at all.

Pastor Shelton told us, "I'm going back home to my conference committee. I need you to give me a telephone number where you can be reached two weeks from today. I will call you whether our committee accepts you or not because I don't believe in leaving people hanging." Of course, he knew that we had a potential call from the Teachers for China project in the works. By the end of school, we were in the last seventy-five people still on the list, and I am thinking, "We are more than likely going to get the call to China, and as of yet, Linda has not given me any indication that she was willing to go."

After the interview with Pastor Shelton, he went home and, a few days later, to his conference committee meeting. In two weeks, he called, saying, "Congratulations, Tommy! The conference committee has given me the okay to extend a call for you and Linda to come and pastor at our conference. Have you made up your mind yet?"

I responded, "No, sir. We have just received a letter saying that we have been selected for the Teachers for China project. How much time can you give us to seek the Lord for His will?"

He replied, "Tommy, I can give you until next Wednesday, but I need to have your answer by noon Wednesday because, if you don't take our call, I need to be able to share with my committee before we leave camp meeting so I can submit another name for their approval."

I told Linda what the situation was, so we prayed and prayed. We looked at the situation, and she was really struggling hard, to the point of tears periodically. Every day, she would come home from work and ask, "Are you praying? Has God told you what to do yet?"

I would answer, "Yes, I am praying, but no, Jesus has not told me what to do!" It came down to Wednesday, the actual day that we had to give an answer to Pastor Shelton. I had gone out for my early morning walk, and I was truly petitioning the Lord hard for his answer. I was laying it all on the line, telling Jesus that I was not going to drag my wife, kicking and screaming to China, but if he wanted us to take the call to China, then in the next few hours, he would have to prevail on her heart to change her mind. Otherwise, I was going to tell Pastor Shelton we would accept the call to Dakota.

We came down to the last hour and a half before noon and I called Linda at work. I said, "Honey, we have got to make a decision now so I can notify Pastor Shelton and Dr. Bascom. Do you feel that God has given you an answer yet?"

She said, "No, I have been praying hard! I have been in the restroom crying and praying, and I just don't know what to do!"

As we were talking, her other extension started ringing, and she put me on hold. In a minute, she comes back to me, saying, "It's Brenda, hold on for a minute, and I'll come right back to you."

So I am on hold, praying, "Lord, I need your answer now! I will not take Linda kicking and screaming. If you want us to go to China, you will have to do something right now! I will go wherever you want me to go, but I am not going to force Linda to go against her will."

Just then, Linda came back on my extension and said Brenda was calling to find out if we had made up our minds yet.

I asked, "What did you tell her?"

Linda replied, "Well, when I picked up the telephone, Brenda asked me the question, and I told her we had not decided yet, but we're going to make the decision now. Brenda then told me, 'Oh Mama, why don't y'all go ahead to China? You know very well the Lord has opened this door and worked it out, step by step. Why don't you just go ahead and take the call to China? It's only for a year, and then when you come back, you can go into pastoring full-time!'"

Hearing Linda repeat what Brenda had just told her, I asked Linda, "What do you think about that?"

She answered, "Well, the more I think about it, the more I am seeing that if we take the call to Dakota, I will always wonder if we should have gone to China. But if we don't take the call to Dakota and go to China, I won't have to worry about asking myself that question."

When I heard her say that, I abruptly asked her, "Honey, did you hear what you just said?" It had not dawned on her even though she was giving me her answer! She had made her decision! I said to her, "You have made the decision that you are willing to go to China!"

Linda responded, "I think that's what we need to do and put this matter to rest."

So I called Pastor Shelton and told him our decision. He was so gracious and understanding about our decision. He said that he was sorry we were not coming to Dakota Conference, but he only wanted us where the Lord wanted us.

Years later, remembering the impression he made on me as a Christian leader and a Southern gentleman, I served on a Gulf States Conference Nominating Committee and placed his name on the list for an open administrative position, which he accepted, and both Pastor Shelton and his wife, Anita, made wonderful contributions to the work there before they retired.

I then went to the religion department and told Dr. Blanco and the other folks who were there, wondering about our decision. And then I called Dr. Bascom.

This whole experience turned out to be one of the most valuable lessons Linda and I have ever had in our Christian journey. We came to realize that even when the children of God are receiving his *living water*, making the decisions they are faced with, on their own, is not always easy or clear. In this life's dead river, we become addicted to making all the decisions on our own, thinking this is totally necessary if we are to be truly free. Yet this is part of the deception and depths of sin in the river we were born into. The only decisions we need to make each day, regardless of the circumstances we face, is to follow what Jesus has already revealed while remaining open and alert for any new information that he reveals along the way. This released us from any unnecessary burdens which truly set us free, and this is when the Lord's *living water* is the most refreshing!

Chapter 44

Over the Pacific Pond

*He gathers the waters of the sea together as a
heap; he lays up the deep in storehouses.*

—Psalm 33:7

As the summer of 1991 progressed, we were busy making preparations to leave in August for China. We tried to research as much as we
could in preparation for meeting the Chinese people. Several friends
suggested that we seek out former missionaries to China, along with
several books, to help prepare us for what most thought was going
to be a tremendous culture shock. There was a series of shots needed
from the health department, some dental work, chiropractic visits,
and passports to obtain. And of course, there were funds for us to
raise to help pay for our tickets overseas, so we mailed out letters to
relatives and friends asking for donations. We took a short trip back
to South Carolina to personally approach some family for funds, and
when we returned to Collegedale, one of my coworkers at the grounds
department had been invited to Three Angels Broadcasting Network
to be interviewed by Danny and Linda Shelton to raise donations for
his mission trip. After I told him we were still short of funds, he called
3ABN, and they invited me to come along with him to be interviewed
as well. While we were there, Danny Shelton asked us to tape several
sermons each to add to their programming and we did.

We also needed to help Brenda make all her arrangements
to live and work for two weeks and then start her fall semester at

Southern College. Before we realized it, our airline tickets from the General Conference had arrived, and on August 10, we were flying to Los Angeles. Meeting the remainder of the teachers there, we took a fourteen-hour direct flight over the Pacific pond to Hong Kong. I never dreamed that I would walk so many laps on the aisles of an airplane, and unfortunately, Linda experienced another bout of claustrophobia but finally managed to go to sleep, and it subsided.

When we arrived in Hong Kong and stepped out of the huge 747 airplane, we immediately understood that two of the biggest problems we would encounter were the tremendous heat and humidity! Being Southerners, Linda and I felt that we were pretty well used to hot summers with high humidity, but Hong Kong and Macau were in the subtropical region where the heat and humidity continued longer during the year. It was terrible! It was oppressive! It made South Carolina seem like Upstate New York. The teachers then boarded several buses for a twenty-minute ride to the Sam Yuk Adventist College in the beautiful lush green mountainous countryside. The college was our gathering point, and we were scheduled to be there for ten days of orientation.

At the orientation, although some of the classrooms and faculty homes had air-conditioning, most classrooms only had fans. Our room had two cots and a small fan. During orientation, we perspired twenty-four hours a day, constantly drinking water to keep from being dehydrated! We lost almost twenty pounds each! You would get out of the shower, and as soon as you were dried off, you were sweating again! Over the next year, I would remember and chuckle many times over the old saying my daddy quoted from his childhood days on the farm: "Perspiration would run off us like sweat!" (Of course, I did not always chuckle when remembering it.)

Some of the college staff were US expatriates, and we became good friends. One couple in particular invited us on Sabbath afternoon to come to their home, so we accepted, enjoying their fellowship and air-conditioning. They were the Tidwells. Ruth was the college librarian, and Charles was an English professor and the registrar. During that school year, the Lord would use them to become our first good friends on that side of the Pacific pond.

We were kept very busy during orientation, learning how to use the textbooks and teaching techniques that earlier teachers had developed over a period of years. Taken through the various pit-falls of those earlier teachers, we were taught how to avoid the same problems and best prepare for leading our classes each day. We also learned about living in the culture, and having a little free time in the late afternoon or evening, we were encouraged to venture out from the college campus in small groups to Hong Kong, to begin acclimating ourselves with the Chinese society. This gave us practice using the local subways, taxis, and local maps. Riding a bus into the city, we would shop for souvenirs to mail home or items we might need to take with us to our various universities. I bought my first pair of Nike tennis shoes for a super low price! We also bought a very good quality camera so we could take pictures and make slides to use in presentations when we came back to the States. Other teachers did the same. This shopping helped us learn how to deal with the people and the money system, as a good bit of dickering was still done in most market places throughout the country. The next day, we would share our successes and failures with each other.

After several days, Dr. Bascom told Linda and me that the Wuhan University, which had originally accepted our applications, had suddenly changed their decision and were going to hire someone else. He said it was because Linda did not have a degree, and though I had a bachelor's degree, the school was able to find two teachers with master's degrees. He explained how the Chinese place a great deal of emphasis on degrees, so they simply wanted the two master's for the same price as my bachelor's. He then explained how he and the East Asia Committee of our church, which had its office in Hong Kong, were working on a placement for us at another university and hoped to have it worked out in a couple of days, so we continued with our orientation classes.

Several days later, Dr. Bascom informed us that all the universities had filled their teaching positions. "However," he said, "we have a small school and church in the Portuguese colony of Macau [pronounced *Ma-cow*] about fifty-five miles from Hong Kong. It is not Mainland China, but 90 percent of the population is Chinese. The church is an 'underground' church with about twenty-five members. We are not permitted to have a church there, but we are licensed to have an English language extension school, from our Hong Kong College. There is a Chinese pastor there, who also serves as the registrar for the school, and at present, two young ladies are there as teachers. Their time is nearly up, and they will be heading back to the US, and so we need two English teachers to take their places." He continued, "There will be no government pressure on you because you are being hired to teach English conversation, and you will be able to teach our faith openly without any problems."

He then asked me, "Do you like to preach?"

I answered, "I love to preach!"

He explained further, "If you are willing to go to Macau and teach, I also want you to hold evangelistic meetings year-round! We have talked to the Hong Kong/Macau Conference president, and he is willing for you to do this and to give you the support you need through the local pastor and the conference office. The Chinese pastor speaks English and can translate for you. I want you to hold four series of meetings in a year." So we told Dr. Bascom we would think and pray about it overnight and talk with him the next day.

We truly believed God was working, and we reasoned that while we were there, we might as well stay. Brenda was in school back in the States, so we would stay and work for the Lord. We took that position to Dr. Bascom, and he told us that because we were going into a different set of circumstances from the other teachers, we would need to stay at the college for a few extra days to familiarize ourselves with the college policies and meet some of the other college and conference staff. This would also give us more time to shop and learn our way around Hong Kong and relax some before we had to start work. A couple of days after the other teachers left, the pastor from Macau would come for us.

We told him, "Great! We are looking forward to it!"

It soon became extremely evident that Linda and I were in one of the great channels of humanity. Throughout Hong Kong, and later into Macau and Mainland China, we came to realize that we knew very little about the people here. In fact, with time, our view appeared to be more and more distorted. The masses we encountered appeared more like a sea, an ocean, rather than a river. Hundreds of thousands and even millions of people were there, moving about in every direction. Yes, they were living the same life we are all born into, but it was more like the great Pacific Ocean as opposed to the Dead River of Montgomery County, Georgia! It took us fourteen hours, flying at the average speed of four hundred miles an hour, to cross that *heap*[236] of waters! And now the two of us found ourselves in the midst of this ocean just like two survivors that suddenly find themselves hanging on to floating debris after their ship sank. What are we going to do? Which direction are we going to go? How are we going to survive, much less, accomplish anything for the Lord?

Well, first of all, we could not afford to forget that not long ago, both of us were part of that vast dead river that now had the appearance of an ocean. Second, we also could not forget while in that condition, we were unable to save ourselves no matter what we tried to do! In fact, we needed to remember that we had already been saved by the Floating Debris we were clinging to! That Debris was Jesus, and his raft of righteousness! Born into the same dead river of humanity as everyone, we tried to drown our Savior! Yet his Heavenly Father helped him to survive on his sinless raft, which was the only way we could be saved and accomplish anything for him! We must continue clinging to Jesus! To survive crossing that huge Pacific pond twice and living from now on, we must hang on to Jesus and his raft of righteousness until we die or Jesus returns to take us home.

Chapter 45

Fai Chi Kei

The poor and needy seek water, but there is none, their
tongues fail for thirst. I, the Lord, will hear them;
I, the God of Israel, will not forsake them.

—Isaiah 41:17

The morning we left Hong Kong for Macau, Pastor Samuel, from the college, took us to the Hong Kong Ferry Terminal, and there, we met the ferry from Macau with Pastor Chan on board. He was a small man and quiet by nature. He spoke English well enough to communicate, but it was very easy for him to be lost if we spoke too quickly or used too many colloquialisms. After saying goodbye to Pastor Samuel, we loaded our luggage and took the high-speed ferry back to Macau.

The pastor escorted us through customs, hailed a cab, and we rode to our apartment building that was about two blocks from the school in Fai Chi Kei (pronounced *Fie-Chee-Kay*), the poorest section of Macau. It was known for its theft, drugs, gangs, and "ladies of the night." Macau is called "the Las Vegas of the East" because of its casinos and grand hotels, but they are in the scenic part of town, overlooking where the river and the harbor meet.

The waterline in Fai Chi Kei was door-to-door shanties made of cardboard boxes, scrap lumber, pieces of rusty tin, and anything else that could be nailed, taped, or tied together so that a person could escape the heat, rain, and the occasional cold. Six hundred thousand people were crammed together on a peninsula and two islands total-ing less than six square miles. Most of these poor souls had come out of Red China by any means they could find to have a chance to escape the communist regime, temporarily left in their home coun-try, but was coming to take over Macau and close its doors to free-dom in a few more years.

We stepped out of the cab onto the filthy streets of Fai Chi Kei, and the stench hit us square in the face! Inside the building, it was even worse—far worse than any of the swampy backwater I ever smelled at Dead River! We could plainly see where garbage had been removed recently from a garbage chute that was in each concrete high-rise apartment building and no doubt swept through the lobby floor and into a dumpster on the street, not five steps out of the front door. Though it was late summer, it was still stifling hot, and the smell from the lobby, dumpsters, and streets were so bad we had to cover our noses. If you did not have a strong stomach, you could very easily become nauseated, and Linda started gagging as we tried to escape into the elevator.

Finally entering an elevator, the pastor took us to the eleventh floor of the twenty-one-story apartment complex. There, he took us into a small apartment across the lobby from the elevator. Stepping through the front door, we entered the largest room in the apart-ment, a combination living room and dining room. There was a bed-room to the right and another bedroom to the far left. Another door was tucked into the front left corner that opened to the bathroom while another door, opposite the front door, opened to the kitchen. Next to the kitchen, the remaining outer wall was a sliding glass door that led out to a tiny walled-in porch, overlooking the street below. The apartment was four hundred and twenty-five square feet with no air-conditioning, and the smells from below had no problem making it up to our floor and above.

Closing the sliding glass door, we sat down around a three feet square dining room table, and the pastor explained that we teachers were each paid the equivalent of $100 US per week. The electricity, rent, and other bills were paid as follows: the apartment was leased by the school for the teachers, and the school provided the rent. The school also paid for the first fifty gallons of bottled gas, which was what we had to cook with on a two-burner hot plate, and any gas over the fifty gallons, we paid for it. It also paid the first 200 patacas (one pataca equaled then about $1.50, US) for the electricity and anything over that amount we paid. We furnished our clothing, food, health and comfort items, plus any other personal expenditure we needed to make. The pastor then took us out to lunch at a local restaurant, and several English students met us there to begin getting acquainted with us.

After lunch, the pastor showed us the school, which was a store front that comprised the first and second floor of another apartment complex. Posters in the store windows advertised the school and its schedule for the coming term. Inside the front door, a small open office sat at the base of the stairs with two chairs, a desk, and a telephone. The remainder of the downstairs was open with movable partitions, chairs, and a few folding tables. It was primarily used as a meeting room with a speaking platform and podium at one end and a piano in the corner. Upstairs, there were two small offices where several desktop computers were set up for word processing, and there were three small classrooms with several tables and chairs, student desks, and blackboards. During the week, most English classes were held there. All total, the school was about one thousand square feet... with air-conditioning! We were presented with the daily/weekly schedule that the students had registered for at the end of the last term. The school was based on a quarterly system.

On Sabbath, the downstairs was used for our Adult Sabbath School, Worship Service, and Fellowship Dinner. The upstairs classrooms were used for Children's Sabbath School classes.

Most of the students were adults, with families, and working a job. In fact, many of them worked two or three jobs, and they would come to school at night to learn conversational English, with the hope that they would one day have enough money and/or a job promotion that would allow them to leave the country before the Communist Chinese government took over Macau.

The school was founded originally by a longtime local Chinese pastor, Dr. Luke. The school had been his heartthrob through the years, and he saw it as a way to establish relationships with the students and their parents on the common ground of wanting to learn English. Through those relationships, these people would be eventually invited to church and its various outreach functions, and if they showed any interest, they would be given Bible studies.

When we arrived, a third of the membership was Chinese, a third was Portuguese, and a third was Filipino. None of the Portuguese were active, so the congregation was basically bilingual; the Chinese speaking Cantonese and the Filipinos speaking English. We soon found that the southern Chinese tended to look down on the Filipinos as a subculture. I equated it very much like the Caucasian and African American situation in America that had existed since our Civil War and the end of slavery.

Because the Philippine economy was so bad, many of their people could not find work in their homeland even though many of them had high school and college degrees. Not finding adequate work to support their families, large numbers of them would immigrate or sign various work agreements in Hong Kong and Macau. By working in those locations, they were reasonably close to home and could afford to visit occasionally. These educated people would have to settle for positions as domestic workers in the homes of wealthy Chinese and Portuguese. They were paid from a lower scale of wages, but it was a lot compared to the wage, if any, they could earn back home.

The Filipinos would band together, renting and dividing an apartment, settling for just enough space to lie down and sleep and have a bathroom to use and bathe in. They would work for years, sending most of their money home to support their family, sometimes numbering twelve or more members, keeping only enough to live on locally. After seeing how most Filipinos lived in Macau, we felt blessed, indeed! Even with Linda and I being bigger folk by stature, compared to the Chinese, our living space was a great blessing! I came to believe this was one of the reasons the Lord put us in a very small apartment at Southern College. It was to prepare Linda for the cramped quarters we were going to have in China.

We had several weeks before the first classes were to begin, so we went about the task of acquainting ourselves as to where the post office, fresh marketplace, and various stores were located. We enjoyed shopping in the open markets, where we bought most of our fruits and vegetables, but we had to learn that most of the vendors would sell to us at a cheaper price than what they had listed on signs, but they wanted us to negotiate with them. It was their custom, and most seemed to enjoy it.

Of course, like any place you go, there were some who would try to take advantage of and cheat us because we were strangers and did not know the language. One of the most common nicknames they had for us was "white ghosts," of course spoken in Cantonese, as they considered us a kind of lower class than themselves. Yet when they found out we were teachers, we were given an extraordinary amount of respect, courtesies, and discounts!

One of the first obstacles we encountered in our new home was that our apartment had no air-conditioner. At that time, it was late summer, but there were several extremely warm months ahead. In fact, we were told it would be high humidity up to Christmas, even if it was not hot, and it was continually miserable! Your clothes would not stay dry unless you were in air-conditioning! We would clean up and dress for our classes, but by the time we walked the two blocks to the classrooms, even at an easy stroll, we were soaked with perspiration. Then we would have to teach in air-conditioned class-rooms because the students expected to be comfortable at school. This began to cause health problems—sore throats, colds, ear infections, and sinus ailments. I asked the pastor what it would take to get an air-conditioner in our apartment. He said, "Oh no, no! The school could not afford an air-conditioner or the additional electric bill! They would not hear of it!"

So I began looking into the cost of a unit myself. After all, we had a very small apartment and the additional electricity could not be too much more. Surely, the school could afford one for us while we were willing to pay the additional electric bill. Yet every time I approached the pastor about the situation, he would not even con-sent to ask the school authorities about buying us a small unit. So after a few weeks of school and our clothing being constantly soaked with perspiration as we began our classes each evening, I sat the pastor down, and we had a little talk. Basically, I told him that if the school could not purchase us a small air-conditioner to make our apartment more tolerable, I would call Dr. Bascom at the General Conference and tell him we were ready to go home because of the conditions we were trying to function in were causing us to be sick! We had agreed to take this assignment at the last minute because the school needed somebody even though we had contracted to go to China. Of course, I was pressuring the pastor to take a step forward as our advocate, and if the college thought they might be losing their teachers, then maybe they would be willing to compromise.

We were also having difficulties sleeping. Yet it was not only because of the heat and humidity but also because of the beds! The only beds that were in the apartment were bunk beds in each bedroom because of space. The pastor was a single fellow and had never been married. I told him, "I am a married man, and I have been married most of my life, and I am going to sleep in the same bed with my wife! The present situation is not conducive to maintaining a good marriage. It is stressful enough being in a new place, having a language barrier, experiencing different cultural customs that we have to learn to be aware of, and so forth! But we have to have things situated where we can at least be comfortable at home! This means we have to have an air-conditioner and a bed that Linda and I can sleep on together!"

He then asked, "Why can't you take the beds down and put them side by side on the floor?"

I responded, "We did try to work that out, but it was terribly uncomfortable with a huge gap in between the mattresses and the bed frames! And putting the mattresses side by side on the floor will not work because they will not stay together during the night!" I then emphatically repeated our demand, "The school has to buy us a bed big enough for us to sleep together and a small window air-conditioner to put in the main room. If they cannot arrange for those two things, we will pack up and go home right away!"

Finally, the pastor went to the school administration in Hong Kong, and they agreed to buy us a small air-conditioner and a double mattress. They would not buy a whole bed but would buy a mattress big enough for us to sleep together. We did have to put it on the floor, which was no problem at all, but it was stuffed with shredded, crushed coconut shells and fibers that were a constant source of discomfort, yet not nearly as bad as the bunk beds for sure! I did have to take extra medication for my back the whole time we were there, but it was better than what we started with. I went shopping and found a window unit within the budget and installed it myself.

Because of this experience, I could not help thinking about how it was my first summer in the river swamp of Georgia. As is the case with most rivers, they are formed by the drainage off the higher ground, and the lowland forest is oftentimes made up of thick brush and trees that form a canopy that restricts both the direct sunlight and air circulation. As a result, the forest atmosphere is heavy with humidity and hot due to the summer heat and lack of fresh air movement. My mobile home was very uncomfortable until I bought and installed an air-conditioner. While we did not live in the same situation in Macau, obtaining an air-conditioner in our apartment made a huge difference in our comfort when at home and making preparations for our classes.

Chapter 46

He Who Hears
Our Prayers

Hear my prayer, O God; give ear to the words of my mouth.

—Psalm 54:2

For the first few weeks in Macau, it was just Linda and me. However, another series of the Lord's miracles allowed Brenda to join us early in our stay. By the time Linda and I left the US in August 1991, we had seen Brenda enrolled, accepted, and moved into the girls' dormitory at Southern College. I made several personal visits to professors and administrators to let them know of Brenda's status. I asked them to check on her from time to time and give her an encouraging word. I let them know that I had given her their names and telephone numbers in case she needed some counsel for any kind of problems that might arise.

There was a communications gap then from the time we left the Los Angeles Airport and arrived in Macau. We had not talked with her for about two weeks at that point. We had been in Macau two days when the pastor let it be known the church had a telephone and we could make collect calls on it. So we decided to call Brenda in her dorm room and surprise her. After working out the time difference, we went to the pastor's apartment to make the call.

Brenda's roommate answered the call, and she immediately informed us that Brenda was no longer at school and was at her grandmother's, Linda's mother, in South Carolina. We inquired further and found that after we left, Brenda had some emotional difficulties. Everything seemed to close in on her, and once again, she tried to take her own life! As a result of that, she was put into the Chattanooga Hospital. After pumping her stomach, the hospital kept her for several days' observation. Her grandmother was notified, and some of Linda's family came to Chattanooga to get Brenda when she was released. The young lady continued saying, "She withdrew from school and went back to South Carolina."

Needless to say, this news broke our hearts, and we were in immediate emotional turmoil! Ending the first call, we then called the home of Linda's mother to check on Brenda. We gave her mother our telephone numbers at the school and the pastor's apartment and then talked with Brenda. After ending the telephone conversation, Linda began declaring to me that we would pack our bags and go home right away, as we needed to be with our daughter at that time!

The more I thought about the situation, the more it bothered me. I began praying, and as I prayed, I could not get away from the thought that our God knows the end from the beginning. He knows everything, and I had no doubt of that fact! Before we left home, the Lord already knew this was going to happen, yet he had already worked a number of miracles to bring us to Macau. And as I thought and prayed about our situation, I could not bring myself to believe that with all God had done to bring us here, we were meant to turn around and go back home! I could not reconcile my mind to do this unless I heard it directly from the Lord! I began to talk to Linda along these lines of thought, and of course, for the moment, that made things even worse as she truly became upset with me. Continuing to pray, I felt I needed some additional godly counsel, and the only thing I could think of was to call Dr. Bascom.

I went to the pastor's apartment and called Dr. Bascom's Maryland office. I explained what had taken place with our daughter, and he was very understanding and compassionate as he listened to me. He said, "Tommy, I can certainly empathize with you and Linda because I have two daughters of my own, and if I were in your shoes, I, too, would certainly be considering coming home to see about my child." He went on to say, "But I also understand your confusion about how God has brought Linda and you to this place at this point in time. I can understand your deep desire to do God's will, regardless of what that will is. I can attest to you that through many similar tragic situations that I have faced, I have been able to rely on our God to answer my prayers. In fact, I want to give you a quotation from the book *Desire of Ages* that I memorized many years ago because I think it will give you courage at this time and hopefully will help you make the right decision as to what to do. I am not sure of the page, but I think it is on page 668.4." He then shared the quotation with me from memory:

> As Christ lived the law in humanity, so we may do if we will take hold of the Strong for strength.
>
> But we are not to place the responsibility of our duty upon others and wait for them to tell us what to do. We cannot depend for counsel upon humanity. The Lord will teach us our duty just as willingly as he will teach somebody else. If we come to him in faith, he will speak his mysteries to us personally. Our hearts will often burn within us as One draws nigh to commune with us as he did with Enoch. Those who decide to do nothing in any line that will displease God will know, after presenting their case before him, just what course to pursue. And they will receive not only wisdom but strength. Power for obedience, for service, will be imparted to them, as Christ has promised. Whatever was given to Christ—the *"all things"* to supply the need of fallen men—was given to him as the head and representative of humanity. And *"whatsoever we ask, we receive of him, because we keep his commandments, and do those things that are pleasing in his sight"* (1 John 3:22).

Dr. Bascom assured me that whatever we decided to do, he and the General Conference would support us, and if we decided to immediately come home, they would do everything they could to get us home as soon as possible. And if we decided to stay, they would support us and our daughter in any way they could. That gave me a lot of comfort! He then had prayer for our family and asked me to go back to our apartment and share the quotation with Linda.

Back in our apartment, I looked up the passage and read it several times to myself and then went into the bedroom and shared it with Linda. I began to explain to her that I felt we needed to pray honestly and truly open our hearts and minds to God's will, claiming the promise in *Desire of Ages* that told us whenever God's people come to him in prayer and need an answer that they might do his will, then he will make his answer known! Claiming that promise in our hearts, I went into the spare bedroom while Linda stayed in our bedroom, and we got down on our knees beside the beds and began to pray individually. We simply poured out our hearts to the Lord, continuing to claim this promise in *Desire of Ages*. No more than several minutes passed while we were on our knees and the doorbell rang. I quickly jumped up and ran to the door, and it was the pastor.

He said that Dr. Bascom had called again and wanted to reassure us that whatever we decided to do, he and the General Conference would support us. The pastor added that after we had hung up, Dr. Bascom said as he was thinking and praying, a third option came to him that he wanted us to add to our consideration. That being if we wanted to stay in Macau and our daughter wanted to join us, the General Conference would see to it that Brenda was flown to Hong Kong, and at each stop along the way, there would be an Adventist pastor or chaplain who would meet her to encourage her, pray with her, and help her through the details of changing flights, handling baggage, and dealing with customs. And after she arrived, we could set up counseling appointments with a psychiatrist and pastor at the Adventist hospital in Hong Kong, if we desire. Again, he wanted us to know that whichever of these three decisions we chose to make, he would support us one hundred percent.

I went into the bedroom where Linda was praying and shared with her what the pastor had just relayed from Dr. Bascom. I could tell right away that Linda did not like that option. Personally, she wanted to go home! She had been miserable for the nearly three weeks we had been overseas. She had not admitted it to me, but she was looking for any opportunity, any excuse, to go back home. I shared with her that I truly thought this was the Lord's answer to our prayers because it meant that not only could we take care of our daughter, but at the same time, we could continue on with the ministry that he had brought us to do.

Again, Linda tried to insist on us leaving and returning to the US because Brenda needed us. I said to her, "Honey, I love you and Brenda very, very much, but we put this situation in God's hands, and he has immediately answered our prayers, giving us his perfect remedy, and I am not about to turn around and go back home, causing the church all this extra expense and trouble when God, in his infinite wisdom, has seen fit to bring us here and make a way so that our daughter can now come and be with us!" I continued, "It is obvious to me that this is God's will for us! Now in this light, if you insist on returning home, I will gladly take you to the Hong Kong airport and put you on an airplane right now to go home. But I cannot, in good conscience, leave Macau when I know exactly what God would have us to do, and it is not going home!"

Linda began to weep again, not hysterically but a weeping of surrender. In a few moments, she admitted to me that she also understood this was the Lord's will for us. She saw it clearly and admitted that she had been looking for an excuse to leave and return home because she did not want to stay in Macau. It was a terrible lifestyle for her—something she had never been forced to deal with and something she thought she would never get used to! But now that she knew God had answered our prayers, she was willing to stay and have Brenda join us.

As I thought more on this situation, it dawned on me that while we had originally accepted a position at Wuhan University, which had not worked out, it resulted in us coming to Macau as an alternative. God knew the end from the beginning. He knew what Brenda was going to do, and we would need a remedy, so by positioning us in Macau, the door was wide open for us to receive Brenda, compared to what the situation would have been with us seven hundred miles into Communist China, having to deal with their political Red tape. Our Lord Jesus was looking out for us in every detail!

After coming to an agreement, we called home and talked with Brenda. She agreed and wanted to come live with us in Macau. We explained our plans to Linda's parents and told them we were going to give Dr. Bascom the go-ahead, along with their contact information, so Brenda could expect a call from him in the near future. Dr. Bascom's office set up the travel arrangements and the contacts along the way, and Brenda had a good trip! There were no problems whatsoever, and she made all her transfers smoothly. We met her at the Hong Kong International Airport and took her by ferry to Macau.

Our Lord Jesus is so good! He constantly amazes me! Every time I think I pretty well understand the Lord, he lovingly puts me back in my place, blowing my mind again at how he is in complete control! He is not only in control when he works things out in our favor or the way we want them, but God is also in control when he makes decisions that we would not have made or do not like! Jesus is able to work out the minutest details in the worst storms of this life so that his people can accomplish what he wants them to accomplish; this is fulfilling the Great Commission! Peter and the other disciples saw this when Jesus was walking on the stormy Sea of Galilee and spoke to them, saying, *"'Be of good cheer! It is I; do not be afraid.' And Peter answered him and said, 'Lord, if it is you, command me to come to you on the water'. So he said, 'Come'. And when Peter was come down out of the boat, he walked on the water to go to Jesus."*[237]

Even in the midst of family difficulties, school troubles, emotional problems, or whatever one can think of as a possible excuse to give up or reason to fail, nothing is too great an obstacle for the One and only Almighty! He, who hears our prayers, will answer in deeds of righteousness. He gives and gives and gives and works and works and works for his people! It is such a privilege, such an awesome, wonderful privilege to know him and to work for him, allowing Jesus to use us through his Holy Spirit! If He wants us to, we can walk on water!

Chapter 47

Iniquity of the Fathers

Visiting the iniquity of the fathers upon the children and the children's children to the third and fourth generation.

—Exodus 34:7

After Brenda arrived, it took a few days for her to get over the long ordeal and subsequent jet lag, but after a few days of rest, I could see the mother-daughter communication was reconnected, and it was a positive development for both of them. Linda no longer felt alone because, in some ways, she and Brenda were more like pals than mother and daughter—each one supported the other. This was an ongoing development, and I know it made the transition of settling into the lengthy school year much easier for Linda. Before long, after learning their way around town, they were willing to go most any-where in Macau without an escort. This helped me greatly because it freed me up to visit church members or work with the pastor in trying to revive the little church.

They made friends with people in the marketplace and in the school, plus the Chinese people seemed to be fascinated with the special mother-daughter relationship that was being demonstrated before them. They learned to count to ten in Cantonese (the long-time dialect of Southern China), and that usually was enough to communicate for any kind of purchases they had to make. Settling into the community, we found several grocery stores that had products we really liked. We even found a store that sold a brand of South Carolina eggs we used back in the US.

Of course, there was a McDonald's, Pizza Hut, and several other nice local restaurants with just about anything you would want to eat. Our favorite restaurant was at the Buddhist monastery across the bay on the island of Taipa. It was a very large facility, and the monks grew most of their own vegetables, and since they were vegetarians, all the food they prepared and sold in the restaurant was vegetarian as well. We would go over there quite often and take some students with us or students would invite us. We could take up to ten people and seat them at one table, and it cost very, very little to feed so many people. It fit right into our budget, so that was one of the reasons it was a favorite place, as well as the food being excellent!

I really think the only negative part about bringing Brenda to Macau was the fact that my and Brenda's relationship had never truly healed from the many years when I was not part of the family. Even though Brenda was a new Christian and was trying to live a life for Jesus, she still had this tremendous struggle to consider me as her father, and she absolutely refused to submit herself to my authority as her father. She said she had the desire, but the willingness to communicate and work together was a constant problem. Additionally, something we did not find out about until a few years later was her bipolar disorder, which we came to see only complicated every aspect of our relationship.

Then there was my problem. I was overly concerned as to how it would appear to others when my daughter wanted to consistently talk back to me when I gave her instructions. I figured they might think, "If I could not manage my child, how would I be able to manage the Lord's church?" We tried and tried to convince Brenda to at least make a gallant attempt to put away these kinds of feelings that she had toward me, hoping it would not poison our relationships with others or hinder the things that we wanted to accomplish within the community. But she and I found it very difficult to get along!

I was as much at fault as she was and probably more. It finally came to the point where the daily stress was terrible! We were bickering back and forth, constantly, day in and day out, having a devastating effect on Linda! It consumed her, and it became very difficult to concentrate on her duties as a teacher with this bad relationship between her daughter and husband growing worse by the day. Finally, in a family meeting, we agreed that something had to give, something had to be done, and we began thinking and praying about our options. We came to the conclusion we needed family counseling as Dr. Bascom had suggested we do once Brenda was settled in Macau.

I talked with him on the telephone, and he suggested that we not go to any of the Chinese pastors or chaplains, primarily because their culture saw these problems with a much different view. Instead, he wanted us to talk with Pastor John Ash, an American, who had been in China and Hong Kong for many years as an employee of the church through the East Asia Committee.

Before I called Pastor Ash, Dr. Bascom gave him a call and asked him whether he would be willing to have regular counseling sessions with the family and individual sessions if he saw the need for them. With all his duties and responsibilities, he was very gracious to juggle his schedule to accommodate us, and so he came to Macau, and we met in our apartment.

As it turned out, there was only the need for a handful of sessions. John was able to make a thorough assessment of what the different problems were (except for the bipolar disorder) in an incredibly short time and then shared his counsel with us. My and Brenda's relationship had to begin again, and we had to go into it recognizing though there had been a lot of time lost and many painful events, these were all in the past. If we needed to express our feelings to each other, then fine, do so in an honest but respectful way. But whether we felt the need to talk about them or not, we had to accept responsibility for causing the pain, apologize, and then let those things go! Jesus did not want us to continue holding things against each other. Just as Jesus had forgiven us, we needed to forgive each other.

This was a major challenge to Brenda because she did not fully trust me anymore. She did not want to let go of the memories and facts of how she and her mother had been terribly hurt through the years when I had left them! Brenda felt that if she forgave me of my wrongs against them, this would mean that I was no longer responsible for those wrongs. She had a lot of these emotions to work through, and it was no easy task for her to accomplish.

John's assessment of me was that I worried about two things. The first worry was the loss of my authority. I was concerned that I was being robbed of my authority as a father and a pastor. My second worry was about how this made me look to everyone else. Borderline obsession had me more concerned with myself than with others, including my own daughter! I was usually trying to demand her respect and obedience rather than earning them through my love and understanding of her. She was an immature eighteen-year-old young woman who had been through years of the traumatic effects of her family being broken up multiple times! When the family was together, she had to live with an alcoholic, unfaithful, argumentative father that she could no longer trust! All this together with a mother, who had become a workaholic, to cope, was a tremendously heavy load of baggage that Brenda carried around through the years!

In the book *Child Guidance*, under the inspiration of the Holy Spirit, the Christian author explains what the Lord meant when he told Moses that the iniquity of the fathers would be visited *upon the children and the children's children to the third and fourth generation.*[238] All those planning to have children would do well to understand and accept the following explanation.

Faulty Training Affects Entire Religious Life

A woe rests upon parents who have not trained their children to be God-fearing, but have allowed them to grow to manhood and womanhood undisciplined and uncontrolled. During their own childhood they were allowed to manifest passion and willfulness and to act from impulse and they bring this same spirit into their own homes. They are defective in temper, and passionate in government. Even in their acceptance of Christ they have not overcome the passions that were allowed to rule in their child-ish hearts. They carry the results of their early training through their entire religious life. It is a most difficult thing to remove the impress thus made upon the plant of the Lord; for as the twig is bent, the tree is inclined. If such parents accept the truth, they have a hard battle to fight. They may be transformed in character, but the whole of their religious experience is affected by the lax discipline exercised over them in their early lives. And their children have to suffer because of their defective training; for they stamp their faults upon them to the third and fourth generation. (CG 275.1)

The Eli's of Today

When parents sanction and thus perpetuate the wrongs in their children as did Eli, God will surely bring them to the place where they will see that they have not only ruined their own influ-ence, but also the influence of the youth whom they should have restrained... They will have bit-ter lessons to learn. (p. 276, CG 275.2)

Oh, that the Eli's of today, who are every-where to be found pleading excuses for the way-wardness of their children, would promptly assert their own God-given authority to restrain and correct them. Let parents and guardians, who overlook and excuse sin in those under their care, remember that they thus become accessory to these wrongs. If, instead of unlimited indul-gence, the chastening rod were oftener used, not in passion, but with love and prayer, we would see happier families and a better state of society. (CG 276.1)

The neglect of Eli is brought plainly before every father and mother in the land. As the result of his unsanctified affection or his unwillingness to do a disagreeable duty, he reaped a harvest of iniquity in his perverse sons. Both the parent who permitted the wickedness and the children who practiced it were guilty before God, and He would accept no sacrifice or offering for their transgression. (CG 276.2)

Society Cursed by Defective Characters

Oh! when will parents be wise? When will they see and realize the character of their work in neglecting to require obedience and respect according to the instructions of God's Word? The results of this lax training are seen in the children as they go out into the world and take their place at the head of families of their own. They perpetuate the mistakes of their parents. Their defective traits have full scope; and they transmit to others the wrong tastes, habits, and tempers that were permitted to develop in their own characters. Thus they became a curse instead of a blessing to society. (CG 276.3)[239]

My sins had taken a severe toll on my child, so much so, Linda and I will never have any grandchildren! However, while a high toll has been paid, God was still good to us again! Even in that particular trial, we were blessed by God's use of John Ash who lovingly, yet honestly, confronted us, giving us some immediate targets to focus on, that Brenda and myself might start building a positive father-daughter relationship. As I said, God was good to us and has continued to help us develop that relationship through the years. Just like the water of rivers and streams is filtered by the sand and soil of their beds, so are the sinful lives of men and women cleansed *with the washing of water by the Word*[240] of God.

Our relationship is still not perfect, but we are now at the point where we can talk about most anything, as long as we remember the things John shared with us back then. The Lord is not finished with us yet but continues to heal us. We thank God for bringing us through that time and many more trying experiences that have given us so many victories since!

Chapter 48

Friends

A friend loves at all times, and a brother [or sister] *is born for adversity.*

—Proverbs 17:17

In a week to ten days, we settled into our class routines, the preparation of our lessons, and getting to know our students. By the time Christmas came, we knew our students very well! In class, we used a combination of vocabulary lists and group conversation. We would give the students a subject for the day and sitting in a circle; they talked to one another using the vocabulary words as they conversed about the subject. We had no real problems with our students because of their keen desire to learn and speak English well. Many of them became friends that assisted us often through our daily lives there.

At night, I taught one advanced and two upper intermediate classes while Linda taught a lower intermediate and several beginners classes. We both had several private students earlier in the afternoons. Most of our students were already quite familiar with the language and were advanced in their understanding; however, the main differences between students were their word pronunciations and conversational sentence structure. All classes were meaningful and fun, and we tried to keep them that way.

As the first session moved along, Brenda started assisting Linda and came to know her students too. One thing that really helped Linda and Brenda adapt was the ladies in their classes enjoyed taking the teachers out shopping or to a restaurant. Sometimes they even took them on small tours around the city.

Each term, we usually had between fifty and sixty students with two-thirds of them being women, mostly adults with families of their own. Many worked multiple jobs to provide a good living for their families, plus many were saving funds to immigrate to other countries when Macau's lease would expire with China. These people wanted to either pay their way, or a family member's way, out of the country before China took over. Their savings would help convince the government of the country they were moving to of their ability to support themselves while helping to obtain a sponsor in the new country. Knowing how to speak English would help them to be sponsored. Once they or a family member was established, that person could then act as the sponsor for their other family members. They were all very hardworking people, working many hours per week, with little time for anything else but to learn English.

As we came to the break between school terms, all the teachers in Mainland China were called from their posts back to the Hong Kong Adventist College where we had our orientation. There we had ten days of R and R (rest and recreation). We spent those days debriefing, sharing, and shopping in Hong Kong. After breakfast and morning worship, we started with the debriefing, which was primarily reporting and making arrangements to deal with any problems we encountered with the school, government, finances, or travel. Sharing took up most of our time, telling how God had been leading and using us in our schools and communities. We would share successes and failures to encourage, as well as help each other understand how different techniques of teaching and witnessing would work or not work in various circumstances. Shopping was primarily for finding items we were unable to find in our separate locations. All these activities were a wonderful time of making new friends and fellowship!

During R and R, Linda, Brenda, and I were introduced to three teachers from Australia: Coral Robbie, Jenny Bearden, and Coralie Shelley. These ladies were not there as part of the Teachers for China project but were in a private endeavor that a Chinese Australian,

Roddy Wong, had undertaken in Zhuhai City. This city bordered Macau at Gongbei, one of the three suburbs that made up Zhuhai. Dr. Bascom had invited Roddy and the ladies to attend the R and R sessions along with our fifty teachers. Since these teachers were going to Zhuhai, Dr. Bascom thought it would be a good idea for the six of us to get to know one another, and we are so glad we did!

After R and R was over and we went back to Macau, Coral, Jenny, and Coralie went to Zhuhai with Roddy. We made plans for one of my students, Stephen, to escort me across the China-Macau border the next Friday, to meet the ladies and bring them to our apartment for the weekend and church services. That first Sabbath they attended our church, Coral was asked to play the piano for Sabbath School and the church service and also take the Sabbath School lesson. Jenny and Coralie took the mission story and talked about their time teaching in Nepal.

The second term in Macau was a happier time, especially for Linda and Brenda, because the Australians were just across the border and most weekends would come to stay with us and help with our Sabbath services. They added so much more to our Sabbaths than they could possibly imagine! The ladies would occasionally prepare an Australian dish for fellowship dinner, and those meals were truly international with Chinese, Australian, Filipino, and American dishes on the table. In the afternoons, we would change clothes and go visiting those who could not attend church or go to one of the small parks for a walk and then back to our apartment for a short nap. After sundown, we would usually go out to one of the restaurants in town and then maybe rent a video to watch at home before turning in for the night. I think back on those times, even today, and wish there was some way we could relive those events that were such a blessing to all. Linda, Brenda, and I truly enjoyed the fellowship we had with the other teachers and college staff during those days overseas.

Though we lost track of Jenny and Coralie after returning to the States, we have maintained a wonderful friendship with Coral Robbie through the years. Being a world traveler, as well as returning to Zhuhai many times to teach for Roddy's clients, she visited us often on her return trips from China to Australia (her plane tickets were always purchased with the ability to include a detour) or to break up her sightseeing trips through the United States or Canada. She has always been much more than a friend! Our Lord Jesus brought her into our lives, giving us a true Christian witness. With her friendship came love, compassion, experience, understanding, and wisdom. She would live with us for months at a time in several of our church districts, and we never grew tired of her being with us. Jesus has blessed us through Coral far more than we have ever blessed her, and we truly look forward to walking the streets of gold and exploring the Lord's vast universe with this dear sister of our faith.

(Unfortunately, at the time of writing this, Coral, almost eighty years old, was diagnosed with colon cancer, requiring surgery. A few weeks after coming home from the hospital, she came down with a serious infection where the surgery was performed. Coral went back into the hospital for intravenous antibiotics; we were praying she would not have to have a second surgery. After three weeks of fighting the infection, she was allowed to come home. However, before this battle ended, Coral had to have three surgeries total but eventually was able to return home and continue raising her grandson.)

Foreigners in Macau were either issued work visas or visitor visas, and since we worked out of the Hong Kong Adventist College, we were considered visitors. This meant we could stay overnight, even rent an apartment, but every fourteen days, we had to leave Macau, and then we could return for another fourteen days, which automatically renewed our visa. Usually, we decided to simply use that time of exiting Macau to go to the Hong Kong College and spend the night. This gave us extra opportunities to visit with the Tidwells or at another couple's home that we met while on R and R. They are Roger and Sunshine Stahl. Roger was an expatriate from Florida, and when he was serving in China years before as a missionary, Sunshine had become one of his students and eventually an Adventist Christian. After a while, they fell in love and were married, and after coming out of China, they decided to live in Hong Kong at the college where he was offered a position teaching English. While in China, Roger had also learned to speak Chinese, so this made him an additional asset to have on staff at the college.

Sunshine has a voice like an angel, a high soprano, and the East Asia Committee, that produced gospel programming for radio in China, used to add her music to their programs and record gospel songs on CDs for listeners who wanted to purchase them. She also was used by evangelists and pastors of the Hong Kong Conference to sing for their evangelistic series. Since we came back to the US, Roger and Sunshine have come to visit us several times, and she gave Sabbath afternoon concerts that blessed our church members greatly.

Some of Sunshine's relatives were still living in China, and most anytime they decided to go for a visit, they would come through Macau and stay the night or the weekend with us, if the Australians were not coming to Macau. But no matter whom we were with, the Lord had supplied us with good Christian friends to worship with, pray with, and spend casual time together during our stay in Macau. In fact, the friendship we experienced with each of these mentioned and others there was like a full cup of the *water of life, clear as crystal, proceeding from the throne of God and of the Lamb.*[241] And we loved every drop of it!

Chapter 49

We Shall Not Be Moved

*There is a river whose streams shall make glad the city of
God, the holy place of the tabernacle of the Most High.
God is in the midst of her, she shall not be moved;*

—Psalm 46:4, 5

When Dr. Bascom asked me if I loved to preach and I told him, "I
sure do," he told me that he was going to send me several copies of
an evangelistic sermon series he had put together for the General
Conference Ministerial Association. He sent them, and I was thrilled
to receive and begin studying them in preparation for beginning our
evangelistic meetings. He told me we could talk about this with the
Chinese brethren, and he was sure they would have resources, such
as advertising posters and brochures, Bible studies, and supplemental
literature necessary for holding such meetings.

He added, "Of course, you might like to run some other seminars such as 'Stop Smoking' or 'Healthful Cooking' classes before or
after each series, but I want you to hold at least three or four evangelistic series during the year you are there. That's your assignment."
He had already mentioned this to the brethren at the college, and
he was planning on talking to the Chinese pastor in Macau about
the venture as he wanted it to be a team effort, and the pastor would
need to be my translator and host.

When we arrived in Macau, I did not push the start of the
meetings because I wanted Linda and me to get our feet firmly on

the ground, learning our way around and preparing for the English classes. But after a few weeks, I decided it was time to go ahead and begin preparations with the pastor to hold the first series of meetings. As we talked, he was very negative about the whole idea, maintaining he tried holding meetings in the past but had very few people attend. It had cost them quite a lot to hold his meetings, which produced no fruit. Little did I know it then, but this would be an excuse of some wherever God sent me to minister, and this was only the first of many excuses given over the rest of our time in Macau for any type of outreach we wanted to have.

As I communicated back and forth with Dr. Bascom, he would always ask me if we had started any meetings yet. I would have to fill him in on whatever the latest excuse or delay happened to be, and this routine grew to be quite frustrating for me and him, especially since I was spending time personalizing the messages he sent me and wanted to begin.

Time continued passing though, and almost before we realized it, we were at the R and R break and half the year was gone. I made up my mind that I was going to have a serious talk with Dr. Bascom at the break and see if there was anything we could do about the lack of cooperation from the pastor and the college. I had kept good notes with dates and excuses, so when I saw him at the R and R, I asked for some private time to go over these details with him. I laid everything out for him to understand and shared not only the problems with the pastor but also with the college administration and the conference office. When Dr. Bascom had originally asked about us holding meetings in Macau, he had spoken with the leaders of the college and the conference, and they had given him the go-ahead for the pastor to help me while promising their budgetary support, yet nothing had been done.

Elder Bascom, being a very forthright individual, decided that at the end of our R and R, he and I should go directly to the college president since Linda and I were technically working as teachers, under the umbrella of their extension school. We brought the president up-to-date with everything that had happened, and Dr. Bascom then asked him for a verbal commitment, and he assured both of us that he would support us to hold meetings with whatever we needed. He added they would seek help from the conference office, so we came away from the meeting extremely encouraged with a renewed motivation to move forward with the soul-winning endeavors!

When we arrived back in Macau, I thought it was strange that our church pastor was not there to greet us because he was usually diligent to do so. We went on to our apartment and unpacked, and then I began going over a list of items I needed to talk with the pastor about for the meetings. After several hours, he showed up, and I asked if we could get together and discuss the meetings. It was obvious that he was very nervous, but he told me we could talk later at school because he presently had several things to handle.

When we met at the school, I scarcely had time to say hello when the pastor started blurting out that the school would be closing early that year and, in the same breath, asking us when we were planning to leave! I had no idea what he was talking about, and I asked him to explain what he meant. As he began answering me, I realized that somewhere between us leaving R and R and that moment, the college had decided to get rid of us! Someone had made a decision that they were going to close the Macau English language school early, and at the beginning of the new school year in the fall, they would reopen as a primary school, and in either case, they would not need our services anymore and since we would be leaving—that meant there would be no meetings held.

The pastor was very anxious for us to give him some kind of date for when we were leaving, and I tried to explain to him what had taken place in our meeting with the college president only the afternoon before, but he kept saying that things had changed at the extension school committee meeting in Hong Kong since Dr. Bascom and I had met with the president. I immediately asked, "Everything changed overnight?"

He responded, "Yes!"

I told him that I could not give him a date before I talked with Dr. Bascom, but when I tried to call him, I could not reach him. He had other teachers in Europe that he needed to visit and was flying there at the moment, so we explained things to his administrative assistant, Treva Burgess, and she said she would be speaking with him after he landed in Europe. Treva would relay my message to Dr. Bascom, and she felt sure that he would call me back that evening.

He did call us that evening, and I do not know how to put it any other way, but he was hot! He told me to call both the college president and the extension school director to confirm what the pastor had told me that afternoon. The next morning, I called both offices and was told they were closed for the day, and no one seemed to know where the administrators were or how they could be reached. That evening, when Dr. Bascom called me, I told him exactly what I was told, so I suggested that it was probably going to take someone with more organizational weight than I had to deal with this problem, and he agreed, telling me for us to sit tight in Macau and not make any moves about leaving until we heard from him. If the pastor wanted to know about our plans to leave, I was to tell him that I was waiting to hear further from Elder Bascom.

Four days later, he called us back and informed us that the school's new plans were legitimate even though he felt like it was totally inconsiderate for us to be treated this way. It seemed obvious to both of us they wanted to get rid of the Pooles, but we did not understand why! The transition to primary school was something they had been talking about and praying over for several years, but I could not help feeling as if it was being used as an excuse. By attempting to implement their plan now, it was merely a way of forcing us to leave early. However, we would stay until the end of the semester because our airline tickets were dated and could not be exchanged, and the school certainly was not willing to reimburse Teachers for China for new tickets, so they decided they would allow us to stay and teach until the end of the term, as originally planned.

As a result of all this confusion, there were going to be no evangelistic meetings, no seminars, and no outreach of any kind! Dr. Bascom instructed us to do the best we could to continue developing relationships with our students and the people in the community that we associated with because we never knew what God might be able to do, a week from now, a month from now, or even after we left Macau. We knew that was true because of how the Lord had led in our lives up to that point in time, and we certainly did not want to leave Macau in a negative manner!

This disappointing situation turned out to be another important lesson learned about working for the Lord. We certainly understood that our Heavenly Father was in full control, but we also knew from past experiences that Satan would do anything and use anyone, even some brethren, to interfere with the gospel work. The devil, that old dragon, knows that while God has the power to do as he sees fit, his character will not allow him to force men and angels to do as he desires. God's character is selfless love, and it is by revealing this pure love for his creation that *the goodness of God leads you to repentance.*[242] And even if some of God's people do not submit their hearts and minds to his primary plans, the Lord will still accomplish his work through someone else and other plans that are just as perfect! "*There is a river, whose streams shall make glad the city of God, the holy place of the tabernacle of the Most High. God is in the midst of her, she shall not be moved.*"[243] God is always in the midst of his plans and purposes and because of this, we, his people, with our eyes fixed on Jesus, shall not be moved either!

Chapter 50

The Work of the Lord

The Lord has revealed our righteousness. Come and let
us declare in Zion the work of the Lord our God.

—Jeremiah 51:10

We continued to work as faithfully as we could through our classes, the church, and our dealings within the community. Implementing a lot of visitation to those who did not come to church very often, or at all, it helped to increase our Sabbath attendance. I had a burden on my heart for the small church, and the more I spoke with the Lord about that burden, the more I believed we were supposed to be doing more! I often felt like we were being defeated by Satan if we were not putting into place some kind of outreach during our last few months. Praying more fervently, God gave me a vision of how we could lift that burden. If we could not hold meetings for the people to attend, then we could take the lessons to them by distributing evangelistic literature! I thought, "Surely the Hong Kong Conference and/or the Adventist College could supply us with literature if we would distribute it!"

In gathering information about the mail service, I discovered that in Macau, it was not against the law to put anything in someone's residential mailbox without postage. It seemed like a wonderful avenue for a literature ministry. We could start using the church on Sabbath afternoons to process the lessons and handle the distribution. All we needed was the literature. I asked our pastor to inquire at the conference and college Evangelism Departments to see if they would provide us with the literature. However, they declined, saying their budgets were too tight.

We then prayed about where we could get the literature in the Cantonese dialect, and it then came to my mind that the East Asia Committee probably had an abundance of literature and lessons on various Bible subjects since their primary purpose was to spread the gospel through Mainland China via radio programs, Bible studies, and health seminars. I telephoned Pastor John Ash and told him about our plans and asked him if it would be possible for us to obtain some literature from the committee. He liked our idea but told me they happened to be very low on literature because they had started updating theirs and had allowed their supply to run down as they prepared to print the new stock. He encouraged me to come over and see what they had on hand and if we thought we could use any of it. Plus, we could talk with others in the office about what they were planning to print (they had their own printing presses) and possibly put in an order while we were there.

Giving us what they could spare, it amounted to almost five thousand pieces of single Bible studies. Thankful for that, we went back to Macau encouraged, but yet this burden would not leave my heart, knowing that a few thousand Bible studies would be gone in no time at all. I kept praying and appealing to the Lord, and one day, I asked Him, "What do you want me to do, Lord? I will do whatever you say, but at the present, I do not understand what that is! I do not speak the language, and whatever you want us to do, we will need funds to pay for the outreach!" I was willing to write some lessons from the sermons Dr. Bascom had sent me, but I would then need someone to translate them into Cantonese. I asked the pastor, but he was unwilling. As I prayed more, the Lord spoke to me and said, "Use your students."

At first, I could not fathom finding any students who could speak and read English well enough to do the translation or be willing to do so! There were no Christian students in my advanced English classes, but then Jesus impressed me to ask them anyway. So the next evening in my advanced class, I told them we were planning on distributing some literature in the community, but not knowing the language, we needed some help. Not going into the details about what kind of literature it was, I did say it was free and would be distributed on a regular basis, covering a variety of subjects, and we wanted to get started right away. I added this would be a very good way to enhance their study of English, and I asked if any of them would be interested in assisting us.

All of them showed very little interest, but one, probably the most open-minded, and who spoke and read English the best. She started smiling and waving her hand vigorously! I was totally shocked, but it was obvious the Holy Spirit was at work again.

Like many students, she had chosen an English name, and hers was Bobo. Bobo was a full-time college student at the University of Macau in the daytime while taking our classes several nights per week, and she was thrilled to begin helping her English teacher with the literature translation!

I asked Bobo and anyone else that was interested, to stay a few minutes after class, and I would discuss more of the details about the project. She was the only one to stay, and I told her these translations were going to be free Bible lessons. Bobo was a Buddhist like most of the others, and she had shown no interest in reading the Bible, but she was very open to the fact that her teacher wanted to share with her people some free lessons about what he believed and what he understood the Bible to teach.

She thought this was not only a nice gesture toward her people but a wonderful opportunity to increase her understanding of the English language. Of course, I was elated because it was the Lord who told me to ask my students, and here was one, that I must admit, I would never have dreamed she would be interested in helping, but she was extremely happy to have the opportunity!

The Lord had clearly answered my prayers and solved the first two challenges of this ministry, so now I asked him where we would find the money to pay for the paper and all the copying that had to be done? I knew our pastor was not going to allow us to use the school's copy machine unless we paid for the expenses. As I figured the cost of the paper and toner, I found out the cost would be considerable, compared to the school's tiny budget. I wondered, "Would the Lord also provide the necessary funds?" There was no reason to doubt that he would since he was leading every step of the way.

After praying about the funds for three days, a letter arrived from a friend named Harry, at Southern College. Enclosed with his letter was a love offering, which I am sure was a sacrificial gift. He was no longer a student but was working full-time at the Grounds Department. Harry was about six years older than me, single, and was extremely frugal with his income, always open to the Lord about using the funds he had to help the Lord's cause. Harry was one of the students that befriended me early on after I arrived at Southern, and we became close as we lived in the same apartments and worked together at the Grounds Department. In fact, Harry had encouraged us to accept the call to China if the Lord opened the door.

We had not been in contact with him since arriving in Macau because he moved off campus, took another job, and we did not have a forwarding address for him. We had no idea that Jesus had impressed Harry that we needed funds for an outreach project before I had taken the problem to the Lord! We knew from experience that it took at least ten days to receive mail from the US and sometimes longer. Yet three days after I had been praying about the need for money, we got a letter from Harry, and in that letter, he tells us he had been praying for us, and he felt led by the Lord that we needed some money for a special project! He had no idea what our project was, but he had checked his reserve evangelism fund and sent us the money order for the balance! Of course, the price of the paper and the toner cost much less in Macau than they would have in the US, so this made the $150 a great windfall with which to start our Fai Chi Kei outreach.

Two weeks later, needing some more funds, we received another letter from a friend, retired US Army Chaplain, Carl Holden of the Ringgold, Georgia, church. Linda and I had worked at and attended Ringgold during our last year at Southern, and we came to know and love Chaplain Holden, who had encouraged us so much. In his letter, he explained how he had been praying for us since before we left the US and, just like Harry, was impressed to send us some money for an outreach project. He had no idea how much we needed or what it was for but said we should use the money however we felt led by the Lord. And just like Harry, at that point in time, we had not been in contact with him or anyone that knew him.

Within three weeks' time, we had received enough money to pay for many reams of paper and plenty of toner for the copy machine! Together, with the help of Bobo, we were able to begin translating the literature we wanted to distribute, knowing God was truly working behind the scenes to help us with his evangelistic project!

All along, I had been telling our pastor what we were praying and what the Lord was impressing me to do, but the pastor said it would be too time-consuming, and he had too much to do; however, when he began seeing the extraordinary answers to prayer concerning this project, it made quite an impression on him. His attitude changed, and he began to take part in the effort. This is a clear, real-life illustration of how important it is that we tell others about the Lord answering our prayers and blessing us as our experiences may encourage them in their Christian walk or like me before meeting Jesus on the highway in Georgia. Louise's prompting about prayer eventually led me to begin praying, and look what has happened since I did! It also demonstrates something that is often said, but not often, truly believed, and that is, this work of salvation is not our work. We have no power to accomplish this work. It is the work of the Lord, and he, out of the graciousness of his heart of love, simply allows us to participate. When we accept God's free gift of salvation, a fountain of eternal life is placed within us, and Jesus allows his *living water* to flow from his fountain, for others to drink! Not too many years after I was born into the dead river of this life, like all people, my heart became hard as rock. Yet over time, Jesus kept sending his messengers with a hammer of love to keep striking my hard heart with his truth. And like the rock in the wilderness, the work was done by the Lord, and *he...split the rock, and the waters gushed out.*[244]

Chapter 51

The Church in Macau

Create in me a clean heart, O God, and renew a steadfast spirit within me. Do not cast me away from your presence, and do not take your Holy Spirit from me. Restore to me the joy of your salvation, and uphold me by your generous Spirit. Then I will teach transgressors your ways, and sinners shall be converted to you.

—Psalm 51:10–13

There is another inspiring story from Macau that needs to be told, and it is about the Filipino members and one in particular named Johnny Gumbuk who had been in this Portuguese colony for at least six years. Like so many Filipinos who had come to Hong Kong and Macau, Johnny was there because of the better standard of living and the higher wages they could earn there, compared to their own country. Many of them possessed college degrees, yet they would come and work nonprofessional jobs, banding together and living in extremely cramped circumstances. It was amazing to see the sacrifices these people would endure just to send 80 percent of their earnings back to the Philippines, usually to support a dozen or more relatives who had little or no income. Johnny was supporting twenty-four family members! These hardworking people would make these sacrifices for many years.

Johnny had been a Seventh-day Adventist Christian most of his life. He was in his early thirties, married, with six children, the oldest being ten. Because of his higher education, he was blessed to obtain a job in an office of the Portuguese government still governing Macau. He lived in an apartment of no more than five hundred square feet, slightly larger than ours, and he shared these quarters with fourteen other Filipino adults and several children.

Entering the apartment and taking two steps brought you squarely against the first of many makeshift partitions. These partitions were usually made out of cardboard boxes or by hanging wires and ropes on which to put scrap cloth and curtains. There was one small bathroom and a kitchen. They all helped one another with caring for the children, cooking, and other chores. They washed their clothes in the bathtub and the bathroom and kitchen sinks while hanging them on clotheslines on the back porch to dry. Some worked at night and some during the day, and all of them slept the best they could in between. Johnny was hoping to save enough to bring his wife and children to Macau to live. Subrenting his apartment enabled him to save a little each month toward that goal.

These working immigrants were almost at the mercy of their employers, the majority of whom were Chinese or Portuguese people. Approximately 80 percent worked as domestic workers, babysitters, gardeners, or construction laborers, and they had to endure quite a lot of persecution. As I came to better understand the circumstances that most of them lived and worked in, I would have to equate their situations with those of African Americans during the 1940s through the 1960s in the US. The Portuguese and the Chinese looked at these immigrants as people who came and had taken up jobs that their family members and friends possibly could have secured. I could not help but wonder, though, why their relatives and friends were not already hired to work those jobs before most of the Filipinos arrived. Yet, in most cases, the Filipinos were willing to put up with all kinds of horrendous conditions to have some steady income. Perhaps the Portuguese and Chinese family and friends were not as willing to work these jobs as the Filipinos were.

Through the years, to gain promotions with better benefits and greater pay, Johnny had allowed the circumstances of daily life to almost totally erode his spiritual life. When he first came to Macau, he was a regular attendee at church, and people were glad to have him there. As time went on, he was instrumental in finding several other Filipino Adventists and bringing them to church, but through the years, Johnny began to compromise his relationship with the Lord more and more. By the time we came to Macau, he and several of the other Filipino members had conceded their faith and participation so much that the little church was struggling to stay alive. Eventually, the pastor and the church began to make compromises to keep Johnny and the other Filipinos participating! They had been the main participants and financial contributors. They had the largest incomes, and although they were not rich by any means, the money they put in the tithe envelopes and offering plate was substantially more than what the Chinese members had to contribute. So of course, the pastor wanted to keep up their attendance, and he changed the services to Sabbath afternoons.

About a year and a half before we arrived, Johnny had received a substantial promotion, and he was required to work Sabbath mornings. As a natural leader to his countrymen who had joined the church, Johnny was the one from whom they took their lead. As he compromised more, they followed his example, and at that point, none of them was attending church at all, and it seemed as if the small church would dry up and die.

That is when the pastor made the concession to stop holding Sabbath School and church service on Sabbath mornings and move them to Sabbath afternoons at 2:00 p.m. to entice Johnny back to church after his morning duties. The pastor figured that if he could get Johnny back, then the other Filipinos would come back as well. This arrangement appeared to alleviate the overall problem of church attendance for a while. But as time went on, with increased compromises against the conscience, the conscience struggles less and less until, finally, there comes a point in time where it surrenders that particular part of one's spiritual conviction. This is how we found the church when we came to Macau. Sabbath School and church service were held on Sabbath afternoon, and still, very few people came to church.

After talking with the pastor enough to understand how the church came to be in that condition, I asked him to start a weekly visitation program, taking me to meet the different members and others who used to attend once in a while. I told him we should try this to see if we could encourage some or all back to church, and he agreed. This did help attendance for a while, and then the pastor and I started giving the sermon on alternating Sabbaths and continuing to visit when someone was absent. This, too, seemed to help the attendance because, after a few weeks, more folks had returned on a regular basis. I think the fact of an American being there piqued their curiosity, but whatever it was, God was blessing, except for the two weeks we were gone for R and R; attendance went down considerably.

The pastor and I had several lengthy conversations about the church's compromise and afternoon services because I was under more and more conviction this state of affairs did not have to be. I had seen Jesus work enough in my own young experience to know he is capable of solving any situation if only his people would enter it in faith! I felt there had been too much compromise, and while the pastor was certainly my senior pastor there and experienced in his particular position, I also knew that God had us there for the purpose of building relationships in the school and edifying the church. If we were not going to hold evangelistic meetings, we were at least going to do all we could to contribute to the spiritual revival of that church!

This meant that some members would have to be confronted with the truth so the Holy Spirit's conviction could begin moving upon the hearts of those who were not living according to the light they had and being the witnesses for God's cause that he wanted them to be! But the pastor did not want me preaching and teaching too strong. Neither did he want me saying too much when we visited the backslidden members. I told him I was not going to beat people over the head with the Scriptures or their sins, but I respectfully let him know that I was not going to run from pointing out the error! In a loving way, I would attempt to build relationships with these members and encourage them to do what Jesus wanted them to do.

As I began to preach and teach the Three Angel's Messages and the English Sabbath School lessons, combined with our visitation, I determined to let the people know that the Lord loved them and we loved them, but there was no way they could be a witness for Jesus and his truth by living as they were living. We encouraged them at every opportunity to live for Jesus!

Quite honestly, I sometimes wondered if there was any positive heart effect taking place although we saw the attendance gradually get better and better. I am sure that having the Australians helped a lot. Coral, Jenny, and Coralie made friends with the members by accompanying some of them to their homes after services or to restaurants with us after Sabbath. And of course, Coral playing the piano for the services also enhanced the spiritual atmosphere, which before then they did not have because no one could play the piano. Spending most every Sabbath with us, worshipping and socializing with our members became a major part of what God used to help strengthen and revitalize the little Macau church.

What was going on with Johnny behind the scenes was truly amazing, though we did not realize it for a good while, except seeing him attend more. Eventually, as all the Filipinos started attending regularly, Johnny was about to take a huge step. He had saved enough money and was going to bring his wife and six children to live in Macau. This was going to bring additional pressure on him to maintain his employment. It was not a matter of sending money back home to aid in the immediate family's support, but once they were with him, all their needs would immediately fall on him. Should they need to visit a doctor or dentist, Johnny had to pay for it. There would be no government welfare assistance like they had back home. As his children would begin school, he would have to purchase costly uniforms for them rather than sending them in everyday clothes. Plus, if he sent them to public school, there were not any English-speaking teachers for the Filipinos; thus, he would have to pay for Catholic School. While bringing his family to Macau would be good for our church, it would increase his personal responsibilities and pressure.

One week in our Sabbath School discussion, we were talking about the importance of taking a stand on the conviction that God places on our hearts. We had a good attendance that day, and all the Filipinos were there. All of them agreed we are to accept that conviction and allow God's love and grace to change and order our lives, thus becoming better representatives of Jesus. They understood this was very important because Jesus is preparing us as his last day people, to stand in the time of trouble as his witnesses to the universe.

This discussion was certainly one of the most heartfelt we had in our class, and Johnny raised his hand to speak. He began by telling us how the Holy Spirit had been placing tremendous conviction on him during the prior three months. Looking at me, he paused and then said, "This has been primarily because of your preaching. I listen closely as you share experiences that you have had in your life, and I know from the way you relate them to us that they were truthful and difficult experiences. They brought you to the point of having to make some difficult decisions that would affect you and your family's lives in a tremendous way. Well, the Holy Spirit has been bringing conviction upon me that I need to take some steps to straighten out my relationship with the Lord. I have come to the conclusion that I should begin taking those steps right away."

Tears came to his eyes! Momentarily, he stopped talking, and there were a lot of smiles and additional tears from those listening. The class stopped and had prayer for Johnny, asking God for more strength and courage and thanking Jesus for all that he had already given.

At the end of the next week's Sabbath School class, Johnny asked us to hold him and his family up in prayer during the following week. Monday, he had an appointment to talk with his boss and let him know that he had recommitted his life to the Lord as a Seventh-day Adventist Christian and that he would no longer be able to work on Saturdays. He would gladly explain to his employer that Saturday was the Lord's Day, according to the Bible, and he was going to follow his convictions about worshipping Jesus on the Sabbath, even if it meant losing his job and being deported. Of course, this was a greater step of faith than normal because he also supported so many other family members back home. Additionally, his boss was a Portuguese Catholic! So we immediately had a special prayer for Johnny and asked him to please keep us informed. After class, I also asked him if he would like me to meet with his boss too. He said it would not be necessary but thanked me just the same.

Much to Johnny's surprise, his boss was extremely impressed with his worker's conviction, and because he was so earnest and had always been such a good employee, the Holy Spirit had gone before him preparing his boss's heart. He told Johnny that he would gladly give him Saturdays off for worship, and he was also going to promote Johnny to a new position that had just been created, which meant a substantial raise in pay with no overtime, involving weekend or weeknight work! By Sabbath, we had spread the word around to most members that God had answered our prayers in a wonderful way, and we were continually praising the Lord as we came together for worship with Johnny and our God!

From that point on, until we left Macau, Johnny Gumbuk was on fire for Jesus! One month before we left, he brought his family from the Philippines, and what a delightful family they were! His wife's name was Leonie, and all six of his beautiful children had names beginning with the letter *J*. Finally, the Adventist Church in Macau had a children's Sabbath School!

Johnny's work ethic reminded me of something I heard Gus Nichols say a number of times, and it proved to bring remarkable results for Johnny and his family. Gus believed that "every Seventh-day Adventist Christian should be the best employee where he or she worked." I agree!

During our last month in Macau, Johnny tried to get a position as a literature evangelist with the Hong Kong/Macau Conference so he could sell Christian books in the evenings, but something prevented him from obtaining a work permit. However, he decided that since he could not do this officially, he would work in an unofficial capacity, just like our church was underground in Macau. He bought the books and literature himself, and two or three nights per week, he would take several of his children to visit other Filipinos whom he had previously built a friendship with, and he would share his love for Jesus with them. After telling his testimony, he would introduce them to the literature and books published by our denomination. If they could afford to buy a book, he would sell it to them, but if they could not afford to buy, he would leave them something to read about Jesus and his love for them, paying for the booklet himself.

I have often thought about Johnny's experience through the years since then and have used his story as a sermon illustration many times. Here was a young man who loved the Lord Jesus but because of trouble and poverty in his home country was compelled to move to a foreign land to obtain work. Separated from his family and friends for a number of years, he basically had to start his life over again, in difficult circumstances with virtually little support from his local church. Receiving very little encouragement to stay faithful to God and lacking the spiritual maturity himself to stay true, over time, he just walked away from practicing what he knew to be biblical truth. Little did he realize the effect his backsliding would have, not only on him but also on his family and his local church. His choices had even led his pastor to begin compromising his faith to accommodate Johnny's work schedule on the Sabbath.

Johnny was living on the other side of the world from us, and God could have used anyone to help him, but Jesus decided, for whatever reason, to use us. I have often told people since then that God loves us so much that he will send someone from the other side of the world, or even an angel from heaven if need be, to help us know and understand his truth,[245] if we are willing to listen! Johnny's story is a perfect object lesson of how God's love is ever seeking an honest heart to take up residence in, as well as the lengths the Lord will go to save anyone even though we should not have to look anywhere else but at the cross. Yet because we are not present at Calvary, oftentimes, the cross of Christ seems too far away for us to see the ultimate expression of God's love for us. And then the Lord somehow magnifies Calvary into a more personal view. Johnny's story is one of those modern-day views for me, and I give all the praise and glory to the Lord Jesus for this wonderful picture of His saving grace! For as Jesus said, *"If anyone thirsts, let him come to me and drink. He who believes in me, as the Scripture has said, out of his heart will flow rivers of living water."*[246]

Chapter 52

Epilogue

As previously mentioned, it had been decided that our language school was closing early and we were to return home in May. Though we could extend our stay, I could not seem to accept this situation as final. I kept telling Linda, "I do not understand why the Lord would do all that he has done to bring us here and then allow the school to close early and send us home! I cannot bring myself to accept this as his will, but I am determined to know if it is!"

Diligently pursuing Jesus in prayer about our circumstances, I continued asking him to make it plain for my simple mind to understand. In fact, since becoming a Christian, praying to know God's will early on, I started using a request that seemed to come quite naturally to me. "Lord, please make your will plain to me, even if you have to hit me over the head with your spiritual two-by-four!" Besides keeping things going at the school so we could finish the full term or even add a summer term, I was thinking that I would need to update the conferences to which I had applied for a church district. I certainly did not want them to forget about us. Linda and I decided to contact them immediately with our current information.

As the time drew closer for our departure, we decided to take our souvenirs and most of our luggage to the Hong Kong College early, where we would store them at Ruth and Charles's house until our departure, thus making the last day of travel from Macau to Hong Kong a lot easier. It also gave us the opportunity to spend a couple of extra weekends with our friends at the college.

Those friends were concerned about the circumstances of the English language school closing early just to get rid of us. Some reasoned, since the school was to reopen as a grammar school, there might be other positions available for us if we wanted to extend our stay in Macau. But as they inquired, they could not find out from anyone if there would be any such opportunities available, so we set our minds on finishing the work at the church and school.

During our final two weeks, I continued to plead with the Lord about making it clear that his will was for us to return to the US at that time…and Jesus did! After our last weekend in Hong Kong, needing to tie up a few loose ends and to collect our carry-on bags for our flight home, we exited the ferry and came into the customs processing section in Macau. To save some time, each of us went through different turnstiles being checked in by different customs agents, and then we were to meet on the other side. During the last nine months of going and coming to the border, there was never a problem or delay. In fact, most of the time, the agents never said a word. They looked at our passports, then at us, stamped our passports, and waved us through. But this time, after looking at our passports, they asked each of us why we had been coming and going so much during the last year. When we hesitated to give a reason, they took us to an interrogation room, and there, another agent began to question us in broken English!

He asked, "You come Macau to gamble?"

I answered, "No. We do not gamble."

Then he asked, "You come work?"

I hesitantly replied, "Well…we come to Macau to teach English."

He did not understand me and was about to ask another question when the pastor was brought in by another agent, and he immediately began interceding for us. I was so glad that he did because I did not want to tell the agent that we were working as employees of the college for fear of getting the school or church into trouble. I thought as long as I could keep from saying that, even if later on they decided to investigate further, they would find that we technically were not employees of anyone in Macau. We were actually employees of the Hong Kong Adventist College, though we lived most of the time in the colony and taught English for the college.

However, the customs agent persisted in asking me, "What you do in Macau when not teach?"

The pastor tried to answer for me, but the agent yelled at him, "Be quiet! Let him answer," pointing at me.

I thought to myself, *Well, if I have to answer, I might as well spill the beans rather than accidentally misstate the truth or appear to be trying to lie.*

Before I could answer, the agent repeated his question with higher volume and some anger.

Matching his volume but with a big smile, I said, "We are preaching and teaching the gospel of Jesus Christ!" And in my peripheral vision, I could see our pastor squirming in his seat like he did not know what to do—get up and run or roll over and play dead! The agent was looking at me as though he thought I was a lunatic, and then his expression turned into the angriest face you could imagine! Standing up abruptly, he began rattling off all kinds of things in Chinese, and I thought he was going to explode and we were going to jail! Even if no one could understand what he was saying, you would have thought we did something terribly wrong!

It was then the pastor was able to break into the conversation, interceding on our behalf while tactfully trying to avoid all possible problems for the school and the church. There was a lengthy heated discussion, and finally, after things settled down, the agent told the pastor they were going to deport us. Thinking quickly, the pastor pointed out that, in fact, we had plane tickets for a certain date only a week in the future and he assured the agent we were about to leave Macau. So the agent wanted to see our tickets to verify what the pastor told him, and the pastor let the agent know that the tickets were in his school safe. So the interrogation ended with the agent taking custody of our passports until we brought him our airplane tickets the next day.

In the morning, I returned to customs with our tickets, and seeing the pastor had told him the truth and the tickets were nonrefundable, plus it was only six more days before we were scheduled to leave, customs was satisfied. Walking back to our apartment, I could not help but have a good laugh at myself, seeing clearly that God had answered our prayers, letting me know it was his will for us to leave Macau. On the final day, as we were leaving, the customs agent stamped our passports, and we were officially deported from Macau.

While traveling back to the United States and visiting with our families in South Carolina, we were assured that we had a ministerial position waiting on us and we would begin pastoring in the Gulf States Conference. Waiting on the conference to return from their camp meeting gave us several weeks to visit with our families in Columbia. In June 1992, we had an interview with the Gulf States administrators in Montgomery, Alabama, and at the end of that meeting, they formally invited us to begin pastoring in the Dothan, Alabama/Bonifay and Marianna, Florida, District.

After serving that district for three and a half years, we were called to St. Elmo/Fairhope, Alabama, District, just outside Mobile, and one year later, I was ordained at our conference camp meeting at Bass Memorial Academy in Lumberton, Mississippi, on May 25, 1996. It was during our service in that district that the conference committee asked me to accept the position of director of the Adventist Community Services/Disaster Response for Alabama, Mississippi, and Northwest Florida. Due to a burden for that ministry being on my heart because of the personal experience I gained during Tropical Storm Alberto in my Dothan district, I accepted the position.

Serving St. Elmo/Fairhope District for six years, we accepted a call to pastor in the Jacksonville/Kinston, North Carolina, District of the Carolina Conference. Jacksonville is home to the United States Marine Corps Expeditionary Forces at Camp Lejeune and the Marine Corps Air Station New River. From October 1971 through October 1973, I served a two-year enlistment in the Marine Corps, part of which was infantry training at Camp Lejeune and permanent duty as an administrative clerk for the depot chaplain's office at Parris Island, South Carolina. This prior service aided me well in the Jacksonville church and community since 75 percent of my congregation was active duty or retired Marine Corps and Navy personnel.

After six and a half years in the Jacksonville/Kinston District, I was medically retired and moved back to Columbia, South Carolina, where Linda and Brenda had been taking care of Linda's ailing mother for the last year I served in North Carolina. In January 2012, Linda's mother died, and as her "personal pastor" (as Agnes used to call me), I held her funeral service, and we laid her to rest next to Linda's deceased stepfather.

On Easter Sunday of 2018, my mother had a stroke, and after a long stay in the hospital and rehabilitation facility, we brought her home for hospice where she died. Assisting her pastor, we laid Mother to rest in August 2018.

Dad's kidneys and heart were already failing him since 2014. When Mother died, Dad elected not to go on dialysis, and our immediate family cared for him through his hospice until he died in December 2018. I held his graveside service, and we laid him to rest beside Mother.

Several years before, we had moved about twenty-five miles northwest of Columbia to the small town of Chapin. After transferring our membership from the Columbia First Seventh-day Adventist Church, we are now members of the recently formed Irmo Seventh-day Adventist Fellowship.

Looking back over my journey down the river of life, only part of it has been told. Yet hopefully enough has been recounted to help anyone see how each person born into this life is faced with the same basic voyage. It is an excursion that may appear to be totally different for each of us. Some enter this river in what appears to be the soundest, most comfortable boat there is, gently ferrying them with all the supplies and equipment needed for a complete and successful trip. While others seem to be tossed into the swift cold water, barely grabbing hold of the first limb that comes floating along, not knowing how far it will take us or if it will even hold us afloat. In either case, we do not realize that before long, there will be the first in a series of deadly rapids that will force us to begin making decisions about the outcome of our lives, attempting to negotiate the treacherous gaps between the rocks and boulders or to paddle to the shore and portage around the danger.

With each decision we make and the result it brings, we can gain knowledge and wisdom or not learn anything and just suffer the consequences. We can record in our travel journal a victory for future reference or undergo the loss, forgetting it immediately, being doomed to repeat it again. The further down this dead river we travel, the greater dangers and deceptions we encounter. Anywhere along this journey, the unexpected can cut it short, but even if we manage to make it to the end, for us, it will be the end forever! This is why it is named Dead River!

The most important decision anyone can make on their journey is to realize they are partaking of a river of death and desire to receive the *living water* that only Jesus can give and then ask for it! In the apostle John's vision in the book of Revelation, an elder told him, "*For the Lamb who is in the midst of the throne will shepherd them and lead them to living fountains of waters.*"[247] The Lord who sat on the throne said to John, "*I will give of the fountain of the water of life freely to him who thirsts.*"[248] "*And he* [the angel] *showed me a pure river of water of life, clear as crystal, proceeding from the throne of God and of the Lamb.*"[249] "*I, Jesus, have sent my angel to testify to you these things… I am the Root and the Offspring of David, the Bright and Morning Star. 'And the Spirit and the bride* [the New Jerusalem full of the people of God] *say, "Come!" And let him who hears say, "Come!" And let him who thirsts come. Whoever desires, let him take the water of life freely.*"[250] Are you thirsty for true, lifegiving water? Then *come* and accept Jesus and all His truth! But don't be deceived! You cannot accept Jesus without accepting all of his truth! You have nothing to lose by doing so! And just like me, you can escape from the dead river of this life to partake of Jesus, the *truth*, the *living water*, as he prepares you for his eternal kingdom!

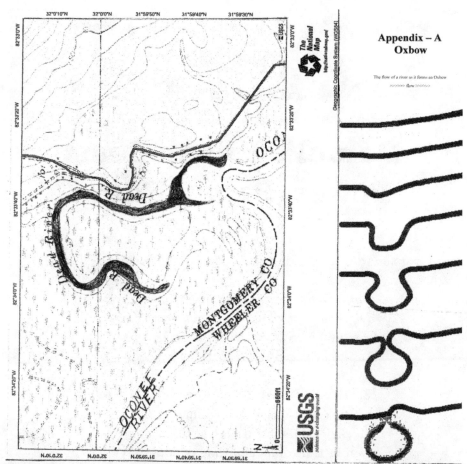

The flow of a river as it forms an Oxbow
>>>>>> flow >>>>>>

The Oconee River is the eastern fork and for almost thirty miles north serves as the present day western border for Montgomery County. As "water seeks its own level across the surface of the globe", so the Oconee cut its original channel, meandering down through the Georgia piedmont and onto the coastal plain, forming an "oxbow" over its last two miles before the forks.

Prior to 1741, the oxbow was open and the river flowed freely through it. But for several years, heavy winter rains fell in north and central Georgia, causing the southern Oconee to flood its surrounding lowlands. By the summer of 1742, extra silt and debris had completely closed off the entrance to the oxbow, while cutting a more direct route to the junction below. In a very short time, beavers dammed up the southern end, cutting the old channel off completely from the Oconee River, leaving a mile and a half of water that became known as "Dead River", due to the lack of current in the oxbow.

Appendix B1

Daniel's Fourth Beast Power, Pagan Rome

(Compare with Revelation's First Beast Power, Rome; pp. 300, 301)

1. *"Came up from the sea"* (Dan. 7:3).
2. *"Different from all the beasts that were before it"* (Dan. 7:7). Combining civil and religious powers, history shows this beast to be pagan Rome that slowly became papal Rome.
3. *The first was like a lion* (Babylon); the second was *like a bear* (Media-Persia); the third was *like a leopard* (Greece); that preceded the fourth (Rome) (Dan. 7:4–7, 2:31–43, 1:1, 8:20–21). Chapter 8 had different symbols but were given in same order and time periods of symbols in previous chapters.
4. *"And it had ten horns."* *"The ten horns are ten kings who shall arise from this kingdom"* (the fourth; 7:7, 24).
5. The fourth beast was *"dreadful and terrible, exceedingly strong. It had huge iron teeth; it was devouring, breaking in pieces, and trampling the residue with its feet... And shall devour the whole earth"* (7:7, 23).

One Little Horn Comes Up among the Ten Horns on the Fourth Beast

6. *"And another shall arise after them,"* coming up shortly after pagan Rome's fall (7:24).

7. *"In this horn, were eyes like the eyes of a man"* (7:8).

8. *"Three of the first horns were plucked out by the roots… And shall subdue three kings"* (7:8, 24).

9. He had *"a mouth speaking pompous words…" "against The Most High"* (7:8, 25).

10. He *"shall persecute the saints of the Most High"* (7:25).

11. He controlled the saints *"for a time and times and half a time."* (7:25).

12. He *"shall intend to change times and law"* (7:25).

13. -------

14. -------

15. Daniel *"watched till the beast was slain, and its body destroyed and given to the burning flame"* (7:11; 2 Thess. 2:3–12; Rev. 19:20 and 20:10).

Appendix B1

Revelation's First Beast Power, Rome

(Compare with Daniel's Fourth Beast Power, Rome; pp. 298, 299)

1. *"Rising up out of the sea"* (13:1, 17:15).
2. *"Seven heads and ten horns and on his horns ten crowns"* (13:1). This power begins as a civil power, then combines with religious power.
3. *"Was like a leopard...a bear...a lion"* (13:2). It carries over some characteristics from the previous three world kingdoms.
4. *"Having seven heads and ten horns...and on his heads a blasphemous name"* (13:1). The first beast is civil or pagan Rome beginning its change to papal Rome.
5. *"And all the world marveled and followed the beast...authority was given him over every tribe, tongue, and nation"* (13:3, 7).
6. ------
7. ------
8. ------
9. *"And he was given a mouth speaking great things and blasphemies..."* (13:5). *"Then he opened his mouth in blasphemy against God, to blaspheme his name, his tabernacle, and those who dwell in heaven"* (13:6).
10. *"It was granted to him to make war with the saints and to overcome them"* (13:7).

11. *"He was given authority to continue for forty-two months"* (13:5). From 538 BC to AD 1798.

12. ------

13. *"So they worshiped the dragon"* (Satan) *"who gave him* [beast] *his power, his throne, and great authority"* (13:4, 2). This entity made to appear as Christianity comes from the devil.

14. *"And I saw one of his heads as if it had been mortally wounded, and his deadly wound was healed"* (13:3).

15. ------

16. *"Let him who has understanding calculate the number of the beast, for it is the number of a man: His number is 666"* (13:18).

Appendix B2

Unwanted Mark

The Papacy, which arose on the ruins of the Roman Empire, differed from all previous forms of Roman power in that it was an ecclesiastical despotism claiming universal dominion over both spiritual and temporal affairs, especially the former. It was a union of church and state, frequently with the church dominate.

The Pope, who calls himself 'King' and 'Pontifex Maximus,' is Caesar's successor.[251]

All the names which are attributed to Christ in Scripture, implying his supremacy over the church, are also attributed to the Pope.[252]

For thou art the shepherd, thou art the physician, thou art the director, thou art the husbandman; finally thou art another God on earth.[253]

The decision of the Pope and the decision of God constitute one decision, just as the opinion of the Pope and his disciple[s] are the same. Since, therefore, an appeal is always taken from an inferior judge to a superior, as no one is greater than himself, so no appeal holds when made

from the Pope to God, because there is one consistory [a meeting place of the minds] of the Pope
himself and of God himself, of which consistory
of the Pope himself is the key-bearer and the
doorkeeper. Therefore, no one can appeal from
the Pope to God, as no one can enter into the
consistory of God without the mediation of the
Pope, who is the key-bearer and the doorkeeper
of the consistory of eternal life; and as no one can
appeal to himself, so no one can appeal from the
Pope to God, because there is one decision and
one curia [court] of God and of the Pope.[254]

All the faithful of Christ must believe that
the Holy Apostolic See [official seat of power
taught to be founded by the Apostle Peter in
Rome] and the Roman Pontiff [the pope] possesses the primacy over the whole world, and
that the Roman Pontiff is the successor of blessed
Peter, Prince of the Apostles, and is true vicar of
Christ, and the head of the whole church, and
father and teacher of all Christians, and that full
power was given him in blessed Peter to rule,
feed, and govern the universal Church by Jesus
Christ our Lord...[255]

We teach and define that it is a dogma
divinely revealed; that the Roman Pontiff, when
he speaks *ex cathedra*, that is, when in the discharge of the office of Pastor and Doctor of all
Christians, by virtue of his supreme apostolic
authority, he defines a doctrine regarding faith or
morals to be held by the universal church, by the
divine assistance promised to him in blessed Peter,
is possessed of that infallibility with which the
divine Redeemer willed that his church should be

endowed for defining doctrine regarding faith or morals: and that therefore such definitions of the Roman pontiff are irreformable of themselves, and not from the consent of the church.[256]

The church has persecuted. Only a tyro [novice] in church history will deny that... One hundred and fifty years after Constantine, the Donatists were persecuted, and sometimes put to death... Protestants were persecuted in France and Spain with the full approval of the church authorities. We have always defended the persecution of the Huguenots, and the Spanish Inquisition. Wherever and whenever there is honest Catholicity [a state of being Catholic], there will be a clear distinction drawn between truth and error, and Catholicity and all forms of error. When she [the Catholic Church] thinks it good to use physical force, she will use it.[257]

On August 24, 1527, Roman Catholics in France, by prearranged plan, under Jesuit influence, murdered seventy thousand Protestants with the space of two months. The Pope rejoiced when he heard the news of the successful outcome.[258]

From the birth of Popery...to the present time, it is estimated by careful and creditable historians, that more than fifty millions of the human family, have been slaughtered for the crime of heresy by popish persecutors--an average of more than forty thousand religious murders for every year for the existence of Popery. Of course the average number of victims yearly was vastly greater during those gloomy years when

Popery was in her glory and reigned Despot of the World; and it has been much less since the power of the popes has diminished to tyrannize over the nations, and to compel the princes of the earth, by the terrors of excommunication, interdiction, and deposition, to butcher their heretical subjects.[259]

The number of the victims of the Inquisition in Spain, is given in *The History of the Inquisition in Spain*, by Llorente, formerly secretary of the Inquisition, pp. 206–208 [Catholic]. This authority acknowledges that more than 300,000 suffered persecution in Spain alone, of whom 31,912 died in the flames. Millions more were slain for their faith throughout Europe.[260]

Under a legate of the pope, their peaceful valleys were invaded, "scaffolds were erected, the instruments of torture rent anew the victims of superstition; then re-appeared all the frightful apparatus which the ministers of tyranny could carry with them. Thousands of heretics, old men, women, and children were hung, quartered, broken upon the wheel, or burned alive and their property confiscated for the benefit of the king and the Holy See.

The Waldenses were burned; they were cast into damp and horrid dungeons; they were smothered in mountain caverns, mothers and babes, old men and women together; they were sent out into exile in the winter night unclothed and unfed, to climb the snowy mountains; they were hurled over the rocks; their houses and lands were taken from them; their children were stolen to be indoctrinated with the religion which they abhorred. Rapacious [plundering] individuals were sent among them to strip them of their property, to persecute and exterminate them. Thousands of heretics or Waldenses [those who believed the Bible or portions of it and not exactly what the pope and his priests told them to believe], old men, women, and children were hung, quartered, or broken upon the wheel, or burned alive and their property confiscated for the benefit of the king and Holy See."[261]

Appendix: p.731. 44. The civil authority may interfere in matters relating to Religion, morality, and spiritual government. Hence it has control over the instructions for the guidance of consciences issued, conformably with their mission, by the pastors of the Church. Further, it possesses power to decree, in the matter of administrating the Divine Sacraments, as to the dispositions necessary for their reception. (Allocution "In Consistorial," November 1, 1850; Allocution "Maxima quidem," June 9, 1862)

[On March 12, 2000, Pope John Paul II admitted the papacy had killed these Christians and others who would not agree to follow the papacy's interpretations of Scripture and commands—so much for the papacy's infallibility and its claim to never err!]

Appendix B3

Boastful Quotations of the Antichrist

Sunday is a Catholic institution, and its claims to observance can be defended only on Catholic principles... From beginning to end of Scripture there is not a single passage that warrants the transfer of weekly public worship from the last day of the week to the first. (*Catholic Press* [Sydney, Australia], Aug. 25, 1900)

You may read the Bible from Genesis to Revelation, and you will not find a single line authorizing the sanctification of Sunday. The Scriptures enforce the religious observance of Saturday, a day which we never sanctify. (Cardinal Gibbons, in *The Faith of Our Fathers*, edition 1892, p. 111)

Question: Which is the Sabbath day?
Answer: Saturday is the Sabbath day.
Question: Why do we observe Sunday instead of Saturday?
Answer: We observe Sunday instead of Saturday because the Catholic Church, in the Council of Laodicea (AD 336), transferred the solemnity from Saturday to Sunday. (*The*

Convert's Catechism of Catholic Doctrine by Rev. Peter Geiermann, CSSR, p. 50, third edition, 1913, a work which received the "apostolic blessing" of Pope Pius X, January 25, 1910)

Question: How prove you that the church hath power to command feasts and holy days?

Answer: By the very act of changing the Sabbath into Sunday, which Protestants allow of; And therefore they fondly contradict themselves by keeping Sunday strictly, and breaking most other feast days commanded by the same church. (*Abridgement of Christian Doctrine* by Rev. Henry Tuberville, DD, of Douay College, France [1649], p. 58)

Question: Have you any other way of proving that the church has power to institute festivals of precept?

Answer: Had she not such power, she could not have done that in which all modern religionists agree with her,—she could not have substituted the observance of Sunday, the first day of the week, for the observance of Saturday, the seventh day, a change for which there is no Scriptural authority. (*A Doctrinal Catechism*, by Rev. Stephen Keenan, p. 174)

The Church is above the Bible; and this transference of Sabbath observance from Saturday to Sunday is proof positive of that fact. (*The Catholic Record*, London, Ontario, Canada, Sept. 1, 1923)

How could anyone dare attempt to change God's holy day?

Answer: 'We ask the papacy, Did you really change Sabbath to Sunday?' ' It replies, Yes we did. It is our symbol, or mark, of authority and power.' 'We ask, How could you even think of doing that?' It's a pertinent question. But the question the papacy officially asks Protestants is even more pertinent. Please read it carefully:

You will tell me that Saturday was the Jewish Sabbath, but that the Christian Sabbath has been changed to Sunday. Changed! But by whom? Who has authority to change an express commandment of Almighty God? When God has spoken and said, "Thou shalt keep holy the seventh day," who shall dare to say, "Nay, thou mayest work and do all manner of worldly business on the seventh day; but thou shalt keep holy the first day in its stead?" This is a most important question, which I know not how you can answer. You are a Protestant and profess to go by the Bible and the Bible only; and yet in so important a matter as the observance of one day in seven as a holy day, you go against the plain letter of the Bible, and put another day in the place of that day which the Bible has commanded. The command to keep holy the seventh day is one of the Ten Commandments; you believe that the other nine are still binding; who gave you authority to tamper with the fourth? If you are consistent with your own principles, if you really follow the Bible and the Bible only, you ought to be able to produce some portion of the New Testament in which this fourth commandment is expressly altered. (Library of Christian Doctrine: *Why Don't You Keep Holy the Sabbath-Day?*, London: Burns and Oates, Ltd., pp. 3, 4).

Appendix B4

Numerical Values in the Latin Papal Title

Numerical Values of Roman Numerals

Vicarius	*Filii*	*Dei*
V = 5	F = 0	D = 500
I = 1	I = 1	E = 0
C = 100	L = 50	I = 1
A = 0	I = 1	_____
R = 0	I = 1	501
I = 1	_____	
U = 5	53	
S = 0		

_____

112

$$
\begin{array}{r}
112 \\
53 \\
501 \\
\hline
666 \\
======
\end{array}
$$

Here is wisdom. Let him, who has understanding calculate the number of the beast, for it is the number of a man: his number is 666. (Revelation 13:18)

Appendix C

Main Differences between Catholic and Protestant Doctrines

Note: These are certainly not all the doctrinal differences between the Catholic Church and Protestantism; however, these are the major differences that brought about the Protestant Reformation and the Catholic Counterreformation.

1. *Authority for doctrine.* "The issue of Sola Scriptura...versus Scripture plus tradition is perhaps the fundamental difference between Roman Catholicism and Protestantism..." The Catholic Church "does not derive her certainty about all revealed truths from the holy Scriptures alone. Both Scripture and tradition must be accepted and honored with equal sentiments of devotion and reverence." Protestants profess to use Sola Scriptura; the Scripture as the only authority for doctrine.[262]

2. *Salvation and grace.* "The Roman Catholic Church views justification as a process, dependent on the grace you receive by participating in the Church." "Protestants often express the idea that salvation is by faith alone, through grace alone, in Christ alone. This assertion views justification as a specific point upon which God declares that you

are righteous—a point where you enter into the Christian life."

"You're saved by grace,"[263] however, the Catholic Church views grace as something that can be earned by participating in any of the rites of the church called sacraments. These are baptism, confirmation, the Eucharist (receiving the bread and wine of Communion), extreme unction, holy orders, matrimony, and penance.[264] However, Protestants see grace as totally a gift of God that cannot be earned.

3. *The Eucharist* (Communion service). "When it comes to the Eucharist,...the Roman Catholic Church holds to the doctrine of transubstantiation—the idea that the edible ritual elements [bread and wine] used during the mass literally become the body and blood of Christ."[265] (Each time is technically another sacrifice of Jesus. [See Hebrews 10:4, 10–12].) "*For it is not possible that the blood of bulls and of goats could take away sins...we have been sanctified through the offering of the body of Jesus Christ once for all. And every priest stands ministering daily and offering repeatedly the same sacrifices, which can never take away sins. But this Man [Jesus], after he had offered one sacrifice for sins forever, sat down on the right hand of God.*"

"In contrast, some Protestants, like Lutherans, hold to [a] perspective called consubstantiation, where Jesus' body and blood are seen as coexisting with the bread and the wine." Martin Luther explained this as "united, but not changed."[266]

"Other Protestants hold to the memorial view—the idea that you're commemorating Jesus' death." This view holds the bread and wine as "symbols"; holy but only symbolic of Christ's body and blood.[267]

4. *Justification.* "Catholics view justification as both a point and a process... Protestants view justification as the moment God declares that a guilty person is righteous [objectively] because of what Christ has done. Sanctification, then, is

the process of being made [subjectively] more righteous throughout your life."[268]

5. *The priesthood.* Catholics believe "that which was reserved just for the magisterium" [ordained clergy], "the ability to bind and loose to forgive and withhold forgiveness through the sacraments and through penance and such, that was just the role of the priest."

    "Protestants see the church as having a horizontal structure" with the "idea of the priesthood of all believers: ...we have the ability to confess our sins to one another, pronounce forgiveness as the Scripture says."[269]

6. *The veneration of the saints and the Virgin Mary.* "Roman Catholics see veneration, not as praying to the Saints and the Virgin Mary, but as praying through them. This is seen as similar to asking a brother or sister in Christ to pray for you." They also believe these "departed saints are also 'able to spill over their overabundance of grace to us'." "The Virgin Mary is seen as 'the mother of our Lord, and there-fore...she is the mother of the church. He [Jesus] is the Creator of all things. So she is the mother of angels. She is the mother of humanity'..." She has also been called "the Queen of Heaven."[270] The remains of saints are considered holy relics and are venerated. Protestants find no biblical authority for this.

7. *Sinless human beings.* The Catholic Church, "through the dogma of the immaculate conception of the Virgin Mary, denies that God in Christ dwelt in the same flesh as fallen man has...,"[271] which elevates her spiritual standing to that of Jesus, making both sinless. It also maintains Mary's virginity after Jesus's birth, throughout her entire life. Protestants hold Mary to be a sinner, and therefore need-ing a Savior like all mankind, with the exception of Christ.

8. *The pope.* The pope is the head of the institution known as "the papacy, which arose on the ruins of the Roman Empire, differed from all previous forms of Roman power, in that it was an ecclesiastical despotism claiming universal

dominion over both spiritual and temporal affairs, especially the former. It was a union of church and state, with the church dominant."[272] The pope is considered the heir of Christ through an unbroken chain of individuals leading back to the apostle Peter holding and exercising all the authorities of both.

9. *Celibacy.* In the Catholic Church, priests are called from men who practice celibacy as answering a call to consecrate themselves totally to the Lord and to humanity.[273] For nuns, it is basically the same. Protestantism does not have nuns nor believes in this obligation for priests or pastors.

10. *Sacraments.* The seven solemn sacraments in the Roman Catholic Church are the following: baptism, confirmation, the Eucharist, extreme unction, holy orders, matrimony, and penance. These sacraments are means of spreading God's grace throughout the church.[274]

Most Protestant churches utilize two of these: baptism and the Lord's Supper (Eucharist). They are considered symbolic rites, participated in by faith, through which God delivers the Gospel.

Notes

1 This was some of the first instructions given to my Homiletics 101 class by our professor, Dr. Douglas Bennett, in September, 1989, at Southern College (presently Southern Adventist University).
2 Romans 1:16, 2:4, 5:8.
3 Romans 5:1; 1 Peter 1:8.
4 Romans 6:23.
5 Psalm 34:8.
6 Jeremiah 2:13, 17:13; John 4:10.
7 John 4:14.
8 Isaiah 12:3.
9 Romans 2:4.
10 Ibid.
11 Ty Gibson, Abandon Ship? (Nampa, Idaho: Pacific Press Publishing Assn., 1997), 57.
12 John 4:10–26.
13 USGS Water Science School, The Water In You: Water and the Human Body, paragraph 1. (Reston, VA. 20192, May 22, 2019), https://www.usgs.gov/special-topics/water-science-school/science/water-you-water-and-human-body.
14 Colossians 1:16–17: "For by Him [the Son of God] all things were created that are in heaven and that are on earth, visible and invisible, whether thrones or dominions or principalities or powers. All things were created through Him and for Him. And He is before all things, and in Him all things consist."
15 Romans 1:19, 20:"Because what may be known of God is manifest in them, for God has shown it to them. For since the creation of the world His invisible attributes are clearly seen, being understood by the things that are made, even His eternal power and Godhead, so that they are without excuse."
16 Hebrews 11:6: "But without faith it is impossible to please Him, for he who comes to God must believe that He is, and that He is a rewarder of those who diligently seek Him." Matthew 17:20: "So Jesus said to them, "'…if you have faith as a mustard seed, you will say to this mountain, "Move from here to there," and it will move; and nothing will be impossible for you'."
17 Deism is the belief in a god that created the world but since then has not participated in its management by natural or supernatural means.

[18] Theistic evolution is the belief that God began with creation and then allowed evolution to further develop that creation since, with His periodic adjustments.

[19] "Henry Pool of Warren County Georgia, 1759–1852," (an article written for the descendants of Henry Pool in the family tree records of Tommy L. Poole, p. 49). Rev. Henry R. Pool, a Baptist minister, was born there in 1759 and, as a young man, married an English woman, Susan Racklett. Soon after their wedding, Henry and Susan sailed for America. They "resided for a short time in Massachusetts and then in Connecticut, later moving to Virginia, into the Carolinas, and finally settling in..." what is now, Warren County, Georgia.

Henry served as a private with Georgia's troops of the Continental Army during the American Revolution. Many years after his death, in an article written in The Atlanta Journal, his last two living daughters said they could "remember being told stories by their mother of their father's bravery in skirmishes fought near Augusta, Georgia; Kettle Creek and Briar Creek, in Georgia; at Camden, King's Mountain, and Cowpens, South Carolina, and at Yorktown, Virginia, where he witnessed the surrender of 'the British Army to General George Washington.'" Other records indicate he also fought at "Cheraw, South Carolina, Charlotte, Guilford's Court House, and Hillsboro, North Carolina."

[20] Godbold was later changed to Godbolt.

[21] Around 1735, John Godbold came from England to settle in the northeastern part of South Carolina known as Mars Bluff. In 1765, his son, James, received a grant of land on which the town of Marion, South Carolina, was built. Around 1852, James's great-nephew, James D. Godbold, moved his wife and twelve children to North Florida, where some of their descendants continue to live and farm today.

[22] My maternal great-great-grandfather, Benjamin Law, was born about 1847, near Live Oak, Florida. On November 30, 1865, he married Nancy Connell, and while raising their (ten) children, they earned a living on their North-Central Florida farm. Their eldest, James Walter Law, was born in the Live Oak, Florida, community on December 20, 1877, and later became my maternal great-grandfather.

[23] Acts 17:24, 26.

[24] Psalm 18:16.

[25] Jethro Kloss, Back to Eden, New Revised Edition (Loma Linda, CA: Back to Eden Publishing Co., 2nd ed., 1988), 623. (Twin Lakes WI: Lotus Press, PO Box 325, 53181. 2009. www.Lotuspress.com).

[26] Genesis 7:11.

[27] Deuteronomy 11:11.

[28] Robert Scott Davis, Jr., A History of Montgomery County, Georgia to 1918 (Roswell, GA: W. H. Wolfe Assoc.'s Historical Publications Division, 1992), 5–6. (Original Montgomery County Historical Society, Inc. Dwight Newsome-CEO, Penny Moses-Sec.)

[29] Ibid, p. 1.

30 Ibid., pp. 1–2.

31 USGS Water Science School, Streamflow and the Water Cycle: "Watersheds and Rivers," paragraph 1. (Reston, VA 20192, June 12, 2019). https://www.usgs.gov/special-topics/water-science-school/science/streamflow-and-water-cycle.

32 1 Samuel 11:7. "An oxbow lake starts as a meander, or curve, in the river. Sediment builds up on one side of the curve, called deposition. The river becomes curvier until the river ultimately loops back onto itself. The river then flows along the straighter path and forms a cutoff. Once the river completes this shortcut, the curve becomes a separate body of water, called an oxbow lake." https://eros.usgs.gov/image-gallery/earthshot/oxbow-lakes. (See appendix A, p. 150.)

33 Hebrews 13:5.

34 Hebrews 4:12.

35 Common expression about how quick someone would start physically fighting.

36 Slang term for recruit basic training in the military services.

37 Slang term for overweight recruit in US Marine Corps Basic Training.

38 Another common expression used to describe a US Marine that has completed basic training with a perfect physical ratio of height to weight.

39 Common expression used to explain a person's weight naked.

40 "The Fabulous Moolah." Mary Lillian Ellison, also known as Lillian Ellisor, was the NWA Women's World Champion Professional wrestler, trainer, and booking agent for other female wrestlers for twenty-eight years, retiring in 2004. She died on November 2, 2007. https://en.wikipedia.org/wiki/The_Fabulous_Moolah.

41 "Donna Christanello." Mary Donna Alfonsi was a female professional wrestler who was trained by and worked for the Fabulous Moolah. She and her frequent ring partner, Toni Rose, won and held the NWA Women's World Tag Team Championship, off and on for a number of years. She retired in 1991 and died on August 21, 2011. (She was also billed as Donna Christianello and Donna Christantello, the name she went by on her official website.) https://en.wikipedia.org/wiki/Donna_Christanello.

42 "Jar Head" is a nickname given to US Marines because of the hair cut worn by many. It looks like someone put a large jar upside down on your head and then shaved the outer portion leaving a small round island of short hair, about an eighth to a quarter of an inch, on top.

43 The White House, office of the press secretary, "President Bush Signs Second Chance Act of 2007—H. R. 1593". (Washington, DC: released April 9, 2008), georgewbush-whitehouse.archives.gov/news/releases/2008/04/20080409-15.html. (Originally stated in the 2004 State of the Union Address by George W. Bush, forty-third President of the United States.)

44 Jonathan A. Czuba et al., Sediment Load from Major Rivers into Puget Sound and its Adjacent Waters, USGS Fact Sheet 2011-3083. (Reston, VA 20192: September 8, 2011). https://pubs.usgs.gov/fs/2011/3083/.

45 2 Thessalonians 2:10–12.

46 "What then? Are we better than they [are Jews better than non-Jews]? Not at all. For we have previously charged both Jews and Greeks that they are all under sin. As it is written: 'There is none righteous, no, not one; There is none who understands; There is none who seeks after God. They have all turned aside; they have together become unprofitable; There is none who does good, no, not one. Their throat is an open tomb; With their tongues they have practiced deceit; The poison of asps is under their lips; Whose mouth is full of cursing and bitterness. Their feet are swift to shed blood; Destruction and misery are in their ways; And the way of peace they have not known. There is no fear of God before their eyes.'"

47 Jeremiah 13:23.

48 Isaiah 1:18–19.

49 John 1:7–9.

50 Job 14:4.

51 John 4:10.

52 2 Timothy 2:15.

53 Isaiah 28:9–10.

54 Psalm 119:98–99.

55 John 4:10.

56 John 3:7.

57 Barrett, Kurian, Johnson, World Christian Encyclopedia (Oxford, England: Oxford Univ. Press, 2nd ed., 2001). "Estimated at least 33,000 denominations." (I asked Google, "What was the number of Christian denominations worldwide in 1982?" This was Google's answer and reference.)

58 2 Thessalonians 2:9–12.

59 Matthew 25:1–13; John 16:1-4; 2 Timothy 3:1–9; 2 Peter 2:1–22.

60 Matthew 4:4.

61 James 2:19–20.

62 John 4:10.

63 Revelation 2:7, 11; 3:5, 12, 21; 22:14.

64 3ABN is located in West Frankfort, Illinois.

65 Frances D. Nichol, ed., Seventh-day Adventist Bible Commentary, vol. 7, "Philippians to Revelation" (Rev. 1:1) "Revelation" (Washington, DC: Review and Herald Publishing Assn., 20039-0555, 1980), 728.

66 Revelation Seminars—A Bible Prophecy Adventure: "Revelation The Open Book Lesson RS-001, (Keene, Texas: Seminars Unlimited, 1983), 4.

67 Ibid, 5.

68 Ibid., 4–5. Quoted from Taylor G. Bunch's quote on these pages.

69 Ibid., 7–8.

70 Daniel 9:24–27.

71 Revelation Seminars—A Bible Prophecy Adventure: "The 'Star' of the Drama of Revelation," Lesson RS002, last note. (Keene, Texas: Seminars Unlimited,

DEAD RIVER TO LIVING WATER

983), 5. "70 weeks times 7 [the number of days in a week] equals 490 days." Ezekiel 4:6, "each day for a year." And Numbers 14:34, "each day for a year…"

72 Ibid, 5. Last note: "Since one prophetic day equals one literal year, then 490 prophetic days equal 490 literal years."

73 In AD 27, after sixty-nine prophetic weeks—483 literal years—Jesus was anointed for his ministry as Messiah at his baptism by the Holy Spirit in the form of a dove (Daniel 9:24; Matthew 3:13–17). In the middle of the seventieth prophetic week, three and a half years after his baptismal anointing, he was crucified, cut off, in AD 31 (Daniel 9:26–27; Matthew 27:33–50). (Literal years: 483 + 3 1/2 + 3 1/2 = 490.)

74 Revelation Seminars—A Bible Prophecy Adventure: "The 'Star' of the Drama of Revelation," Lesson RS-002, p. 6, second note. "(Ezra 7:7, 12, 13) points out that the decree [for starting this time prophecy] was issued in the seventh year of King Artaxerxes. History shows that the king began to reign in 464 BC. His seventh year would thus be 457 BC…in the fall of the year." Lesson RS-014, p. 7, second note and chart/question no. 15, "It is most sobering to realize that the judgment has been in session in heaven for well over 100 years" (Keene, Texas: Seminars Unlimited, 1983), (Acts 7:59, 8:4).

75 Daniel 9:24.

76 Acts 7:59.

77 Daniel 9:27.

78 Titus 1:2; Hebrews 6:18.

79 Hebrews 12:29, "For our God is a consuming fire." Exodus 24:17; 1 John 1:5.

80 Revelation 19:20; 20:9, 10, 14, 15.

81 Jeremiah 25:30–33; Acts 1:9–11; 1 Thessalonians 4:16, 17; Revelation 1:7.

82 Isaiah 40:10, 62:11; Revelation 22:12.

83 "Let there be lights in the firmament of the heavens…let them be for signs and seasons, and for days and years" (Genesis 1:14). (Joel 2:30, 31) "And I will show wonders in the heavens and the earth: blood and fire and pillars of smoke. The sun shall be turned into darkness, and the moon into blood, before the coming of the great and awesome day of the Lord" (v. 32). (Matthew 24:3–14) "When He opened the sixth seal…there was a great earthquake; and the sun became black as sackcloth of hair, and the moon became like blood. And the stars of heaven fell to the earth…" (Revelation 6:12–13). The Lisbon, Portugal Earthquake, Nov. 1, 1755. "The greater part of that city was destroyed with the loss of between 60,000 and 90,000 lives. The sea rose to fifty feet above its ordinary level. The great earthquake of 1755, extended over a tract of at least four millions of square miles… It pervaded the greater portions of the continents of Europe, Africa, and America" (Revelation Seminars—A Bible Prophecy Adventure: "The Four Horsemen of Revelation," Lesson RS-009, Exhibit no. 2, p. 1.) (Robert Sears, "Wonders of the World In Nature, Art, and Mind" [New York: published by Robert Sears, 1843], pp. 50, 58.) The Dark Day was May 19, 1780. It was not an eclipse but a day of supernatural darkness.

President Timothy Dwight of Yale said, "Candles were lighted in many houses. The birds were silent, and disappeared. The fowls retired to roost. It was the general opinion that the day of judgment was at hand." Bible Readings for the Home, "Signs of the Times," question no. 9, notes, paragraph 1, (Mountain View, CA: Pacific Press Publishing Assn., 1944), 320. (Quoted in Connecticut Historical Collections, compiled by John Warner Barber, (2nd ed., New Haven: Durrie & Peck and J. W. Barber, 1836), 403). The Moon Turned Red as Blood. "The moon which was at its full, had the appearance of blood." This happened the night of the Dark Day, May 19, 1780. Revelation Seminars—A Bible Prophecy Adventure: "The Four Horsemen of Revelation," Lesson RS-009, Exhibit no. 2, p. 2. (Edwin M. Stone, History of Beverly, Massachusetts, Civil and Ecclesiastical (Boston: James Monroe and Company, 1843).

The Stars Fall from Heaven on November 13, 1833. "The morning of November 13,1833, was rendered memorable by an exhibition of the phenomenon called shooting stars, which was probably more extensive and magnificent than any similar one hitherto recorded... Probably no celestial phenomenon has ever occurred in this country, since its first settlement..." Revelation Seminars—A Bible Prophecy Adventure: "The Four Horsemen of Revelation," Lesson RS-009, Exhibit no. 2, p. 2. (E. H. Hitchcock, "On the Meteors," American Journal of Science and Arts 25, no. 2 (New Haven: January 2, 1834): 354).

Frederick Douglass, My Bondage and My Freedom, p. 186. "I witnessed this gorgeous spectacle, and was struck with awe... I had read that the stars shall fall from heaven, and they were now falling." Bible Readings for the Home, "Signs of the Times," question no. 10, notes, paragraph 1, (Mountain View, CA: Pacific Press Publishing Assn., 1944), 322. (New York and Auburn: Miller, Orton, and Mulligan, 1855), 186. Written by Geoffrey C. Ward and Dayton Duncan; directed by Stephen Ives; executive producer, Ken Burns; narrated by Peter Coyote, The West. (Florentine Films, Walpole, New Hampshire and WETA-TV/PBS, Arlington, Virginia). This dramatic/documentary film premiered on PBS, September 15, 1996. It tells of a Lakota Sioux tribal historian named Lone Dog who kept records through the years of what happened to his people by painting the various events on buffalo hides. In the early morning hours of November 13, 1833, he and his people were awakened by the great light of falling stars that filled the dark prairie sky.

[84] Matthew 24:5; Revelation 13:1–10.
[85] Isaiah 14:12–15; Ezekiel 28:2, 12–19; Matthew 4:1–10; Revelation 12:3, 4, 7–9; 20:1–3, 7, 8, 10.
[86] Genesis 3:1–5; Revelation 12:4–17, 20:7–10.
[87] John 14:15; Revelation 12:17, 14:12, 22:14.
[88] Acts 1:11, 7:49.
[89] Revelation 21:2.
[90] Revelation 21:1.

91 Matthew 24:30–31.
92 John 5:28–29; Revelation 20:5–6.
93 John 5:28–29; Revelation 22:12.
94 1 Thessalonians 4:16–17.
95 Revelation 20:7–10, 14.
96 Revelation 20:5–7.
97 1 Corinthians 6:2; Revelation 20:4.
98 Nahum 1:9.
99 Jeremiah 4:23–26; Revelation 20:5.
100 2 Thessalonians 1:7–9; Revelation 20:1–2, 5.
101 Revelation 21:1–4.
102 Revelation 20:11–15.
103 Isaiah 65:17; Revelation 21:1–2, 5.
104 Titus 1:2.
105 John 17:17.
106 Psalm 34:8.
107 Isaiah 44:3.
108 Revelation 22:1.
109 Revelation Seminars—A Bible Prophecy Adventure: "Revelation's Seal of God," Lesson RS010, (Keene, Texas: Seminars Unlimited, 1983), 1.
110 Revelation 14:9, 11.
111 Revelation Seminars—A Bible Prophecy Adventure: "Revelation's Seal of God," Lesson RS010, (Keene, Texas: Seminars Unlimited, 1983), 2.
112 Ibid, 2–3.
113 Office of the South Carolina Secretary of State, Notary Public Online Manual, "Seals and Stamps" (Columbia, South Carolina: 2014), §26-1-5(18), p. 4. "A seal or stamp must include the notary's name, The words 'notary public' and the words 'State of South Carolina." https://sos.sc.gov/sites/default/files/Documents/Mail%20In%20Service/Notaries/South%20Carolina%20Notary%20Public%20Reference%20Manual.pdf.
114 Revelation Seminars—A Bible Prophecy Adventure: "Revelation's Seal of God," Lesson RS010, (Keene, Texas: Seminars Unlimited, 1983), 2–3.
115 Exodus 20:8–11.
116 Revelation Seminars—Bible Prophecy Adventure: "Revelation's Seal of God," Lesson RS010, pp. 2–3, (Keene, Texas: Seminars Unlimited, 1983). Exodus 31:17; Ezekiel 20:12; Revelation 4:10–11.
117 Ezekiel 20:20.
118 Ibid, 20:12.
119 Revelation 12:17, 14:12.
120 Revelation Seminars—A Bible Prophecy Adventure: "Revelation's Seal of God," Lesson RS010, (Keene, Texas: Seminars Unlimited, 1983), 3.
121 Revelation 7:3.
122 Ibid.

123 Revelation Seminars—A Bible Prophecy Adventure: "Revelation's Seal of God," Lesson RS010, (Keene, Texas: Seminars Unlimited, 1983), 3.
124 Genesis 2:1–4.
125 Revelation Seminars—A Bible Prophecy Adventure: "Revelation's Seal of God," Lesson RS010, (Keene, Texas: Seminars Unlimited, 1983), 4.
126 Genesis 2:2–3.
127 Psalm 23:2–3.
128 Genesis 2:2–3.
129 Exodus 16:1, 23–30.
130 Luke 4:16.
131 Matthew 24:20.
132 Matthew 28:1; Mark 16:2, 9; Luke 24:1; John 20:1, 19; Acts 20:7; 1 Corinthians 16:2.
133 Isaiah 66:23.
134 Psalm 1:3.
135 Ezekiel 20:20.
136 Romans 3:20.
137 Galatians 3:23–24.
138 Colossians 2:17.
139 Ibid, verse 16.
140 Matthew 22:37, 39; John 14:15.
141 James 2:17–22.
142 Bible Readings for the Home, "The Change of the Sabbath," question no. 16, (Mountain View, California: Pacific Press Publishing Assn., 1944), 443. Dr. Augustus Neander, The History of the Christian Religion and Church, translated by Henry John Rose (London: Gilbert and Rivington, 1841), 186. "Opposition to Judaism introduced the particular festival of Sunday very early, indeed, into the place of the Sabbath... The festival of Sunday, like all other festivals, was always only a human ordinance, and it was far from the intentions of the apostles to establish a divine command in this respect, far from them, and from the early apostolic church, to transfer the laws of Sabbath to Sunday. Perhaps at the end of the second century a false application of this kind had begun to take place; for men appear by that time to have considered laboring on Sunday as a sin." Encyclopedia Britannica, 9th ed., article "Sunday," (New York: Henry G. Allen and Company, January 1, 1888). "The earliest recognition of the observance of Sunday as a legal duty is a constitution of Constantine in AD 321, enacting that all courts of justice, inhabitants of towns, and workshops were to be at rest on Sunday (venerabili die Solis), with an exception in favor of those engaged in agricultural labor." [Sunday was the venerable day of the sun, the day of the week that pagan religions worshiped the Sun god].
143 I saw again, in my mind's eye, the article in my ninth-grade world history book, about Emperor Constantine's law changing the seventh-day Sabbath to the first day of the week.

144 Bible Readings for the Home, question no. 16, (Mountain View, CA: Pacific Press Publishing Assn., 1944), 443. (Dr. Augustus Neander, The History of the Christian Religion and Church, translated by Henry John Rose. (London: Gilbert and Rivington, 1841), 186.

145 "Sunday, 'Christian Usage paragraph 7. https://en.wikipedia.org/wiki/Sunday. "In 363, Canon 29 of the Council of Laodicea prohibited observance of the Jewish Sabbath (Saturday), and encouraged Christians to work on the Saturday and rest on the Lord's Day (Sunday). The fact that the canon had to be issued at all is an indication that adoption of Constantine's decree of 321 was still not universal, not even among Christians. It also indicates that Jews were observing the Sabbath on the Saturday." [Council of Laodicea, "Canon 29," (Rome: Catholic Church, AD 363)]

146 Revelation 14:9.

147 Revelation 7:2.

148 Galatians 5:5.

149 2 Corinthians 10:5

150 Galatians 5:5.

151 Galatians 2:16.

152 Pastor Doug Batchelor, Amazing Facts Topical Study Guide No. 6, "Written in Stone, 'Your Questions Answered'", no. 3, 2011. Holy Bible—Prophecy Study Edition, NKJV (Nashville, TN., Thomas Nelson Publishing, 1982), 1537.

153 2 Timothy 1:9.

154 Romans 3:20.

155 Acts 4:12.

156 Titus 3:7.

157 Hebrews 11:39, 2.

158 Pastor Doug Batchelor, Amazing Facts Topical Study Guide No. 6, Written in Stone, "Your Questions Answered", no. 3, 2011. Holy Bible—Prophecy Study Edition, NKJV. (Nashville, TN., Thomas Nelson Publishing, 1982), 1537.

159 Romans 3:20.

160 Galatians 3:24.

161 Romans 3:20.

162 Romans 10:4; Ephesians 2:14–15; Colossians 2:14, 16–17.

163 Francis D. Nichol, ed., S. D. A. Bible Commentary, vol. 6, (Romans 1:5), "Obedience to the faith." (Washington, DC: Review and Herald Publishing Assn., 1956), 472–473. (Romans 16:26

164 Ibid, (Romans 10:4), "Christ is the end of the law." (Washington, DC: Review and Herald Publishing Assn., 1956), 596.

165 Ibid, vol. 7, (James 2:14), "Faith." (Washington, DC: Review and Herald Publishing Assn., 1956), 520.

166 Colossians 2:16–17.

167 Francis D. Nichol, ed., S. D. A. Bible Commentary, vol. 7, (Colossians 2:17), "Which are a shadow." (Washington, DC: Review and Herald Publishing

Assn., 1956), 206. Annual Sabbaths, e.g., Day of Atonement, Pentecost, Feast of Tabernacles, etc., were shadows or types of the reality (Christ) to come in the various ministries of Jesus that was fulfilled according to the Messianic prophecies. In Romans 5:14, Paul describes Adam as a type or figure (tupos) of him who was to come, Christ. However, nowhere in Scripture is the seventh-day Sabbath described as a shadow or type (tupos). Only ceremonial/annual Sabbaths were considered shadows or types.

[168] 1 John 2:18, 22; 2 John 7; 2 Thessalonians 2:3, 8; Revelation 13.

[169] Matthew 24:15.

[170] Francis D. Nichol, ed., S. D. A. Bible Commentary, vol. 4, "Introduction to Daniel," 3. Historical Setting, paragraph 2. (Washington, DC: Review and Herald Publishing Assn., 1956), 745. Vol. 7, "Introduction to Revelation", 3. Historical Setting, paragraph 1. (Washington, DC: Review and Herald Publishing Assn., 1956), 720.

[171] Daniel 2:31–35, 37–45.

[172] Daniel 7:3–7.

[173] "Sunday," "Etymology," paragraph 3 and "Pagan correspondence," paragraph 1, https://en.wikipedia.org/wiki/Sunday.

[174] Ibid., "Christian Usage" paragraph 4. https://en.wikipedia.org/wiki/Sunday. "On 7 March 321, Constantine I, Rome's first Christian Emperor, decreed that Sunday would be observed as the Roman day of rest" (paragraph 5).[2] "On the venerable Day of the Sun let the magistrates and people residing in cities rest, and let all workshops be closed. In the country, however, persons engaged in agriculture may freely and lawfully continue their pursuits; because it often happens that another day is not so suitable for grain-sowing or vine-planting; lest by neglecting the proper moment for such operations the bounty of heaven should be lost'." Eviatar Zerubavel, The Seven Day Cycle: The History and Meaning of the Week (Chicago: University of Chicago Press, 1989), 45.) Philip Schaff, History of the Christian Church: Vol. II: From Constantine the Great to Gregory the Great AD 311–600 (New York: Charles Scribner, 1867), 380, note 1.

[175] Revelation 13:12.

[176] Revelation 13:5–6.

[177] "Heruli," "Intro," paragraph 2. https://en.wikipedia.org/wiki/Heruli, "From the late 4th century AD the Heruli were one of the peoples" dominated by the empire of Attila the Hun. "By 454…they established their own kingdom on the Middle Danube, and…also participated in successive conquests of Italy…with their last kingdom eventually dominated by Rome." "Religion," paragraph 2. "By the time of Justinian…many Heruli had become Arian Christians…[Emperor] Justinian appears to have pursued a policy of attempting to convert them to Chalcedonian Christianity." "Intro," paragraph 3. "The Heruli disappeared from history around the time of the conquest of Italy by the Lombards" (AD 568–570). Alexander Sarantis, "The Justinianic Herules," Florin Curta,

(ed.), Neglected Barbarians. (Turnhout, Belgium: Brepols Publishers, 2010), 361–372.

[178] "Ostrogoths," "Intro" paragraph 1. https://en.wikipedia.org/wiki/Ostrogoths "In the 5th century, they followed the Visigoths in creating one of the two great Gothic kingdoms within the Roman Empire... After the death of Attila and collapse of the Hunnic empire represented by the Battle of Nedao in 453, the Amal family of Theodoric the Great began to form their kingdom in Pannonia... In 493 Theodoric the Great established the Ostrogothic Kingdom of Italy... Following the death of Theodoric,...eventually tempting the Byzantine Emperor Justinian to declare war on the Ostrogoths in 535... The war lasted for almost 21 years and caused enormous damage across Italy, reducing the population of the peninsula. Any remaining Ostrogoths in Italy were absorbed into the Lombards [Italians], who established a kingdom in Italy in 568. "Gothic War and end of the Ostrogothic Kingdom." "The Gothic War between the Eastern Roman Empire and the Ostrogothic Kingdom was fought from 535 until 554 in Italy, Dalmatia, Sardinia, Sicily and Corsica...with... the apparent reconquest of Italy by the Byzantines. Their official religions were "Arian and Chalcedonian Christianity." https://en.wikipedia.org/wiki/Gothic_War (535-554), 1.5—"Gothic War and end of the Ostrogothic Kingdom (535–554)." https://en.wikipedia.org/wiki/Ostrogothic_Kingdom, Samuel Cohen, "Religious Diversity In Jonathan J. Arnold; M. Shane Bjornlie; Kristina Sessa (eds.), A Companion to Ostrogothic Italy, (Leiden, Boston: Brill Publishers, 2016), pp. 503–532.

[179] "Vandals," "Intro," paragraph 1. https://en.wikipedia.org/wiki/Vandals. "The Vandals were a Germanic people who first inhabited what is now southern Poland... By 439 they established a kingdom which included the Roman province of Africa as well as Sicily, Corsica, Sardinia, Malta and the Balearic Islands." "Sack of Rome, AD 455," paragraph 1. "After Attila the Hun's death, however, the Romans could afford to turn their attention back to the Vandals, who were in control of some of the richest lands of their former empire [para 2]. In an effort to bring the Vandals into the fold of the Empire, Valentinian III offered his daughter's hand in marriage to Genseric's son. Before this treaty could be carried out, however, politics again played a crucial part in the blunders of Rome. Petronius Maximus killed Valentinian III and claimed the Western throne. Diplomacy between the two factions broke down, and in 455 with a letter from the Empress Licinia Eudoxia, begging Genseric's son to rescue her, the Vandals took Rome, along with the Empress and her daughters Eudocia and Placidia." "Intro," paragraph 3. "Their kingdom collapsed in the Vandalic War of 533–34." "Turbulent End paragraph 3, "in 534 Gelimer surrendered to the Byzantine conqueror, ending the Kingdom of the Vandals..." Paragraph 4. "In the words of Roger Collins: 'The remaining Vandals were then shipped back to Constantinople to be absorbed into the imperial army'." "In March 534... Gelimer surrendered to Belisarius and accepted the Romans' offer of vast estates

in Galatia." "Pharas, chief of the Heruli, in a friendly letter to Gelimer, speaks of the Roman Emperor Justinian's offer if he will surrender. "That generous prince will grant you a rich inheritance of lands, a place in the senate, and the dignity of patrician:" Though offered the rank of a patrician, he refused it because he was not willing to change his Arian faith. Encyclopedia Britannica Online, retrieved 8 March 2014. Roger Collins, "Vandal Africa, 429–533" The Cambridge Ancient History—Late Antiquity: Empire and Successors, AD 425–600 (Cambridge Univ. Press, 2000), 124–126. https://en.wikipedia.org/wiki/Gelimer, paragraph 4. 4Edward Gibbon, Decline and Fall of the Roman Empire, chapter XLI: "Conquests of Justinian, Charact of Balisarius, Part II" (London: Strahan and Cadell, 1776–1788).

180 "Arianism," https://en.wikipedia.org/wiki/Arianism. "Arianism is a Christological doctrine attributed to Arius (c. AD 256–336), a Christian presbyter from Alexandria, Egypt. Arian theology holds that Jesus Christ is the Son of God, who was begotten by God the Father with the difference that the Son of God did not always exist but was begotten within time by God the Father, therefore Jesus was not co-eternal with God the Father."

181 Bible Readings for the Home, "Jesus Living In the Priest," Rev. P. Millet, S. J., (English translation by the Rt. Rev. Thomas Sebastian Byrne, D. D., Bishop of Nashville), (Mountain View, California: Pacific Press Publ., 1944), 220. (New York: Benziger Brothers, printers to the Holy Apostolic See, 1901), 23–24. "Should Jesus Christ come in person from heaven into a church to administer the sacrament of reconciliation [forgiveness of sins], and should He say unto a penitent, 'I absolve thee,' and should a priest sitting at His side in the tribunal of penance pronounce over a penitent the selfsame words, 'I absolve thee,' there is no question that in the latter case, as in the former, the penitent would be equally loosed from his sin."

182 Ibid., 219. "From the Civilta Cattolica," quoted in the 'Vatican Council,' March 18, 1871, by Leonard Woolsey Bacon. (American Tract Society edition), 220.

183 Ibid., 219. Prompta Bibliotheca, vol. 6, article, "Papa", ("The Pope"), Lucius Ferraris. (First published in Bologna, Italy: 1746, 26).

184 The Catholic Worship Service, "Mass in the Catholic Church," https://en.wikipedia.org/wiki/Mass_in_the_Catholic_Church.

185 Bible Readings for the Home, notes, paragraph 3, (Mountain View, California: Pacific Press Publ., 1944), 220. Dictates of Hildebrand (Dictatus papae) is a compilation of twenty-seven statements of powers of the pope. "Annals of Baronius," 1076, vol. XI, col. 506. See Gieseler's "Ecclesiastical History," third period, div. 3, par. 47, note 3; and Mosheim's "Ecclesiastical History," book 3, cen. 11, part 2, chap. 2, par. 9, note.

186 A Biblical Prophetic Year. https://en.wikipedia.org/wiki/Prophetic_Year#:~:text=In%20scripture%2C%20Prophetic%20Years%20of,messiah%20as%20per%20Daniel%209.

187 Daniel 7:25.

[188] Pastor Doug Batchelor, Amazing Facts Prophecy Study Guide 20, The Mark of the Beast, question no. 4, Holy Bible—Prophecy Study Edition, NKJV, (Nashville, TN: Thomas Nelson Publishing, 1982), 1631.

[189] Ibid.

[190] Bible Readings for the Home, question no. 9, notes, Augsburg Confession, Article XXVIII. (Mountain View, CA: Pacific Press Publ., 1944), 440. https:// elemunah.com/end-times-headlines/quotes-of-roman-catholic-persecution/.

[191] Bible Readings for the Home, question no. 8, notes, paragraph 2, lines 12–15. (Mountain View, California: Pacific Press Publ., 1944), 223.

[192] Frances D. Nichol, ed., S. D. A. Bible Commentary, vol.7, "Philippians to Revelation," (Rev. 13:3) "Was healed." (Washington, DC: Review and Herald Publishing Assn., 20039-0555, 1980), 817.

[193] Ibid.

[194] Sylibus on Revelation—RELB 426, "Vicarius Filii Dei—'Vicar Of The Son Of God'," intro and no. 2, (first time using this title for the Pope in "Donation of Constantine"), compiled by Dr. H. Douglas Bennett, (Collegedale, TN: School of Religion, Southern Adventist University [formerly Southern College], revised November 1988), 39–42. (Catholic Encyclopedia, vol. IV, "Vicar of Christ").

[195] Ibid, no. 3, p. 39.

[196] Ibid.

[197] Ibid, no. 4 and no. 5, p. 39.

[198] Ibid, no. 6, p. 39.

[199] Ibid, no. 7, p. 39.

[200] Ibid, paragraph 5, p. 42.

[201] Frances D. Nichol, ed., S. D. A. Bible Commentary, vol.7, "Philippians to Revelation," (Rev. 13:18) "Number of the beast." (Washington, DC: Review and Herald Publishing Assn., 20039-0555, 1980), 823.

[202] https://en.wikipedia.org/wiki/Roman_numerals, Roman Numerals, paragraph 1. (Gordon, Arthur E., Illustrated Introduction to Latin Epigraphy (Berkley: University of California Press, 1982), ISBN 0-520-05079-7).

[203] https://americasbesthistory.com/index.html, "Timeline," (Pottstown, PA). October 19, 1781, British forces surrender to American forces and their French allies at Yorktown, Virginia. September 3, 1783, John Adams and American delegation sign the Treaty of Paris officially ending the Revolutionary War between US and Britain. January 14, 1784, US Congress ratifies the Treaty of Paris. On March 4, 1789, the new American government was established under the US Constitution. February 1, 1790, the US Supreme Court convenes for first session. On March 4, 1791, Vermont becomes the 14th state. On May 17, 1792, the New York Stock Ex-change began. On October 13, 1792, the cornerstone of the Executive Mansion (called the White House since 1818) was laid. On September 18, 1793, the cornerstone of Capitol Building was laid. On July 10, 1797, the first US Navy ship was launched (USS United States). July 14, 1798, the Alien and Sedition Acts made it a federal crime to publish

malicious statements about the United States government and extended power to the president to control immigration plus imprison and deport aliens who oppose the government. As of the completion of these events, and others, the new nation of the United States of America had been established by 1798.

204 See the US Constitution's First Amendment that contains what is called the Establishment Clause, which declares what is known as a separation of church and state concerning freedom of religion.

205 Kitty van der Heijden and Alberto Pallecchi, "With 1.2 Billion Members, the Catholic Church Can Lead on Climate Action" (Washington, DC: World Resources Institute, July 26, 2018). https://www.wri.org/blog/2018/07/12.

206 Ephesians 1:13–14.

207 Isaiah 37:31–32; Revelation 12:17.

208 Psalm 27:5; Daniel 12:1.

209 Revelation 1:10.

210 Mark 2:27–28; Luke 6:5.

211 Genesis 2:2–3.

212 Isaiah 66:23.

213 Matthew 5:17–18.

214 Romans 3:20.

215 Romans 3:31.

216 Acts 5:29

217 Leviticus 23:3, 32; Jeremiah 17:21, 22.

218 Genesis 2:2, 3.

219 Ezekiel 46:3.

220 Proverbs 16:7.

221 Proverbs 11:14.

222 1 Kings 2:10 (KJV)

223 John 11:11.

224 John 11:14.

225 This man was misquoting 2 Corinthians 5:8, and additionally, like many Christians today, he was taking one misquoted or misunderstood verse and allowing it to outweigh dozens of other clearer verses on the same subject. These false doctrines are fooling many people, especially Christians who do not read their Bible carefully and should know better. They are setting themselves up to be eternally lost by trying to communicate with dead relatives, friends, and other saints! His weight of scriptural evidence was totally backward, and his mind was all but closed about reexamining what the weight of scriptural evidence actually said. In the same chapter, in verse 2, Paul says that "we groan earnestly desiring to be clothed with our habitation which is from heaven." What is the clothing he is talking about? He mentions it in verse 1, "a building from God, a house not made with hands, eternal in the heavens." The clothing he is talking about is the glorified body to be given us at the resurrection. When we die, we are not glorified then! It happens only at the second coming of Jesus.

In verse 2, he is telling us that he desires so much to obtain that new clothing that he groans for it! Then in verse 6, he admits knowing that "while we are at home in the body [the body we have now] we are absent from the Lord." Then in verse 8, he clearly says that he would "rather be absent from the body and to be present with the Lord." In other words, he would much rather skip the dying part (which leaves him sleeping in the grave until Jesus comes) and go directly to heaven! If any of us had the choice, we, too, would desire the same thing! We would rather not wait until Jesus comes to take us to heaven! We would all prefer to go to heaven as soon as we die. But that will not happen. We who die before Jesus returns will have to wait in the grave until the Resurrection Day, yet it will only seem like a moment of time has passed since we closed our eyes in death and are awakened by the trumpet sound and the voice of Jesus calling us back to life! The interpretation of going to heaven or hell at death is a false teaching that came from the Greeks and is substantiated by historical records of their religions.

[226] Psalm 69:14–15.

[227] Matthew 11:7.

[228] Matthew 6:8.

[229] Revelation 7:17.

[230] This is the term Dr. Jack Blanco used on several occasions when referring to the events of my past life.

[231] Proverbs 15:9.

[232] Proverbs 28:9.

[233] Acts 2:17–18.

[234] Malachi 3:10–11.

[235] Luke 18:29–30.

[236] Psalm 33:7.

[237] Matthew 14:27–29.

[238] Exodus 34:7.

[239] E. G. White, Child Guidance, chap. 47, "Lax Discipline and Its Fruitage" (Washington, DC: Review and Herald Publishing Assoc., 1954), 275–277.

[240] Ephesians 5:26.

[241] Revelation 22:1.

[242] Romans 2:4.

[243] Psalm 46:4–5.

[244] Isaiah 48:21.

[245] John 14:6; 1:1, 2, 14, 17:17.

[246] John 7:37, 38.

[247] Revelation 7:17.

[248] Revelation 21:6.

[249] Revelation 22:1.

[250] Revelation 22:16–17.

251 Developed by ASI Missions, Bible Readings, Happiness Digest Series, "The Kingdom and Work of Antichrist," note, paragraph 2, (Silver Spring, MD: Better Living Publications, 1990), 82. Adolf Hamack, What Is Christianity? (New York: G. P. Putnam's Sons, 1903), 270.

252 Bible Readings for the Home, p. 218, question no. 3, notes, paragraph 2. p. 219, paragraph 1. (Mountain View, California: Pacific Press Publ., 1944). Cardinal Robert Bellarmine, S.J, "On Councils: Their Nature and Authorities," book 2, chapter 17, translated by Ryan Grant, (Paris: 1614).

253 Ibid, paragraph 2, p. 219. From oration of Christopher Marcellus in fourth session of Fifth Lateran Council, Labbe and Cossart's "History of the Councils," published in 1672, vol. XIV, col. 109.

254 Ibid, paragraph 7, p. 219. Writings of Augustinius de Acona, printed without title page or pagination, question 6, "On an Appeal From the Decision of the Pope."

255 Ibid, paragraph 8, p. 219. "Petri Privilegium," in section on "The Vatican Council and Its Definitions," by Henry Edward Manning, archbishop of Westminster (Roman Catholic), London, Longmans, Green & Co., 1871, p. 214.

256 Ibid, paragraph 9, p. 219; paragraph 1, p. 220; Id., p. 218.

257 Ibid, question no. 4, paragraph 3, p. 221. The Western Watchman (Roman Catholic) of St. Louis, December 24, 1908.

258 "The Western Watchman (Roman Catholic) of St. Louis," November 21, 1912. Quotes of Roman Catholic Persecution, August 15, 2021. https://elemunah.com/end-times-headlines/quotes-of-roman-catholic-persecution/.

259 John Dowling, The History of Romanism (New York: Edward Walker Publishing, 1845), 541–542. https://archive.org/details/historyofromanis00dowl/page/542/mode/2up?q=p541.

260 Bible Readings for the Home, question no. 4, paragraph 2, 1944, p. 221.

261 R. W. Thompson, The Papacy and the Civil Power, (New York: Harper & Brothers, Publishers, Franklin Square, 1876), p. 416.

262 Dr. Mikel Del Rosario, "7 Key Differences Between Protestant and Catholic Doctrine," no. 2 "Tradition," (Dallas TX: Voice-Dallas Theological Seminary, 2014), https://voice.dts.edu/article/7-key-differences-between-protestant-and-catholic-doctrine-del-rosario-mikel/. [this article is quoting the Catholic Catechism].

263 Ibid, no. 3, "Salvation and Grace."

264 Ibid.

265 Ibid, no. 4, "The Eucharist."

266 Ibid.

267 Ibid.

268 Ibid, no. 5, "Justification."

269 Ibid, no. 6, "The Priesthood of Believers."

270 Ibid, no. 7, "The Veneration of Saints and the Virgin Mary."

271 Bible Readings for the Home, "The Fall of Modern Babylon," question no. 14, notes, paragraph 1, lines 4 and 5. (Mountain View, California: Pacific Press Publishing, 1944), 256. "The False Christ," J. Garnier, London, George Allen, 1900, Vol. II, pp. 94–95.

272 Ibid, "The Kingdom and Work of Antichrist," question 1, note, p. 218. (Daniel 7:24

273 Catechism of the Catholic Church, chapter 3, article 6: "The Sacrament of Holy Orders," VI. "Who Can Receive This Sacrament?, 1579," United States Catholic Conference Inc. (New York: Bantom Doubleday Dell Publishing Group Inc., 1994), 440.

274 Ibid, chapter 3, article 9: "I Believe in the Holy Catholic Church," paragraph 1, III. "The Mystery of the Church," "The Universal Sacrament of Salvation, 774," p. 222.

About the Author

Tommy Poole was born in Jacksonville, Florida, and raised in Columbia, South Carolina. After graduating from high school in 1970, he married his childhood sweetheart, Linda Caulder. In 1971, he enlisted for two years in the US Marine Corps. In 1973, Linda and Tommy were blessed with their only child, Brenda Ann.

In the fall of 1987, Tommy had a personal experience with Jesus Christ and, several years later, felt God's call into the gospel ministry. He returned to college and, in 1991, received a bachelor of arts degree in religion from Southern College (now Southern Adventist University). That year, Tommy and his family accepted a call to teach English in Macau with the Teacher's for China Project, where he also assisted with the pastoral duties in the local church.

In 1992, Tommy was called to the Gulf States Conference, where he began pastoring churches in Dothan, Alabama; Bonifay, Florida; and Marianna, Florida. In 1995, he was called to pastor churches in St. Elmo and Fairhope, Alabama, where he also took over the duties as conference disaster response coordinator for Alabama, Mississippi, and the Florida panhandle.

In 2001, Tommy was called to the Carolina Conference, where he pastored churches in Jacksonville and Kinston, North Carolina, until he was medically retired in 2007. The Pooles returned to Columbia, staying for several years to assist aging parents until their deaths. Since that time, Tommy, Linda, and Brenda made their home in the small community of Chapin, South Carolina, moving their church membership to the Irmo, South Carolina SDA Fellowship Church, where Tommy now serves as an elder for the congregation.

CPSIA information can be obtained
at www.ICGtesting.com
Printed in the USA
BVHW041248110723
667064BV00001B/46

9 798887 314303